159220

Ranking Faiths

Ranking Faiths

Religious Stratification in America

James D. Davidson and Ralph E. Pyle

ROWMAN & LITTLEFIELD PUBLISHERS, INC.
Lanham • Boulder • New York • Toronto • Plymouth, UK

Published by Rowman & Littlefield Publishers, Inc.
A wholly owned subsidiary of The Rowman & Littlefield Publishing Group, Inc.
4501 Forbes Boulevard, Suite 200, Lanham, Maryland 20706
http://www.rowmanlittlefield.com

Estover Road, Plymouth PL6 7PY, United Kingdom

British Library Cataloguing in Publication Information Available

Library of Congress Cataloging-in-Publication Data
Davidson, James D.
  Ranking Faiths : Religious stratification in America / James D. Davidson and Ralph E. Pyle.
    p. cm.
  Includes bibliographical references and index.
  ISBN 978-1-4422-0853-7 (cloth : alk. paper) — ISBN 978-1-4422-0855-1 (electronic)
    1. Religion and social status—United States—History. 2. Social stratification—United States—History. 3. United States—Religion. I. Pyle, Ralph E. II. Title.
  BL2525.D42 2011
  306.60973—dc22

                                                                      2010029032

⊗™ The paper used in this publication meets the minimum requirements of American National Standard for Information Sciences—Permanence of Paper for Printed Library Materials, ANSI/NISO Z39.48-1992.

Printed in the United States of America

Contents

Preface

If you have ever been to the Grand Canyon, or have seen pictures of it, you have seen the layers of colored rock stacked on top of each other: first red, then gray, then orange, then black, then beige, and so on. If you have ever seen the movie *Titanic* or a picture of that luxury liner, you know that the passengers had a choice of accommodations: first class (the most luxurious and most expensive), second class (less luxurious and less expensive), and third class (least luxurious and least expensive). If you have ever looked at the graphics in the bottom left-hand corner of the front page of *USA Today*, you have probably seen rows of people figures, ranked by the number of children they have, their calorie intake, the hours they spend listening to the radio, and so on. These are all images of stratification: in one case, the stratification of rock, in another, the stratification of cabins on a ship, and in yet another, the stratification of people.

Sociologists study the stratification of people—by examining lots of things, such as how much education they have, what kinds of work they do, how much money they make, how many and what kinds of civic groups they belong to, and so on. Then, we look to see if the people in the upper strata are different from people in the lower strata on the basis of other things, such as race, ethnicity, class, gender, and religion. If they are different on race, we call that racial stratification. If some nationality groups rank higher than others, that's called ethnic stratification. When rich kids rank higher than poor kids on something like SAT scores, that's called class stratification. Gender stratification occurs when men rank higher than women on something or women rank higher than men on something else. When the members of some religious groups have more access than members of other faiths do to things like good educations, good jobs, and good incomes, we call that religious stratification.

This book is about religious stratification in America. We decided to do a book on this topic for a reason. As people who are interested in inequality, we have noticed that people who study stratification tend to use a conflict perspective. We view society as pretty unstable, due mainly to conflicts between racial groups, ethnic groups, classes, and the sexes, all of which want to maximize their own well-being, even if they harm others in the process. We have always thought it was odd that monographs, journal articles, and textbooks on stratification make almost no mention of stratification based on religious affiliation. They suggest that religion is simply one of many means that elites use to justify their lofty status and to convince others that their lower station in life is fair, given their personal limitations and cultural deficiencies. People in the dominant group portray themselves as the righteous and "the elect," who are entitled to the blessings God has bestowed on them, and everyone else as people who aren't as successful in life because, frankly, they don't deserve it.

On the other hand, as people who specialize in the study of religion, we are aware of many books and journal articles showing how religious groups rank in terms of the socioeconomic status of their members. For example, the leading textbooks in the sociology of religion contain chapters indicating that the members of some religious groups are more educated, more prosperous, and more influential than people belonging to other faiths. However, when it comes to interpreting these findings, religion scholars don't use conflict theory. Instead, we rely on functionalist theory (which says that religion contributes to well-being of society by offering people in different social strata beliefs and practices that are appropriate for their station in life) and/or Weber's thesis that belonging to some religious groups (especially Protestant denominations rooted in Calvinist theology) is more conducive to worldly success than belonging to other faiths (such as traditional Catholicism).

Thus, there is a disconnect. Specialists in the study of stratification have found conflict theory useful in explaining stratification based on race, ethnicity, class, and gender, but have not used it to study stratification based on religious affiliation. Meanwhile, specialists in the study of religion have documented religious group differences in socioeconomic status, but don't use a conflict approach to link their analyses to studies of inequalities based on race, ethnicity, class, and gender.

As people who are interested in both religion and stratification, we thought we would try to do something about this curious situation. To that end, we decided to use a conflict approach to study religious stratification in America. If we succeed, our work might encourage others who study stratification to give more serious consideration to religious affiliation, and it might encourage others who study religion to give more serious consideration to conflict theory.

But, as we see it, this is much more than an intramural exercise among sociologists. It also is our way of calling Americans' attention to a type of inequality that is often overlooked and not well understood. We want to show that—like stratification based on race, ethnicity, class, and gender—stratification based on a person's religious affiliation has been part of the American experience since colonial times. We want to explain how it developed, how it has persisted and changed over the years, how it has affected our society, and what Americans can and should do about it.

Chapter 3 is an edited and revised version of our article "The Origins of Religious Stratification in Colonial America," which was published in the *Journal for the Scientific Study of Religion*, volume 42, March 2003, pages 57–75. Some parts of that article also appear in chapter 1. Chapters 1 and 6 contain data and text that were first published in Davidson's article "Religious Stratification: Its Origins, Persistence, and Consequences," *Sociology of Religion*, volume 69, Winter 2008, pages 371–95.

We want to thank our wives, Anna and Aloka, for their kindnesses when they must have felt that we were wedded to this book and not them. We also are grateful to Deborah Coe, Rachel Kraus, Kris Morgan, Scott Morrissey, and David Reyes, who have worked with us on specific parts of our analysis. We also extend thanks to colleagues, students, and other people who have contributed to this volume by listening to our presentations, asking penetrating questions, reviewing our papers, and offering constructive criticisms and suggestions. We also thank Sarah Stanton, Janice Braunstein, and Jin Yu for their professionalism and patience in the production of this book. Finally, we are grateful for our parents who, without knowing it, planted the seeds that grew into this project.

1

Ranking Faiths

Although the United States prides itself on being a land of equal opportunity, in fact, some people have always had more access to resources such as higher education, wealth, and political power. To this day, whites have more social, economic, and political influence than blacks. Throughout U.S. history, people with northern European (Anglo-Saxon) backgrounds have had more power, privilege, and prestige than people with other ethnic ancestries. People who are born into wealthy families have always had more access to first-rate educations, lucrative careers, and political offices than people who are born into poverty. Despite recent gains, women still have fewer opportunities for worldly success than men.

Thus, American society is stratified in many ways: by race, ethnicity, class, and gender. With whites still having more opportunities than blacks, the persistence of racial stratification cannot be denied. The fact that Anglo-Saxons have had the upper hand on other nationalities shows that ethnic stratification has been a part of our nation's history. The fact that inherited wealth gives rich people advantages over the poor shows that class stratification is still an important part of America's social fabric. Men's disproportionate control of resources calls our attention to the tenacity of gender stratification.

The effects of race, ethnicity, class, and gender are well documented by sociologists. They have written many books about racial stratification, ethnic stratification, class stratification, and gender stratification (e.g., Anderson and Massey 2004; Crompton and Mann 1986; Geschwender 1978; Huber 1986; Nerad 1999). All of the major textbooks in the field of stratification also include chapters on race, ethnicity, class, and gender (e.g., Aguirre and Baker 2008; Hurst 2007; Kerbo 2006; Landry 2007; Marger 2009; Rossides 1997).

1

The same cannot be said about the effects of religion and the existence of religious stratification. Although sociologists of religion have produced numerous books and articles showing that religious groups differ in terms of their members' educations, occupations, and incomes (e.g., Johnstone 2007; Kosmin and Keysar 2006; Smith and Faris 2005), scholars specializing in the study of social stratification pay little or no attention to religious stratification. For example, none of the major textbooks in the field of stratification have chapters on religious stratification. In fact, they make almost no reference to religion as a factor in the unequal distribution of power, privilege, and prestige. Based on the content of these texts, one could easily get the impression that there is no such thing as religious stratification.

When we ask colleagues who share our interest in social inequality why they pay so little attention to religious stratification, they give us one or more of the following explanations:

1. Our society is increasingly secular. Religion may have been an important part of public life at one time, but it isn't any more.
2. Religious affiliation has gone from being a largely ascribed and permanent status to being largely a matter of personal choice, so if religion has any adverse effects on people's access to resources, they are free to switch religions or drop out of religion altogether.
3. Religion is not as visible as race and gender and, therefore, is not as useful as a consideration when it comes to allocating social rewards and benefits.
4. If there is any relationship between religion and resources, it is (a) because resources affect people's religious affiliations, not because religious affiliation affects people's resources, or (b) it can be explained away by controlling for other factors, such as education.
5. Even if religious stratification existed at earlier points in U.S. history, it is no longer an important part of American society.

Although there is some empirical evidence to support each of these assertions, the weight of the best and most recent evidence tilts the scales toward five alternative assumptions.

1. Religion continues to be an important influence in modern society.

For a long time, European and American scholars argued that the modernization of society was contributing to the demise of religion (e.g., Bellah 1970; Berger 1967; Dobbelaere 1981; Wilson 1966). With tongue in cheek, Hadden (1987) argued that this secularization thesis had become an article of faith in sociological theory and research. Then, in one of his most important contributions to current scholarship, Hadden presented a very compelling body of evidence challenging the secularization argument. Finke and Stark (1992) and Warner (1993) then took Hadden's thesis to the next level, arguing that the secularization thesis does not apply to the United States, which—they showed quite convincingly—has become more religious (not less) over time. The prevailing view these days is that religion continues to be an important factor in our society. Its influence is documented daily on television, in the newspapers, on talk radio, on the Internet, and in social research on religion's impact on family life, economic growth, the law, health and medical care, political discourse and voting, and work (Barro and Mitchell 2004; Christiano et al. 2008; Ebaugh 2006; Dillon 2003).

2. Religious affiliation is still largely an ascribed and permanent status.

Factors such as race, ethnicity, religion, and gender used to be considered objective realities and inherited attributes that had inescapable effects on people's lifestyles and life chances. In recent years, it has become fashionable in some academic circles to view social reality as a social construct, to emphasize the active and creative role individuals play in shaping their own lives, and to see people as consumers who shop for identities and roles the same way they shop for cars and household appliances (Gergen 2009; Heiner 2009; Taylor 2009). These approaches have led to subjectivist views of race, ethnicity, and gender (e.g., Aguirre and Baker 2008) and a growing interest in seeing religion as a voluntary matter and religious affiliation as a personal choice (Ammerman 2003; Cimino and Lattin 2002; Pew Research Center 2010). This approach is bolstered by evidence showing that one-fourth of Americans change religions at some point in life, usually when they are relatively young (typically before they are thirty-five years of age) and especially when they marry someone who was raised in another faith (Hoge et al. 2001; Kosmin and Keysar 2006; Fischer and Hout 2006; Roof and McKinney 1987). For example, former president George W. Bush was raised Episcopalian, but became a United Methodist when he married Laura Welch, a United Methodist. His brother Jeb Bush, also raised Episcopalian, converted to Catholicism to share the faith of his wife, Columba Garnica Gallo, who grew up Catholic.

However, the emphases on "social construction," "agency," and "rational choice" do not come to terms with other research showing that, to this day, the vast majority of Americans inherit their religion from their parents and never change faiths. Nelsen (1988), for example, shows that well over 90 percent of teenagers growing up in families with two Protestant parents or two Catholic parents take on their parents' religion. He also found that the sons and daughters of two parents who have no religious preference (Nones) tend to become Nones. When parents are of different faiths, children are most likely to take on the religious affiliation of their mothers, though not in all cases. More recently, Smith and Denton (2005) also have documented adolescents' tendencies to take on the religious identities and ideas of their parents. Other studies confirm the fact that three out of four Americans never leave the religion they inherited from their parents (Fischer and Hout 2006; Keister 2005; Kosmin and Keysar 2006). Even when there might be good reasons for them to change faiths or drop out of religion altogether, most people remain affiliated with the religion of their childhood throughout their lives. Thus, for most Americans, religious group membership is far more ascribed and permanent than it is voluntary.[1]

3. Religion is quite visible.

There is not much research on the extent to which people accurately perceive or correctly predict other people's race, ethnicity, class, gender, or religion. We don't know of any empirical basis for saying that religion is any harder to identify than other attributes.

Without research, most of us are tantalized by cases of mistaken identity. John Howard Griffin's book *Black Like Me* (1976) taught us that a white man can pass as a black man, and James O'Toole's book *Passing for White* (2003) reminds us that light-skinned blacks are often considered white. It is not uncommon for Latinos to be mistaken for Italians, or for Irishmen to be mistaken for Scots. The question "Is that a boy or a girl?" indicates an inability to tell the difference between male and female in some individual cases. Non-Asians acknowledge having difficulty telling the difference between Koreans, Filipinos, Japanese, and Chinese people. Some people find it hard to tell an Episcopalian from a Presbyterian, or a Hindu from a Buddhist. And some Jews have changed their names to pass as WASPs.

We grant that some group traits are more identifiable than others. Skin color and sexual attributes are very identifiable to most people. But, in our experience, people who say that religious affiliation is not visible still make reasonably accurate decisions about people's religious affiliations. Based on the language students use in the essays they submit with their applications for graduate school, our academic colleagues have little or no difficulty telling the difference between an applicant who is a fundamentalist Protestant and one who is an atheist. They also are quite willing to assume that an Italian male who graduated from Marquette is a Catholic. When a woman who grew up in Mississippi says she was "born again" at vacation Bible school, they are quite rightly prepared to assume that she is Baptist. If a job candidate has an English name and refers to his prep school's headmaster as "rector," their assumption is that he is Episcopalian. If a coed's curriculum vitae says she is from Iran and is living in Dearborn, Michigan, while attending graduate school, they would accurately assume she is Muslim. Sure, they might be wrong every now and then, but more often than not, they will be right.

4. Religion has important effects on people's access to resources, even after other factors are taken into account.

We do not deny that conditions such as education, occupation, and income affect some people's religious affiliations (McCloud and Mirola 2009; Roof and McKinney 1987). Many of us know someone who, in the course of being upwardly mobile, has switched from an evangelical Protestant sect to a mainline Protestant denomination, or has gone from being a Reform Jew to being a Unitarian-Universalist. These cases—in which increasing access to resources is the independent variable and religion is the dependent variable—account for a portion of the correlation between religion and resources.

Another portion of the correlation is due to the fact that religion is linked to other factors that increase access to resources. For example, mainline Protestants tend to be white and highly educated (Roof and McKinney 1987; Smith and Faris 2005), and being white and highly educated increases one's chances of becoming wealthy (Keister 2000). When race and education are taken into account, the correlation between religion and resources is reduced a bit (Keister 2005).

However, even after these other factors are taken into account, religion continues to have effects. Some of its effects are indirect, through variables such as the division of labor in families, attitudes about education, family values, and economic values (Beyerlein 2004; Hertel and Hughes 1987; Keister 2008; Sherkat 2007; Lehrer 1999). Others are direct effects on outcomes such as education, labor force participation, social contacts that can provide information, and opportunities that can enhance wealth ownership, asset accumulation, and net worth (Burstein 2007; Homola, Knudsen, and Marshall 1987; Keister 2000, 2003, 2005, 2008; Pyle 1996, 2006). Thus, even after factors such as race and education are controlled, religious affiliation has significant effects of its own on people's access to social, economic, and political resources.

5. Religious stratification has always been and continues to be an important part of our society.

This claim can be verified in several ways. Historical documents, church records, and national telephone surveys provide information about the number of different religious groups in the United States at various points in time, as well as the size of these groups and the religious composition of the U.S. population. Public records provide the names of public officeholders, including all U.S. presidents, cabinet officers, Supreme Court justices, and members of the Congress. Through historical accounts and public records, one can identify who the nation's business leaders and wealthiest people have been at various periods of time. Websites and university histories record the names of people who have served as presidents of the nation's leading colleges and universities. The U.S. census, which is conducted every ten years, and national surveys provide data on the educational achievements, occupational status, and incomes of the American people in general. Historians and social scientists also have produced excellent descriptions of important cities and towns, including the religious backgrounds of the cultural elites, business elites, and political elites in these settings. Several more contemporary studies have used the *Who's Who in America* to locate the religious backgrounds of America's elites. In recent decades, it has become possible to calculate the socioeconomic status and discover the religious identifications of representative samples of American citizens.

Using these various sources of information, we have made connections between people's religious backgrounds and their access to important social resources. In some studies (Davidson and Pyle 2005; Pyle 2006), we have analyzed data on religion and the socioeconomic status of Americans in general. In others, we have investigated the religious affiliations of economic, political, and cultural elites (see appendix 1 for details). With regard to religion and power, we have documented the religious affiliations of the people who signed the Declaration of Independence, were delegates to the Constitutional Convention, were Speakers of the House in the thirteen original colonies, have been cabinet officers and Supreme Court justices, have been president of the United States, and have been identified as political leaders or political elites. With regard to religion and privilege, we have confirmed the religious affiliations of business leaders at both the local and national levels and the occupational status and income characteristics of people who belong to different religious groups. With regard to religion and prestige, we have gathered data on the religious ties and educational attainment of Americans in general, Ivy League presidents, and other cultural elites. Let's take a look at just some of the data documenting the history of religious stratification in America (other data are reported in later chapters).

RELIGIOUS STRATIFICATION IN THE COLONIAL PERIOD

In the twelfth and thirteenth centuries, about 15 million people lived on the land that we now know as North America, and "tens of millions" more lived in Central America, and South America (Feagin and Feagin 2008, 136). These indigenous people lived in tribal communities that had different topographies, different economies, and different worldviews. These "Native Americans" have been described as "extremely religious," believing in a Creator, evil forces, and an afterlife and participating in a variety of religious practices asking the Creator for help and trying to ward off evil (Feagin and Feagin 2008, 137).

Then, Columbus landed in San Salvador in 1492, Ponce de Leon arrived in Florida in 1513, St. Augustine was settled by 1565, Jamestown became a settlement in 1607, and the Pilgrims landed in Plymouth in 1620. In the next 150 years or so, people belonging to many different religious groups settled in the thirteen original colonies (Finke and Stark 1992). During the colonial period, the largest groups were the Congregationalists, who settled in the northeast, the Presbyterians, who settled in the middle colonies, and the Anglicans, who settled in the South. Other sizable Protestant groups included the Baptists, the Quakers, the Dutch Reformeds, and the Methodists. There also were small numbers of Moravians, Mennonites, Huguenots, Catholics, and Jews.

Unitarianism was taking root among Congregationalists such as Charles Chauncy and a growing number of other educated colonists, such as John Adams and John Quincy Adams. Because these people increasingly considered themselves Unitarians, met in Unitarian congregations, and made church-related decisions as Unitarians (Cooke 1910), we consider Unitarianism a colonial religion, even though the congregations did not unite into a single denomination until 1825. Similar schisms were occurring in other groups. The Methodist Episcopal Church (aka Methodists) split off from the Church of England in 1784. The Protestant Episcopal Church (aka Episcopalians) separated from the Church of England in 1789. By 1793, German Reformeds had separated themselves from Dutch Reformeds.

By the time of the Revolutionary War, the signing of the Declaration of Independence, and the ratification of the U.S. Constitution, some of these religious groups had accumulated more power, privilege, and prestige than others.

Power

An examination of the religious affiliations of the founding fathers provides a clear indication of religious stratification in the colonies. Table 1.1 shows that 95 percent of the signers of the Declaration of Independence and 85 percent of the delegates to the Constitutional Convention belonged to just three Protestant denominations: Anglican, Congregational, and Presbyterian. Anglicans alone accounted for over 60 percent of the signatures on the Declaration and almost half (47.5 percent) of the participants at the Convention. Congregationalists ranked second, and Presbyterians were third. Together, these groups were 17.5 times more likely than all other groups combined to sign the Declaration and 5.7 times more likely to participate in the Conven-

Table 1.1.   Religious Representation of America's Founding Fathers

	Signers of the Declaration of Independence[a]		Delegates to the 1787 Constitutional Convention[b]	
Religion	N	Percent	N	Percent
Anglican (Episcopalian)	34	60.7	19	47.5
Congregationalist	13	23.2	8	20.0
Presbyterian	6	10.7	7	17.5
Quaker	1	1.8	2	5.0
Roman Catholic	1	1.8	2	5.0
Dutch Reformed	—	—	1	2.5
Methodist	—	—	1	2.5
Baptist	1	1.8	—	—
Total	56	100	40	100

[a] Stokes (1950, 464).
[b] Olmstead (1960, 217).

tion. They also were way overrepresented in these settings (85 to 95 percent) relative to their numbers in the total population (about 9 percent).[2] Other groups, which were highly popular among the people, were hardly represented among national political elites. For example, Baptists, who had more adherents than Anglicans at the time, were not even present at the Constitutional Convention.

Privilege

There was a considerable concentration of wealth in the colonies. It is estimated that "the top 1 percent of free households owned about 13 percent of the wealth" (Beeghley 2005, 166). Congregationalists were well positioned among economic elites in New England. On the eve of the Revolution, two-thirds of rich merchants of Boston were Congregationalists (Baltzell 1982). Almost all of Boston's fifty leading families during the seventeenth and eighteenth centuries were Congregationalists. Anglicans were overrepresented among wealthy individuals in New York City in the 1750s (Meyers 1943, 58–59), and they dominated economic relations in the Southern provinces (Longmore 1996).

Quakers were highly visible among the wealthiest 2 percent of New Jersey residents in the middle of the eighteenth century (Purvis 1980, 597), and they were disproportionately represented among wealthy Philadelphians at the end of the colonial period (Nash 1968). The 1769 Philadelphia tax list showed that Quakers, who constituted no more than one-seventh of Philadelphia's population, accounted for more than half of those who paid taxes in excess of one hundred pounds (Tolles 1948, 49).

Presbyterians were fast rising in influence in the late colonial period and were beginning to achieve visibility among people of importance in all regions. In Pennsylvania's Chester and Lancaster counties, Presbyterians were overrepresented in the upper tax brackets by 1782 (Bonomi 1986, 96). By the time of the Revolution, Presbyterians stood on the threshold of being one of the most elite of the new nation's denominations.

Prestige

Education has always been one of the leading indicators of prestige. People with the most education have always been granted more honor and respect than people with fewer years of schooling. What, then, were the religious affiliations of the most highly educated colonists?

A majority of the "university men" in seventeenth century New England, and other colonies no doubt, came from England, where most had attended Oxford and Cambridge universities (Stout 1974). Both schools were affiliated with the Church of England and only Anglican communicants were allowed to matriculate. Another one-third of New England scholars had graduated from Harvard, which was founded by Congregationalists in 1636 (Stout 1974). Thus, Anglicans and Congregationalists were disproportionately represented among the colonies' educational elites.

The prominence of these groups persisted into the eighteenth century, largely through their own efforts. Congregationalists saw to it that their Calvinist brand of Protestantism was incorporated into public elementary and secondary schools intended for lower status children in New England. In Virginia, Anglicans saw to it that such public schools were under the control of the Archbishop of Canterbury and the Bishop of London (Butts and Cremin 1953). Attempting to solidify their elite status even further, especially in areas where religious diversity prevented them from enforcing religious conformity in the public schools, these elite faith groups created private secondary schools of their own through endowments, denominational funding, and entrepreneurship (Butts and Cremin, 1953).

These Latin schools and academies were seen as stepping stones to higher education. Some well-to-do colonists sent their sons back to England, so they too could attend Oxford and Cambridge. Others, wanting their sons to go to such schools but not wanting to send them all the way to England, played a major role in the formation of institutions of higher learning in the colonies (Barck and Lefler 1958). As a result, six of the nine leading colleges founded

between 1636 and 1769 were associated with just three Protestant denominations: the Congregational Church (Harvard, 1636; Yale, 1701; Dartmouth,
1769); the Church of England (William and Mary, 1693; Columbia, 1754);
and the Presbyterian Church (Princeton, 1746). Most of the presidents and
leading faculty at these schools—such as Yale's Thomas Clap, William
and Mary's Hugh Jones, Columbia's Samuel Johnson, and Harvard's John
Winthrop—were members of (and, in many cases, ministers in) the same
elite denominations (Coe and Davidson 2010). So were the graduates, most
of whom went on to careers in Protestant ministry, public service, medicine,
education, commerce, and the military (Cremin 1970; Vine 1978).

Overall Ranking

Thus, at the end of the eighteenth century, religious groups were differenti-
ated on the basis of their representation in the social, political, and economic
hierarchies of the new nation (see figure 1.1). Anglicans, Congregationalists,
and Presbyterians, which were about 9 percent of the total population, clearly
were the Upper stratum in colonial life, so much so that Baltzell (1964) later
dubbed them "the Protestant Establishment." Quakers and Unitarians also
were overrepresented in some spheres of colonial influence but can best be
described as members of the Upper Middle stratum. Other Protestant groups
were less prominently positioned in the Lower Middle stratum, but ranked
ahead of Catholics, Jews, Others, and people with no religion, who, taken

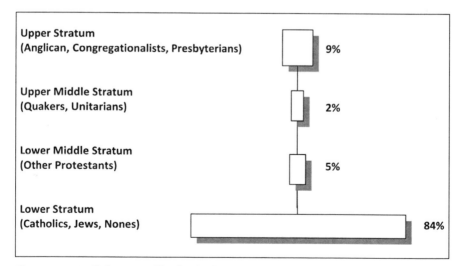

Figure 1.1.   Religious Stratification in the Colonial Period

together, comprised the Lower stratum even though they far outnumbered the groups in higher strata.

RELIGIOUS STRATIFICATION IN THE 1800s

The nation's religious composition changed dramatically in the next one hundred years. Unitarianism officially became a separate denomination when the American Unitarian Association was founded in 1825. The Church of Jesus Christ of Latter-day Saints (aka Mormons) emerged from the "burned over district" of upstate New York in 1830. The Christian Church/Disciples of Christ came into being in 1832. The Methodists, Presbyterians, and Baptists not only grew in size (Finke and Stark 1992), they also divided into separate groups along racial and regional lines. For example, the Methodist Episcopal Church, South, separated from the Methodist Episcopal Church in 1844. The Southern Baptist Convention was formed in 1845. The Presbyterian Church in the Confederate States of America split off from the Presbyterian Church in the United States of America in 1861 and, later, became the Presbyterian Church in the U.S.A. Black denominations such as the Union American Methodist Church (1813) and the African Methodist Episcopal Zion (1820) sprung up before the Civil War, but there was a veritable explosion of new black denominations in the thirty years following the war. By the end of the 1800s, there were many more religious groups than there had been in the colonial period.

In addition to the formation of new groups, several groups that were only a small percentage of the colonial population increased their memberships. Baptists and Methodists increased to 4.3 million members in 1850 and 13 million members in 1890, mainly as a result of their evangelistic efforts (Finke and Stark 1992). Catholics and Jews benefited from increased immigration. The Catholic population, which was only about 40,000 at the end of the colonial period, increased to 195,000 in 1820, jumped to 650,000 in 1836, then skyrocketed to 12 million in 1900 (D'Antonio et al. 2001). There were only 2,000 to 3,000 Jews in the colonies, but enough to establish congregations in New York (1656), Newport, Rhode Island (1677), Savannah (1733), Philadelphia (1745), and Charleston, South Carolina (1750). The Jewish population was still only about 5,000 in 1820. However, with the immigration of Jews from Germany, it grew to about 50,000 in 1850 and 250,000 in 1880. With the immigration of East European Jews, the Jewish population jumped to about 1 million by 1900.

What effects, if any, did these changes have on the pattern of religious stratification that emerged in the colonial period? Let's see.

Power

Between 1800 and 1899, twenty-three men served as presidents of the United State (see table 1.2). Fifty-two percent of the presidents belonged to just two Protestant denominations: Episcopal and Presbyterian. Thirty percent of the presidents were Episcopalians; 22 percent were Presbyterians. Considering the fact that these two groups were only about 5 percent of the total U.S. population at this time, they clearly were overrepresented in the White House during this period in our history.

Three presidents were Unitarians. Three others were Methodists. Three were Nones. One president was a Disciple of Christ, and one was Dutch Reformed. Unitarians and Dutch Reformeds had more presidents in the first half of the century; Methodists and Nones had more in the second half. There were no Catholics, Jews, or people of any other faiths among nineteenth century presidents.

In the midst of the continuing political dominance of the Protestant Establishment, there were some indications of change. Episcopalians and Presbyterians were 63 percent of all presidents in the first half of the nineteenth century and 46 percent in the second half. Relative to their numbers in the total population, there were ten to twelve times as many Episcopalian and Presbyterian presidents as one would expect in the first half of the century and eight to ten times as many in the second half. Episcopalians had more access to the presidency in the first half, whereas Presbyterians had more in the second half.

Privilege

There was a marked increase in the concentration of wealth during the 1800s (Beeghley 2005, 166–67). Recall that the top 1 percent of households controlled 13 percent of the wealth in the colonial period. By the 1860s, and from that point to the end of the century, the top 1 percent controlled between 26 and 29 percent of the wealth.

Who were these richest of all Americans? What were their religious affiliations? (See table 1.3.) A study of leaders in the textile, railroad, and steel industries between 1870 and 1879 (Gregory and Neu 1962, 199–200) shows that these business elites were most likely to be Episcopalians (25 percent) and Congregationalists (22 percent). Presbyterians ranked third (14 percent), followed by Unitarians (10 percent), and Quakers (8 percent). Methodists (6 percent) and Baptists (4 percent) were farther down the list. An additional 11 percent belonged to a variety of other Protestant denominations (6 percent) or were Protestant but did not specify their denomination (5 percent). There were no

Table 1.2. U.S. Presidents, 1800–1899, by Religious Affiliation

	Total N	Total %	1800–1849 (%)	1850–1899 (%)
Episcopalian	7	30	45	15
James Madison (1809–1817)				
James Monroe (1817–1825)				
William Henry Harrison (1841)				
John Tyler (1841–1845)				
Zachary Taylor (1849–1850)				
Franklin Pierce (1853–1857)				
Chester Arthur (1881–1885)				
Presbyterian	5	22	18	31
Andrew Jackson (1829–1837)				
James Polk (1845–1849)				
James Buchanan (1857–1861)				
Grover Cleveland (1885–1889, 1893–1897)				
Benjamin Harrison (1889–1893)				
Unitarian	3	13	18	8
John Adams (1797–1801)				
John Quincy Adams (1825–1829)				
Millard Fillmore (1850–1853)				
Methodist	3	13	—	23
Rutherford B. Hayes (1877–1881)				
Ulysses S. Grant (1869–1877)				
William McKinley (1897–1901)				
Nones	3	13	9	15
Thomas Jefferson (1801–1809)				
Abraham Lincoln (1861–1865)				
Andrew Johnson (1865–1869)				
Disciples of Christ	1	4	—	8
James Garfield (1881)				
Dutch Reformed	1	4	9	—
Martin Van Buren (1837–1841)				
Total	23	99	99	100

Table 1.3. Religious Affiliations of American Industrial Leaders in the 1870s

Religion	%
Episcopalian	25
Congregationalist	22
Presbyterian	14
Unitarian	10
Quaker	8
Methodist	6
Baptist	4
Other Protestant	6
Protestant Unspecified	5
Catholic	—
Jewish	—
Total	100

Source: Gregory and Neu (1962).

Catholics or Jews. Episcopalians, Congregationalists, and Presbyterians were 1.5 times more likely to be business leaders than members of all other religious groups. These three denominations were far overrepresented relative to their numbers in the total population. One of the leading analysts of America's upper class also noted that there was an "affinity between the gentleman-businessman of the 'Gilded Age' and the Episcopal Church" (Baltzell 1958, 229).

The dominance of Episcopalians, Congregationalists, and—to a lesser extent—Presbyterians was reflected in many urban centers. For example, Philadelphia's moneyed class in the same period (including leaders in banking, shipping, real estate, textiles, chemicals, iron works, coal, canals, railroads, steel, oil, department stores, and utilities) was largely made up of Episcopalians and Presbyterians (Baltzell 1958, 70–129, 223–61). There was a "growing influence of the Episcopal Church upon the Victorian upper class" (Baltzell 1958, 247).

Prestige

One of the leading indicators of prestige has to do with the types of schools people attend or work at as faculty or administrators. Private education is admired more than public education, and there are no more prestigious schools than those which make up the Ivy League. Harvard, Yale, and Dartmouth have Congregational roots; Columbia was started by the Church of England; Princeton is Presbyterian; Brown is Baptist; Cornell and the University of Pennsylvania are nonsectarian.

One way to estimate the stature of religious groups in the 1800s is to determine the religious affiliations of the presidents of Ivy League schools (Coe and Davidson 2010). Between 1800 and 1899, these schools had a total of fifty-four presidents. Table 1.4 shows their religious affiliations.

Twenty-six percent were Episcopalians, 22 percent were Congregationalists, and 17 percent were Presbyterians—eight to ten times more than one might expect considering the size of these groups in the total population. Nearly twice as many members of these groups were Ivy League presidents, as compared to members of all other religious groups. Seventeen percent were Unitarians, and 13 percent were Baptists. The overall pattern was pretty stable throughout the century.

Thirteen of the fourteen Episcopalians (93 percent) were presidents of Columbia and Penn. The other one was at Cornell. Ten of the fourteen Congregationalists (83 percent) were presidents of Dartmouth and Yale. The other two were at Columbia and Cornell. Five of the nine Presbyterians (55 percent) were presidents of Princeton. Two others were presidents at Dartmouth, one was at Penn, and one was at Columbia. All nine of the Unitarians were presidents of Harvard, and all seven of the Baptists were presidents of Brown. The one Reformed president was at Penn, and the one Disciple was at Cornell. No Other Protestants, Catholics, Jews, or Nones were Ivy League presidents in the nineteenth century.

It is not surprising that the religious affiliations of the presidents tended to be the same as the church that founded the institution. Schools were often required to hire "their own kind." But that was not always the case, and the cases where it was not reveal the stature of the elite denominations. Whenever Dartmouth's president was not a Congregationalist, he was a Presbyterian. When Columbia's president was not an Episcopalian, he was either a Con-

Table 1.4. Ivy League Presidents, 1800–1899, by Religious Affiliation

	N	1800–1849 (%)	1850–1899 (%)	Total (%)
Episcopalian	14	27	25	26
Congregationalist	12	23	21	22
Presbyterian	9	19	14	17
Unitarian	9	19	14	17
Baptist	7	8	18	13
Reformed	1	4	—	2
Disciples of Christ	1	—	4	2
Unknown	1	—	4	2
Total	54	101	100	101

Source: Coe and Davidson (2010).

gregationalist or a Presbyterian. Penn had eleven presidents during the 1800s. Five were Episcopalians, two were Presbyterians, one was Reformed, and the religion of the other is unknown. Cornell had three presidents between its founding in 1865 and the end of that century. One was an Episcopalian, one was a Congregationalist, and the other a Disciple of Christ. Thus even when schools were not required to hire Episcopalians, Congregationalists, or Presbyterians, they tended to do so. The only exception was Harvard: when its president was not a Congregationalist, he was a Unitarian.

Combining these data, we see that the groups that comprised the Upper stratum in the colonial period continued to be dominant religions in the nineteenth century. Other Protestants, such as Methodists and Baptists, ranked lower, but these groups still had more stature than Black Protestants, Catholics, Jews, and Nones.

RELIGIOUS STRATIFICATION FROM 1900 TO THE PRESENT

America's religious landscape has continued to change in the past 110 years. In the early 1900s, the changes were largely due to the influx of Catholic and Jewish immigrants. The Catholic population, which stood at 12 million in 1900, was 20 million by 1920. The Jewish population, which was about 1 million in 1900, was about 2 million in 1920. The rapid increase in these non-Protestant groups triggered a nativist reaction that culminated in the Immigration Act of 1924. That act all but stopped the in-migration of people from eastern and southern Europe (the main sources of Catholic and Jewish immigrants) and Asian and Middle Eastern countries (the main sources of Hindus, Buddhists, and other eastern religions). What was a flood of immigrants was reduced to a trickle between 1924 and 1965. Except for the in-migration of some Jews from Germany and some Puerto Ricans to the mainland, this period was one of religious consolidation, not religious diversification.

That all changed in 1965, when President Lyndon Johnson signed a new Immigrant Act. This one reopened the doors of immigration and in came millions of newcomers. The largest percentage of the new immigrants has been Hispanic Catholics from Mexico, Puerto Rico, Cuba, and Central and South America. Other groups have included Protestants and Catholics from the Pacific Rim. Large numbers of Hindus and Buddhists also have arrived from a variety of Asian nations. Muslims have come to the United States from the Middle East. Today, Protestants are on the verge of being less than half of the total population for the first time in U.S. history. Catholics, Jews, Others, and Nones are almost a majority of all Americans. Catholics alone are about one-quarter of the total population. Nones are about 15 percent. Jews are about 2 percent. Muslims, Hindus, Buddhists, and others are about 8 percent. Clearly, the diversity of the nation's religious landscape has increased. What has happened to its historical pattern of religious stratification? First, let's look at data on the religious affiliation of American elites, then some data on the connection between religion and socioeconomic status for the general population.

Elites

Episcopalians, Presbyterians, and—to a lesser extent—Congregationalists continue to be overrepresented among presidents of the United States and presidents of Ivy League schools, but they no longer have the virtual lock they once had on these positions. In the early 1900s, there were five to ten times as many members of these religious groups in these positions. Now there are about twice as many.

Between 1900 and 1959, 44 percent of U.S. presidents were members of the Protestant Establishment (Presbyterians Woodrow Wilson and Dwight Eisenhower, Episcopalian Franklin Roosevelt, and Congregationalist Calvin Coolidge). Since 1960, 30 percent of presidents have been affiliated with Protestant Establishment denominations (Episcopalians Gerald Ford and George H. W. Bush and UCC/Congregationalist Barack Obama). The increasing number of "outsiders" includes two Baptists (Jimmy Carter and Bill Clinton), two Disciples of Christ (Lyndon Johnson and Ronald Reagan), one Methodist (former Episcopalian George W. Bush), and one Catholic (John Kennedy).

Between 1900 and 1959, 63 percent of Ivy League presidents were Episcopalians, Presbyterians, or Congregationalists. Since 1960, only 17 percent have been. The growing number of Others includes ten Jews, three Catholics, a Mormon, a Quaker, a Methodist, a Church of the Brethren, an Eastern Orthodox, a None, and fourteen people whose religious affiliations are unknown.[3]

Other studies of elites also point to both continuity and change. Fry (1933a and 1933b) recorded the names and religious affiliations of every person listed in the 1930–1931 edition of *Who's Who in America*, which is considered the best single source of information about America's elites (see table 1.5).[4] Episcopalians, Presbyterians, and Congregationalists clearly were the dominant groups. Episcopalians ranked highest with 22 percent of all listees, 6.3 times more than their percentage in the total population. Presbyterians ranked second at 20 percent (3.3 times what one might expect). Congregationalists ranked third at 11 percent and 5.6 times their representation in the population. Together, these three groups accounted for 53.5 percent of all listees.

Unitarians and Quakers came next. Unitarians were only 6 percent of all listees, but there were twenty times as many of them in *Who's Who* than one might expect. There were even fewer Quakers, but they too were over-

Table 1.5.   Religious Affiliations of Individuals in *Who's Who in America* (percent)

Religious Group	1930–1931[a]	1950–1951	1970–1971	1992–1993
Protestant Establishment				
Episcopalian	21.94	23.12	20.22	18.04
Presbyterian	20.31	18.39	19.62	13.91*
Congregationalist/UCC	11.29	8.84	5.91	3.19*
Other Elite				
Unitarian-Universalist	5.98	4.03	3.60	2.39*
Quaker	1.09	1.75	1.50	.65
Catholic	4.45	8.41	13.21	23.12*
Jewish	1.31	2.54	6.91	12.32*
Other Protestant				
Baptist	8.97	6.21	5.11	4.71*
Disciples	2.05	2.36	2.20	.36*
Lutheran	2.41	2.71	3.70	6.01*
Methodist	14.50	15.50	14.21	9.57*
Reformed	1.00	.44	.30	.36
Other[b]				
Mormon	.39	.27	1.10	1.52*
Christian Science	.69	.70	.60	.22
All Others	3.62	4.73	1.81	3.63
No Affiliation Listed	43.86	48.49	69.01	65.66

[a] The 1930–1931 figures are reported by Fry (1933a).
[b] Reported by Ament (1927).
* 1930–1992 difference significant $p < .001$.

represented (4.8 times as many). Christian Scientists were even smaller (less than 1 percent), but there were slightly more of them (1.3 times as many) in *Who's Who* than one might expect. All other groups were underrepresented. Methodists came closest to parity (.88), followed by Jews (.73), Reformed (.72), Disciples (.67), Baptists (.55), Lutherans (.33), Mormons (.33), and Catholics (.13).

The rankings were very similar in 1950–1951. Half of the listees were Episcopalians, Presbyterians, and Congregationalists. These groups were still overrepresented, as were the Unitarians, Quakers, and Christian Scientists. For the first time, Methodists were slightly above parity at 15.5 percent of all listees. None of the other groups had more than 10 percent of the listees, and all of them were underrepresented relative to their numbers in the population.

The 1970–1971 rankings were a little different. Episcopalians (20.2 percent) and Presbyterians (19.6 percent) were still the largest groups and were still overrepresented. Congregationalists' numbers slipped noticeably, although they—like Unitarians, Quakers, and Christian Scientists—were still overrepresented. Methodists were slightly above parity once again. Catholics were up to 13.2 percent of listees but had not reached parity. Baptists, Lutherans, Reformeds, and Mormons continued to be small in numbers and underrepresented. The biggest change involved Jews, who now were 6.9 percent of all listees and 2.4 times more likely to be in *Who's Who* than in the total population.

By 1992–1993, Episcopalians, Presbyterians, and Congregationalists had slipped to 35.1 percent of all listees, but remained overrepresented. Though small in numbers, Unitarians, Quakers, and Christian Scientists were still overrepresented. Methodists declined percentage wise and slipped slightly below parity, while Lutherans continued their steady climb up the ranks. The biggest gainers were Jews (who now were 12.3 percent of all listees, six times more than one might expect) and Catholics (who were nearly one-fourth of all entries and were closing in on parity).

Population as a Whole

The other way to describe religious stratification is to estimate the socioeconomic status of people who belong to various groups. The evidence in table 1.6 shows the ranking of nineteen religious groups at the end of the twentieth century and the beginning of the twenty-first (Davidson 2008). The Privilege column reports each group's ranking in terms of the median household income of its members. The Power column indicates each group's presence in the 107th Congress (2001–2002). The Prestige column shows the percentage of each group's members who are college graduates. The last column indicates each group's overall ranking or total score on all three dimensions.

Episcopalians, Jews, Presbyterians, and Unitarians ranked the highest. They were followed by Hindus, the United Church of Christ, Methodists, Mormons, Catholics, and Lutherans. A third stratum consisted of Nones, members of the Church of Christ, Adventists, the Assemblies of God, Baptists, and Buddhists. Muslims, the Church of God, and Jehovah's Witnesses were at the bottom. This profile is similar to other recent rankings of religious groups.

There is considerable consistency across the three dimensions. This consistency is most apparent in the Upper stratum, where all four groups score high in all three domains. For example, Episcopalians averaged $55,000 in income. There were four times as many Episcopalians in Congress as one would have expected based on their numbers in the total population. And 56 percent of Episcopalians were college graduates. Essentially, the same pattern occurs among Presbyterians. They averaged $50,000 per household,

Table 1.6. Religious Stratification, 2001

Stratum	Inc[a]	Privilege R[b]×W[c] = S[d]	Cong[e]	Power R[b]×W[c] =S[d]	Coll[f]	Prestige R[b]×W[c] = S[d]	Total Score
Upper							
Episcopal	55	1 × 3 = 3	4.0	1 × 2 = 2	56	1 × 1 = 1	6
Jewish	72	1 × 3 = 3	7.0	1 × 2 = 2	58	1 × 1 = 1	6
Presbyterian	50	1 × 3 = 3	3.0	1 × 2 = 2	51	1 × 1 = 1	6
Unitarian Universalist	58	1 × 3 = 3	3.3	1 × 2 = 2	72	1 × 1 = 1	6
Upper Middle							
Hindu	51	1 × 3 = 3	0.0	4 × 2 = 8	67	1 × 1 = 1	12
United Church of Christ	41	2 × 3 = 6	2.0	2 × 2 = 4	49	2 × 1 = 2	12
Methodist	48	2 × 3 = 6	1.7	2 × 2 = 4	36	3 × 1 = 3	13
Mormon	40	3 × 3 = 9	3.0	1 × 2 = 2	30	3 × 1 = 3	14
Catholic	47	2 × 3 = 6	1.1	3 × 2 = 6	33	3 × 1 = 3	15
Lutheran	49	2 × 3 = 6	0.8	3 × 2 = 6	36	3 × 1 = 3	15
Lower Middle							
None	46	2 × 3 = 6	0.1	4 × 2 = 8	34	3 × 1 = 3	17
Church of Christ	34	3 × 3 = 9	1.0	3 × 3 = 6	30	3 × 1 = 3	18
Seventh-day Adventist	30	4 × 3 = 12	2.5	2 × 2 = 4	29	3 × 1 = 3	19
Assembly of God	38	3 × 3 = 9	1.0	3 × 2 = 6	24	4 × 1 = 4	19
Baptist[g]	33	3 × 3 = 9	0.8	3 × 2 = 6	22	4 × 1 = 4	19
Buddhist	38	3 × 3 = 9	0.0	4 × 2 = 8	42	2 × 1 = 2	19
Lower							
Muslim	31	4 × 3 = 12	0.0	4 × 2 = 8	46	2 × 1 = 2	22
Church of God	26	4 × 3 = 12	0.0	4 × 2 = 8	15	4 × 1 = 4	24
Jehovah's Witnesses	24	4 × 3 = 12	0.0	4 × 2 = 8	12	4 × 1 = 4	24

Note: Within strata, groups with the same scores are listed alphabetically.
[a] Inc = median household income (rounded to nearest $1,000) in 2000. Data from Kosmin and Keysar (2006, 153).
[b] Rank within this dimension (1 = Upper, 2 = Upper Middle, 3 = Lower Middle, 4 = Lower).
[c] W = weight (3 for privilege, 2 for power, 1 for prestige).
[d] S = score.
[e] Cong = percent in 107th Congress/percent in society. Data from www.adherents.com.
[f] Coll = percent college graduates. Data from Kosmin and Keysar (2006, 157).
[g] There are differences between American, Southern, and Black Baptists, but Kosmin and Keysar (2006) do not distinguish between these types in the calculations on income and education, and www.adherents .com does not in its calculations on the religious affiliations of members of Congress.

there were three times as many in Congress as one might have expected, and 51 percent were college graduates. There also is considerable consistency among lower status groups. Muslims, the Church of God, and Jehovah's Witnesses scored low on all three dimensions. For example, the median income for members of the Church of God was $26,000 (less than half the median of groups in the Upper stratum). The Church of God had no members in the 107th Congress, and only 15 percent of its members were college graduates. Jehovah's Witnesses averaged only $24,000, also had nobody in Congress, and had very few members who had graduated from college.

There is a bit more inconsistency in the other strata. For example, Mormons' educational and income rankings were modest, yet there were three times as many Mormons in the 107th Congress than one might have expected based on Mormons' representation in the total population. On the other hand, Hindus ranked high in privilege ($51,000 median income) and prestige (67 percent college graduates), but were low in power (with no members in Congress). Buddhists ranked highest in prestige (42 percent college grads), lower in privilege ($38,000 median income), and lowest in power (no members in Congress). Nones were prosperous ($46,000 median income) and fairly highly educated (34 percent are college graduates), but they were underrepresented in the Congress (only one-tenth as many members as one might have expected).

But, even in these middle ranks, there is more consistency than inconsistency. The United Church of Christ is a good example. Its members were above average in education (49 percent college grads) and income ($41,000), and they were twice as likely to be in Congress as one might have expected. For Catholics, Methodists, Lutherans, Baptists, the Church of Christ, and the Assemblies of God, scores on any one dimension were within one rank of their scores on the other dimensions.

Thus, there has been a transition from an Old Upper stratum made up of Episcopalians, Congregationalists, and Presbyterians to a New Upper stratum made up of Episcopalians, Jews, Presbyterians, and Unitarian-Universalists. The four groups in the New Upper stratum sit atop a vertical ranking of other groups that have less access to power, privilege, and prestige.

THREE KEY QUESTIONS

Given the evidence showing that religious stratification arose in the colonial period, it is only natural to wonder about the conditions under which it developed. What were these conditions and how did they combine to produce an unequal ranking of religious groups so early in our history? Also, given the evidence that religious stratification persists but also has changed over time, we need to explore the forces that have produced these outcomes. For example, why does it appear that religious inequalities were larger in the colonial period and early 1800s than they are now? Why have some groups remained high in the rankings throughout U.S. history? Why have some groups remained low for 250 to 300 years? And why have some groups slipped in the rankings while others have improved over the years? Finally, what effects has religious stratification had on the society as a whole? To what extent and in what ways has it contributed to the well-being of the society? To what extent and in what ways has it caused problems that otherwise might not exist? Do its effects vary with changes in the magnitude of religious inequalities?

When we turn to the experts for explanations, we run into another problem. The people who specialize in the study of social stratification have not investigated these questions, so they don't have answers, and the people who specialize in religion and have studied religious group rankings have answers that are not very helpful. Instead of linking their interpretations to the conflict approach that researchers use to explain other types of stratification, religion scholars tend toward a functionalist view of religious group rankings. In a nutshell, they tend to see society as a social system made up of social institutions (marriage, education, religion, politics, economy) that contribute to society's equilibrium by meeting basic societal needs. They assume that leadership positions in these institutions are more important than other social positions, that these positions require the most talented members of society, and that higher wages and benefits are useful in getting the right people into these leadership positions and rewarding them for working for the well-being of the society as a whole. It is said that the people who occupy these leadership roles need rational and refined lifestyles that are compatible with their station in life. Protestantism's emphasis on work as a calling and the importance of self-discipline are seen as key elements in such a lifestyle. One might learn these things early in life as members of mainline denominations, or discover that the religious message emphasized in mainline denominations reinforces a rationalized view of the world that is suited to the life experiences of those in the middle strata. People of lesser means join religions offering beliefs and practices that are more suited to their life situations. Thus, religious differences in socioeconomic status are seen as arising out of society's need for order, as persisting because they reflect core cultural values, and as having functional consequences for the society as a whole.

Here's the problem. The vast majority of sociologists, including those who study stratification, abandoned this point of view years ago (Davidson and Pyle 2005). Their criticisms were that the functionalist argument makes unsubstantiated claims about society's need for order, does not account for social change and unrest, and justifies the status quo, including racism, sexism, and other inequalities (Ritzer 2010, Turner 2002, Ryan 1981). Also, as we have said elsewhere, Weber's thesis that Protestants are better suited for worldly success "treats religious groups as separate entities, which they are not (historically, theologically, or sociologically)," "blames the victims, which we are not willing to do in studies of race, class, and gender," and lacks empirical support (Davidson 2008, 373).[5]

Thus, we have a reality—religious stratification—that specialists in social stratification have tended to overlook (even deny) and which specialists in religion acknowledge but tend to interpret in terms of outdated theories and unverified hypotheses. Seeing this conundrum as a worthwhile challenge, we thought it would be fun to explore the origins, persistence and change, and consequences of religious stratification (something experts in stratification would not be inclined to do) by using conflict theory (something experts in religion would not be inclined to do). The risk would be doing something that neither group would like. On the other hand, the reward could be causing scholars who study stratification to give more consideration to the existence of religious stratification, and prompting scholars in the study of religion to make more use of conflict theory when they try to explain its origins, its persistence and change, and its consequences for society. We decided to go ahead with the project and let the chips fall where they may.

CONCLUSION

So far, we have stated our assumptions about religion's continuing role in modern society and presented evidence that religious stratification has been an important part of American life from colonial times to the present. We also have asked key questions about its origins, how it has persisted and changed over the years, and how it has affected our society. Here's the rub: specialists in the study of social stratification do not have any answers to these issues, and the explanations in the study of religion are antiquated and seriously flawed. We have taken this dilemma as a challenge: to increase interest in the study of religious stratification and to do so using an approach that could provide a more unified understanding of inequalities based on race, ethnicity, class, gender . . . and religion. Let's begin our journey by outlining that approach.

2

Our Approach

In chapter 1, we presented evidence showing that religious stratification has been a part of America's social fabric from the colonial period to the present. At the end of that chapter, we posed three questions: (1) How did religious stratification arise in America? (2) How has it persisted and changed? and (3) What have been its consequences for our society? The goal of this chapter is to explain our general approach to these questions.

ALTERNATIVES

Sociology offers us two general theories of stratification: functionalism and conflict theory (Hurst 2007; Kerbo 2006; Rothman 2005; Ryan 1981).[1] Broadly stated, functionalism presumes that society is a social system made up of interdependent parts, called social institutions. These institutions contribute to society's equilibrium by meeting basic societal needs, such as the need for knowledge (education), meaning (religion), affection and procreation (family), goods and services (business), and social coordination (government). If these institutions are to perform these functions, society must make sure that leadership positions in each sphere are held by its most talented members strictly on the basis of merit (without regard to extraneous or particularistic characteristics such as race, ethnicity, class, gender, and religion). One way to lure the most talented people into key positions in areas such as politics, business, and education is to attach socially significant rewards to these positions. These rewards include lofty incomes, substantial health benefits, lucrative retirement

packages, and social esteem. Once the most talented people are in leadership positions, these rewards provide incentives for leaders to do their
best on behalf of the society as a whole. From a functionalist perspective,
then, social inequality benefits the whole society because it helps society
locate its brightest and best, it puts them in positions through which they
can contribute to social order and equilibrium, and it rewards them for
persisting in these roles.

Conflict theorists have a very different view of society, seeing it as inherently unstable, often teetering on the brink of chaos. From a conflict point of
view, the source of this instability is the conflicting interests of social groups
that seek to maximize their own well-being, even if they harm other groups.
Traditionally, conflict theorists have stressed the importance of the divisions
between economic classes, but they also have examined conflicts between
races, ethnic groups, and the sexes. Those groups that succeed in gaining the
upper hand over others cultivate social policies and practices that serve their
own interests and work to the disadvantage of their competitors. Without
regard to merit or social stability, access to leadership positions in society
becomes tilted toward members of advantaged groups and away from others. In the process, some groups accumulate ever more influence, wealth,
and honor, while others have ever less access to these rewards and benefits.
These inequities breed social tension and alienation and, thus, destabilize
society. From this perspective, social inequality is intrinsically unfair and
social stratification is inherently dysfunctional.

The functionalist approach dominated the study of stratification through
the 1950s, when it was severely criticized by Tumin (1953) and others,
such as Mills (1956). It also was found wanting as social researchers tried
to explain the social turmoil of the 1960s. It didn't explain the actions of institutional leaders, who made decisions that were contrary to the well-being
of the society. Nor did it explain the actions of youth and minorities, who
participated in a variety of social movements that mocked national leaders,
questioned prevailing social policies, rallied behind countercultural figures,
and advocated radical changes in the American way of life.

As the limitations of functionalist theory became more and more apparent,
sociologists increasingly turned to the conflict approach. Some people—
including many in the sociology of religion—equated conflict theory with
Marxism, which they did not care for, so they clung to functionalism as
tightly as they could. However, most had a broader view of conflict theory
and embraced it. As younger scholars (who were products of the 1960s) came
into the field, they were predisposed to conflict theory. Over the past several
decades, scholars have developed several forms of conflict theory (some
Marxian, others Weberian) and have used them to study different types of

social inequality, with the emphasis being on race, class, and gender (Landry 2007; Ritzer 2010; Turner 2002).[2]

MAKING CHOICES, BLENDING IDEAS

For the same reasons that a majority of sociologists no longer use functionalist theory to study stratification, we do not think it is a useful launching pad for our analysis. We think the conflict approach is a better starting point. Because the Weberian version of conflict theory has produced many robust explanations in studies of stratification based on race, ethnicity, class, and gender, and because it is more suited to the study of religion, we have adapted it to our study of stratification based on religion.[3]

Our approach begins with conflict theory's focus on social groups. It permits the study of racial groups, ethnic groups, classes, and the sexes, but—unlike Marxian versions of conflict theory—it also makes room for religious groups. It assumes that religious groups—like the others—are important in their own right (not merely by-products of other social forces). It also borrows conflict theory's idea that all groups act on their self-interests, but it adds the notion that they also act in terms of their values (which may or may not coincide with their interests). Thus, it invites us to think about how groups and their members try to maximize their access to resources, and how they might encounter resistance from members who question the legitimacy of pursuing this goal. These provisions alone encourage more informed and nuanced analyses of religious groups than are possible with Marxian versions of conflict theory. In contrast to approaches that treat groups as relatively autonomous units and concentrate on their inner dynamics (as Weber [1958] did in *The Protestant Ethic and the Spirit of Capitalism*), ours imports conflict theory's emphasis on the interrelationships between groups. It highlights the role that power plays in these relationships, as groups try to shape the society according to their worldviews and worldly self-interests, build alliances with compatible groups, and attempt to overcome opposition from groups that have conflicting goals and objectives. Later in this chapter, we will explain how these ideas relate to the origins, persistence and change, and consequences of religious stratification. Before we do that, we need to define some key concepts.

Religious Groups

We use the term "religious groups" to refer to all of the faiths, churches, denominations, sects, and cults that are part of America's religious land-

scape. We chose this term, rather than the more common term "denomination," to be theologically neutral and inclusive. It encompasses Protestantism, Catholicism, Judaism, Islam, Buddhism, Hinduism, the Church of
Jesus Christ of Latter-day Saints (Mormons), the Universal Life Church
(aka Moonies), and many other faith groups. Some of these large groups
are subdivided into denominations (such as Episcopalians, Baptists, and
Presbyterians) or branches (such as Reform, Orthodox, Conservative, and
Reconstructionist Jews). Some of these subdivisions contain even more
specific groupings, such as American Baptists, Southern Baptists, and
independent Baptists. Our analysis will move between larger and smaller
subgroups, depending on the topic we are exploring at the time and the
availability of data.

We have included all of the historically significant and currently important
groups for which there also is enough data to draw reliable conclusions. Our
analysis includes groups that have deep roots in American history (e.g., the
Episcopal Church, which separated from the Church of England in 1789) and
others that are much younger (e.g., the Assemblies of God, which was
founded in 1914). It also includes groups that were brought to the United
States by immigrants (e.g., Islam, Catholicism, Hinduism), and others that
grew out of American soil (e.g., Mormons, Disciples of Christ, all of the
various black Protestant denominations). It does not include groups that have
played lesser roles in U.S. history (e.g., witchcraft) or for which there is insuf-
ficient national data (e.g., Native American religions).

Because the American experience includes so many different groups, some
categorizations and clarifications are needed. By using categories, we background some theological and organizational differences and foreground other
ones. Within Protestantism, we sometimes differentiate between "mainline"
Protestants and "evangelical" Protestants. This distinction highlights the differences between groups that have church-like qualities and those that have
sect-like qualities. Groups with church-like qualities (e.g., Episcopalians,
Presbyterians) tend to tolerate theological diversity within the group and affirm society, whereas groups with sect-like qualities (e.g., Southern Baptists,
Nazarenes) emphasize compliance with traditional group norms and tend to
reject society (Demerath 1965; Roberts 2004). At other times, we distinguish
between groups within these categories. Three mainline groups (i.e., Episcopalians, Presbyterians, and members of the United Church of Christ) are
considered "liberal," while all others are considered "moderate," with the
difference being in the extent of their internal diversity and their willingness to affirm society. Some evangelical groups (e.g., Southern Baptists)
are considered "fundamentalists" because they stress "right belief," whereas
others (e.g., the Assemblies of God) are considered "pentecostals" because

they emphasize the importance of the Holy Spirit in people's lives (Albanese 2007; Roof and McKinney 1987).

We alert readers to the fact that many groups are offshoots of other groups, and others are the result of mergers. These schisms and mergers produce name changes and, sometimes, odd nomenclature, which we try to clarify as we go along. For example, the Episcopal Church was an offshoot of the Church of England (Anglicanism), which was an offshoot of the Roman Catholic Church, which was an offshoot of Judaism. On the other hand, the United Methodist Church came into being in 1968 when the Methodist Church merged with the Evangelical United Brethren, which resulted from the merger of the Evangelical Church and the Church of the United Brethren in Christ. In 1957, the United Church of Christ was formed when the Evangelical and Reformed Church merged with the Congregational Christian Churches.

Race and ethnicity enter into our analysis when they define particular religious groups (e.g., the African Methodist Episcopal Church), or when they include large subgroups (e.g., German or eastern European Jews, Irish, Italian, or Latino Catholics).

Religious groups organize themselves in different ways: some more hierarchically, others more democratically. Most have some sort of state, national, and/or international structure (e.g., archdioceses, presbyteries, conferences, lobbying organizations) and a local presence (e.g., parishes, congregations, mosques, temples, and their equivalents). Although groups vary in the amount of authority they grant to these units, as a rule, they are responsible for coordinating the groups' internal affairs and pursuing their values and interests in society. These organizational variations affect the groups' capacities to build alliances with other groups and to lobby on behalf of their own values and interests.

The groups also have members. Historically, membership has been ascribed. People have inherited the religious affiliations of their parents, in much the same way they have inherited their race, ethnicity, class, and gender. Like these other traits, religious affiliation also has remained permanent throughout the course of people's lives.

As we said in chapter 1, some recent scholarship emphasizes the voluntary nature of these traits. To be sure, there is an element of choice in each of these attributes. For example, some people try to hide their racial identity or emphasize one aspect of their ethnic ancestry over another, and some people do change religions. When this happens, we need to consider people's religious affiliation during childhood and their religious affiliation in adulthood. Their religious upbringing affects their lifestyle and their life chances. It sets their lives in motion, and it has effects that are discernible long after they join another church. But we put these childhood influences in the background of our analysis and focus on the extent to which people's religious adherence during their adult years affects their access to social resources, such as political office.

Without denying the voluntary nature of some religious commitments, we call attention to the fact that the vast majority of people inherit their race, ethnicity, class, gender, and their religion (Nelsen 1988; Smith and Denton 2005), and three out of four people never leave the religion they inherited from their parents (Kosmin and Keysar 2006; Fischer and Hout 2006; Keister 2005). They do not switch religions or drop out of religion even when others might see that as the wise thing for them to do. Thus, for most Americans, religious group membership is far more ascribed and permanent than it is voluntary.

Generally speaking, membership in religious groups involves some more or less formal recognition by the groups (or group leaders) that individuals have fulfilled the group's membership requirements and that the group considers the individuals members. Membership requirements vary widely, from very exclusive groups that have very demanding requirements to very inclusive groups with less stringent requirements. As a rule, groups keep records of their members' names, addresses, and other information that might be needed.

Membership also includes the expectation that people will abide by the teachings of their group throughout the course of their lives. As we noted earlier, some groups (such as sects and cults) have very strict standards regarding such conformity. They have a variety of means by which they try to transmit their values and norms to their members, they insist that their members accept these principles, and they dismiss or excommunicate those who fail to do so. Other groups (such as denominations and churches) are more lenient. They permit a greater range of beliefs and practices, and they are reluctant to expel members from the group. Stricter groups produce higher levels of agreement than more lenient groups do. But even in stricter groups, individuals vary in the extent to which their beliefs and practices are aligned with group expectations. These individual variations are even more pronounced in less demanding groups (Glock and Stark 1965, 1966; Smith and Denton 2005; Stark and Glock 1968).

Obviously, when there is consensus on group norms, there is likely to be consistency in the group's behavior. For example, if church leaders and church members embrace a theodicy of "good fortune" (which treats inequality as just and fair), they will support public policies that perpetuate social inequality (Weber 1946b). If they favor a theodicy of "social justice" (which views inequality as unjust and unfair), they will work in unison for a more equal distribution of social resources (Davidson and Koch 1998; Davidson, Mock, and Johnson 1997; Davidson and Pyle 1999). When there are gaps between church leaders and church members, or among members, on such matters, various parts of the group may find themselves pursuing conflicting goals. For example, if church leaders espouse a theodicy of good fortune but church members prefer a theodicy of social justice, or leaders advocate social justice but members stress good fortune, the parties will find that they are at odds with each other on many issues related to public policy. When such gaps and conflicts arise in our analysis with regard to religious stratification, we will examine their implications.

Finally, we also need to consider people who do not belong to or identify with any particular religion. This category includes atheists who deny the existence of a god and don't want to be a part of any religious group, agnostics who aren't sure about the supernatural or the value of belonging to a particular religion, and believers who—for their own personal reasons—are not involved in organized religion. Like other researchers, we call all of these people "Nones."[4]

Scarce Resources

We are interested in people's access to three scarce resources: power, privilege, and prestige. Power is the ability to achieve one's goals or impose one's will on others, even in the face of opposition. It is a largely political term, but it is not limited to partisan politics. It includes all forms of political activity, such as participation in lobbies and social movements seeking various types of social reform, but especially election and appointment to public office. Privilege is an economic concept that includes the income people earn through work and the financial value of all other assets (such as one's home, automobiles, insurance policies, savings accounts, stocks, and bonds) that comprise one's wealth. Prestige refers to the social honor and respect that are attached to attributes such as the amount of education one attains, the type of work one does, where one lives, and the civic groups and social clubs one belongs to. For example, phrases like "he's got class" and "she's white trash" are clear indications of how people's lives are judged by others.

Some researchers have focused on one of these domains more than the other two. Dahrendorf (1959) called special attention to power and authority. Marx and Engels (1959, 1964) shined the spotlight on economic structures and processes. Warner and his colleagues (1942, 1943, 1949, 1963) put status in the foreground of their analyses. Following Weber's (1946a) lead, we consider all three domains. In chapter 1, for example, we examined people's access to leadership positions in the political arena (power), the business world (privilege), and the cultural domain (prestige). In forthcoming chapters, we will present additional evidence concerning the religious affiliations of public officer holders, such as U.S. presidents, cabinet officers, and Supreme Court justices. When we turn our attention to the economic sphere, we will examine the religious affiliations of the nation's corporate elite and people with various occupations. With regard to culture, our analysis focuses on the religious affiliations of college and university presidents and people with different amounts and types of education.

We assume that each domain is at least to some degree independent from the others. Each one stands on its own. No one is entirely reducible to any of the others. Thus, leadership positions in politics are not simply a function of success in business sphere. Leadership in business is not coterminous with either political or cultural prominence. And leadership in cultural enterprises is not the same as political and economic advantage.

However, we do not assume that the three domains are completely independent, or of equal importance. In our view, the economic arena is the most potent because it has considerable bearing on people's access to power and prestige and, ultimately, on their life chances. Power ranks second. Although the political arena is a sphere of its own, access to power sometimes is a function of privilege. Power also has implications for prestige that cannot be explained solely in terms of wealth, and its own effects on a person's life chances. Prestige ranks third. Cultural influence is often accorded to persons who have little or no privilege or political power, and it can affect one's access to both power and privilege. Yet leadership positions in the cultural arena are not necessarily reserved for leaders in politics and business.

Religious Stratification

The two components we have discussed so far—membership in religious groups and scarce resources—are related, with religious affiliation being the independent variable and access to resources being the dependent variable. Quite apart from other factors (such as race, ethnicity, class, and gender), religious affiliation affects people's access to power, privilege, and prestige. The extent to which it does can vary over time, but as we showed in chapter 1, it has had at least some effect from the very beginning of our society to the present. Thus, it has always been possible to put religious groups into four strata—Upper, Upper Middle, Lower Middle, and Lower—indicating their access to resources such as education, wealth, and political power.[5] This vertical ranking is called "religious stratification."

The amount of religious stratification at any given time is indicated by the Upper stratum's (or "elite" groups') access to resources relative to all other ("nonelite") groups' access to the same resources and by elite groups' access to resources relative to their percentage in the total population (i.e., the extent to which they are overrepresented among people with access to particular resources). Because religious stratification has been a fact of life in our society from the colonial period to the present, we want to know how it arose, how it has persisted and changed over the years, and how it has affected our society.

ORIGINS

Noel's (1968) theory of the origins of ethnic stratification in the American colonies provides a very compelling point of departure for our analysis of religious stratification. According to Noel, if the early stages of intergroup contact include ethnocentrism, competition, and differential power, ethnic stratification will result. Adapting this framework to fit our concern with religion, we argue that religious prejudice, competition, and differential power served as the necessary and sufficient bases for the emergence of religious stratification in colonial America (see figure 2.1).

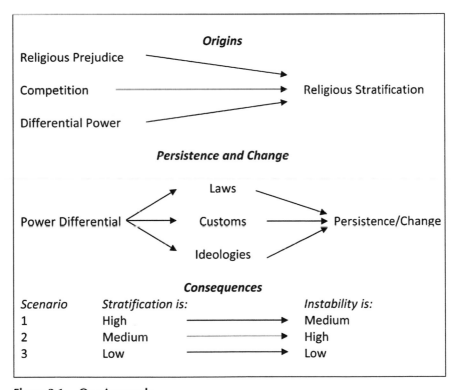

Figure 2.1.   Our Approach

First, we assume that religious prejudice provides the groundwork for a system of religious stratification. Religious prejudice is not a necessary correlate of religious commitment. In other words, religious groups are quite capable of viewing their differences with mutual respect, even admiration. However, when religious attachment is accompanied by feelings of superiority and inferiority, religious prejudice does tend to occur (Glock and Stark 1966; Hunsberger and Jackson 2005). When religious affiliation involves loyalty to one group and antipathy toward others, religion serves as a potential battle line along which people divide (Coleman 1956).

Religious prejudice by itself need not lead to religious stratification. The presence of competition structured along religious lines is an additional factor required for the emergence of stratification. Competition involves interaction between religious groups that are striving to achieve the same scarce goals (Menendez 1985). The competition may be for land, political office, civic freedoms, cultural influence, or any other resource that is mutually desired by competing groups. The more valuable the resources, the more intense the competition. The more intense the competition, the greater the likelihood that it will result in a system of religious stratification.

Religious prejudice and competition will not lead to a system of religious stratification unless some groups are able to get the upper hand on others. The ability to impose one's will on others is affected by the relative size of the groups, their organizational bases, and their other resources, such as the number of groups that support their values and interests. As a rule, a larger, better organized group with more resources will dominate smaller, less well organized groups with fewer resources.

Religious prejudice, competition, and differential power are mutually reinforcing. Competition often leads to harsh negative feelings among groups, which serves to reinforce the competition between groups (Turner and Singleton 1978). Power also influences prejudice. Groups with superior resources often portray subordinate groups in a negative fashion, thus perpetuating prejudice. Prejudice can perpetuate an imbalance of power, as negative beliefs legitimate the inequality and hamper efforts to equalize resources (Aguirre and Turner 2001). Power differentials also limit competition, which has the effect of increasing dominant groups' ability to impose their will on others.

In sum, religious prejudice identifies who the religious minorities are likely to be; competition offers the incentive for their subordination; and differential power promotes a structure of religious inequality. When all three of these conditions are present, religious inequality will become institutionalized in the form of religious stratification.

Institutionalization has three components: laws, customs, and ideologies. Laws are codes of conduct that indicate what types of behavior are legally acceptable and legally unacceptable. Laws are stipulated by local, county, state, and national legislative bodies and enforced by the police and the courts. We are interested in laws that call for or prohibit the use of religious affiliation as a criterion for the allocation of power, privilege, and prestige. Customs are recurring patterns of behavior. Our concern is with customs that increase or decrease religious groups' access to scarce resources. Finally, we are interested in the ideological foundation of religious stratification. We will examine cultural myths, beliefs, and values touting the superiority of elite religious groups and the inferiority of others' religions, or proclaiming the equality of all religious expressions.

In the next chapter, we use this framework to document the existence of religious prejudice, competition, and differential power in colonial America. We show that, by the American Revolution and the signing of the U.S. Constitution, religious adherence had become so embedded in the laws, ideologies, and customs of the colonies that there was a clear ranking of religious groups in terms of their access to social, economic, and political resources. Anglicans, Congregationalists, and Presbyterians ranked higher than all other groups. Unitarians and Quakers ranked below these three groups. Other Protestant denominations (such as Methodists and Baptists) formed a third stratum. Catholics, Jews, and people with no religious preference ranked lowest of all.

PERSISTENCE AND CHANGE

Once religious stratification exists, it can persist over time, and/or it can change. Under what conditions do these different outcomes occur? When and why does religious stratification persist, and what causes it to change over time? Is religious stratification as pronounced now as it was in the colonial period? Or, is it less pronounced? Why?

A functionalist perspective assumes that religious stratification persists and changes in response to developments in the society's core values and cultural patterns. As long as the core culture persists, so will the original pattern of stratification. If and when the cultural foundation of the society changes, new patterns of stratification are likely to emerge.

The contours of this view are found in much of the literature on religion in America. Modernization theory, for example, contends that in advanced societies universalistic processes of occupational allocation have increasingly displaced an ascriptive basis for inequality (Parsons 1971). In other words, as societies modernize, particularistic factors such as race, religion, and gender are no longer as important as they once were in influencing one's social placement. Groups that were formerly excluded from high ranking positions based on their ascribed status are freed for inclusion as full members of society. According to this view, whatever ascriptive barriers that remain are being eliminated. Thus, ascriptive bases for stratification are giving way to an open-contest system that rewards individuals in proportion to the special talents and abilities that they possess.

Modernization theorists argue that an increasing emphasis on meritocratic principles of occupational selection signaled the demise of the Protestant Establishment of the colonial period (Lemann 1992). They claim that by the mid-twentieth century, religiously rooted ingroup-outgroup distinctions were no longer as important as they once were in the selection of individuals for professional and managerial positions. In their view, insider ties are no longer a guarantee of superior social placement.

Baltzell (1976) argues that after World War II, meritocracy replaced class advantage as the determinant of movement into the elite ranks. Baltzell suggests that by the 1960s prestigious colleges became elitist meritocracies. Lemann (1992) agrees that meritocracy was the mechanism that brought the WASP establishment down. Owing to the implementation of meritocratic admissions at elite schools, children of the Protestant Establishment have had less access to positions of power and influence after midcentury.

Many analysts suggest that the cultural hegemony of Protestant values began to decline with the ratification of the First Amendment, which precluded any possibility of a religious establishment at the national level. Handy (1984), on the other hand, believes that a decline in Protestant power in America started after World War I, and he refers to the period between 1920 and 1940 as the "second disestablishment." Handy suggests that during this time, Protestantism was undergoing a spiritual decline, while the Roman Catholic Church was increasing its power in America. Handy agrees with Theodore H. White, who wrote that "American Protestant culture dominated politics until 1932—when all of it broke down in the marketplace" (quoted in Handy 1984, 181). Carroll and Roof (1993) also maintain that the social and cultural influence of mainline Protestant denominations began to wane after the 1920s. They note that "religious and secular changes have undermined the hegemony for denominations that once enjoyed considerable influence and status as 'custodians of the culture'" (1993, 23). During the 1940s and 1950s analysts began to speak of a tripartite division (triple melting pot) of Americans into three major religious blocks of Protestant, Catholic, and Jew (Herberg 1960). The implication was that America was not a Protestant nation. Some scholars began referring to a "post-Protestant" phase in America's development (Berger 1986). These analysts suggested that religious pluralism and an increase in the numbers of those with no religious preference signaled movement away from an earlier period when WASP elites were the dominant force in America.

Some observers (e.g., Hammond 1992) believe we have entered a third phase of disestablishment, which suggests an end to an historic linkage between Protestantism and power in American life. They point to laws expanding religious pluralism. James Fallows has suggested that the G.I. Bill "shifted power within the country, through a dramatic expansion of the college-educated class" (1988, 83), providing new opportunities for white ethnics to move up the ladder of success. In 1960 the nation elected its first Catholic president. The social movements of the 1960s are seen as further steps in the direction of religious, as well as racial, ethnic, and sexual equality.

We disagree with this overall perspective and the hypotheses it leads to. From our conflict perspective, once a clear ranking of religious elites and nonelites is established, it takes on a life of its own. The laws, ideologies, and customs favoring elites are so highly institutionalized and so effectively transmitted that people tend to take them for granted. Simply by conforming to the prevailing culture, elites (even those who are not talented and well trained) come to have greater access to society's resources than nonelites (including those who have leadership attributes). In short, the original pattern tends to reproduce itself.

Within this highly institutionalized structure of inequality, dominant groups act on the basis of their values and interests, which tend to overlap. As the principal architects of the society, elite groups tend to believe the prevailing social order and dominant culture are just and that they have a responsibility to preserve them. They also believe they deserve and should protect the advantages they have over subordinate groups. According to Weber (1946b), their theodicy of good fortune treats their worldly resources as blessings from God and, thereby, reinforces their worldly self-interests. Thus, they try to preserve laws, ideologies, and customs that accomplish these goals and/or adopt new ones that will have the same effect. There are always some elites whose values do not line up with their self-interests. Guided by a theodicy of social justice, they question existing social arrangements, which they believe result in unfair advantages for "insiders" and undeserved disadvantages for "outsiders" (Davidson and Koch 1998; Davidson and Pyle 1999; Davidson, Mock, and Johnson 1997). These dissident elites imagine a society with more egalitarian values and more inclusive social practices, but in their heart of hearts, they realize that the central tendency for elites is to preserve the laws, ideologies, and customs that have brought them so many advantages.

Nonelites, on the other hand, have a very different set of values and interests. Their central tendency is to believe that the prevailing social order and dominant culture are unfair and stacked against them. They imagine a more egalitarian society in which they and their children would have just as much access to resources as other religious groups do. Guided by a theodicy of social justice, their instinct is to overturn the laws, ideologies, and customs that sustain the current society and replace them with ones that are fairer and more inclusive—all of which would be in their best interest. However, there are always some nonelites whose values conflict with their worldly self-interests. Favoring a theodicy of good fortune, these people believe in the fairness of the "host" society and that, if they embrace its policies and wait for their turn, they will be as successful in life as those who rank above them at the moment. These people often gain leadership roles in nonelite religions and use these opportunities to inspire others, but they often encounter resistance from non-elites whose instincts are to question the legitimacy of the dominant society and seek laws, ideologies, and customs that will improve their lot in life.

Thus, elite and nonelite religious groups are not autonomous units; they are inseparable. Each party takes the other one into account as it acts, and each one's actions have implications for the other one. They are locked into a power relationship that involves considerable tension over their respective values and self-interests. To the extent that elites prevail over nonelites, the original system of religious stratification will persist. To the extent that non-elites prevail over elites, the original pattern is likely to change.

What determines which group will prevail? The outcome depends on the power differential between the elites and the nonelites (see figure 2.1). The differential is measured in terms of three factors. The first is group size, as indicated by a group's total membership or its membership as a percentage of the total population. All other things being equal, larger groups should have a power advantage over smaller groups. The second consideration is a group's organizational capacity. By that we refer to a group's organiza-tional infrastructure, including local congregations, ministerial associa-tions, church-sponsored schools and colleges, mission activities, and other organizational structures designed to enhance the institution's viability. The third factor is resources. This variable concerns a group's access to power, privilege, prestige, and alliances with members of other religious groups who share their values and/or interests. Thus, we will report data on the ebb and flow of religious group memberships, the expansion and contraction of religious organizations, and fluctuations in resources such as alliances with other groups.

Based on what we already know about immigration over the course of U.S. history, it is reasonable to hypothesize that the overall power differential is not as large as it once was, but that it still favors the historically elite religious groups. If so, elites should be able to preserve most of the laws, ideologies, and customs that were the pillars of the original ranking of religious groups. At the same time, assuming that the overall power gap has closed somewhat, we should find fewer legal and social barriers to nonelite progress.

Research on racial, ethnic, class, and gender stratification shows that non-elites and their allies have had more success in changing laws than they have had in changing long-standing customs and ideologies (Boger and Wegner 1996; Carr and Kutty 2008; Christiansen and Hoge-Esch 2006; Crosby et al. 2007). The civil rights and women's movements have succeeded in passing laws that make discrimination illegal, but segregation and cultural biases persist. The main reason for this is that efforts to change laws are usually made in the legislative bodies and courts, where reason and order are the norms and one only has to persuade a small number of people. Changing customs and ideologies involves other settings, where the emotions and conflicting self-interests of many more people are at stake.

Assuming the same thing is true in the case of religious stratification, even if laws favoring religious elites are struck down, proelite customs are likely to persist in the all-important spheres of politics, business, and education. These customs include political appointments favoring religious elites, hiring and promotion practices in the business world that have the same effect, and religious favoritism in educational institutions. Also, unlike scholars who contend that the pro-mainline Protestant ideology that developed in the colonial period has been supplanted by a multicultural ideology, we expect to find that the pro-Protestant bias remains a powerful cultural force in our society but now coexists—uncomfortably—with a more egalitarian or multicultural alternative.

Thus, we expect to find that the overall level of religious stratification has declined, but that religious groups in the upper stratum still have sizable advantages over nonelite groups in lower strata. We also expect to find some changes in the rankings of some groups, but a greater tendency toward continuity in the social hierarchy. The timeline for any changes remains to be seen.

CONSEQUENCES

Our final question is: So what? Does religious stratification really matter? Does it have any impact on society? If so, what kinds of effects does it have?

According to Kingsley Davis and Wilbert Moore (1945)—and other scholars working in the functionalist tradition—stratification does matter. It has consequences. Moreover, they argue, it is functional for society. It allows society to achieve its goals, one of which is social stability. In line with this view, Baltzell (1964, 48) claimed that "the WASP upper class [that] remained more or less in control of the American elite throughout the first three decades of [the twentieth] century . . . was perhaps inevitable, and, as it served to maintain a continuity of tradition at the level of leadership, it was a healthy thing for society as a whole."

Melvin Tumin (1953) and others working in the conflict tradition also believe that stratification matters, but that it produces social problems and destabilizes the society. Tumin describes eight ways in which stratification is problematic or dysfunctional for society. It

1. limit[s] the discovery of the full range of talent available in a society
2. set[s] limits upon the possibility of expanding the productive resources of the society
3. provide[s] the elite with the political power necessary to procure acceptance and dominance of an ideology which rationalizes the *status quo*
4. distribute[s] favorable self-images unequally throughout a population . . . [and] limit[s] the development of this creative potential
5. encourage[s] hostility, suspicion, and distrust among the various segments of a society and thus [limits] the possibilities of extensive social integration
6. distribute[s] unequally the sense of significant membership in the population
7. distribute[s] loyalty unequally in the population, [and]
8. distribute[s] the motivation to participate unequally in a population.

In Tumin's view, then, stratification does not contribute to the stability of the society; it fosters instability. It is not functional; it is dysfunctional. As we read the literature on race, ethnic, class, and gender stratification, the evidence supports Tumin's view. As all of the leading stratification texts show, instead of contributing to social equilibrium, these types of stratification foster social instability.

Religious stratification should have the same effect. Instead of being "a healthy thing" for the society, as Baltzell argued, its consequences should be negative. Rather than dealing with each and every one of the negative effects Tumin mentioned (some of which are virtually impossible to document, such as reaching society's potential), we concentrate on what we consider to be the basic difference between the functionalist and conflict perspectives: instead of contributing to social order, religious stratification leads to disorder; instead of fostering social stability, it produces social instability.

Thus, stratification's negative consequences are indicated by the absence of social integration and the presence of social problems that would not exist if it were not for religious inequality. The absence of integration is seen in the lack of ecumenical activities, cosponsorships, and partnerships that would unite elite groups and nonelite groups. The presence of problems is indicated by behaviors aimed at marginalized religions (e.g., hate groups, hate literature, killing, kidnapping, vandalism) and behaviors directed toward elite groups (e.g., protests, marches, self-defense organizations, boycotts, riots, strikes). The severity of these behaviors is indicated by the number of people who are killed or maimed, the amount of property that is destroyed, the number of police and fire personnel who are called upon to restore order, and the cost of the investigations and the prosecutions that follow. The more frequent these behaviors and the larger these numbers are, the more serious the problems are.

The severity of these problems varies with the amount of religious stratification in the society. Although the temptation is to hypothesize a straight, linear relationship between the two, the connection is more complex than that (Carter 2007; Ostby 2005, 2007). Medium to high levels of religious stratification should produce more problems than low levels, but there are good reasons to believe that medium levels of inequality will produce more problems than high levels. When there are medium levels of inequality, there is likely to be considerable tension related to the laws, ideologies, and customs having to do with religion's effects on access to resources. In other words, the rules of the game will be contested in virtually every arena (the courts and the streets), leading to almost constant turmoil. The legal, ideological, and behavioral issues are likely to be much clearer to both elites and nonelites when inequality is more pronounced. Under these conditions, elites have the situation under control and have no need to attack nonelites. Nonelites, on the other hand, understand the rules of the game and have almost no opportunity to change them.

Thus, we imagine three sets of circumstances (see figure 2.1). In the first scenario, religious stratification is very pronounced. The social, economic, and political gaps between elites and nonelites are huge. Elite groups have far more than their fair share of resources; nonelites have far less. These inequalities are so highly institutionalized in the laws, customs, and ideologies of the society that elites and nonelites alike take their respective stations in life for granted. Both groups simply do what they think is right and natural for people in different social strata. As they go about their lives, religious stratification fosters divisions between them. Because the inequality is so extreme and prevailing laws, ideologies, and customs are so highly institutionalized, these divisions tilt toward the absence of solidarity more than they do toward the presence of disorder. Although there are occasional flare-ups, religious stratification's destabilizing effects tend to be muted.[6]

In the second scenario, religious stratification is an undeniable social fact, but it is less pronounced. Elites have more access to resources than nonelites, but the gap between the two is not quite as large as in the first scenario. Elites are more nervous about their lot in life, and nonelites are less inclined to accept their status as a permanent condition. Under these conditions, tensions between elites and nonelites are likely to increase. As elite groups try to solidify their loftier status and nonelites challenge the prevailing social arrangements, the frequency of disruptive behaviors and the magnitude of social problems increase. Religious stratification's destabilizing effects become more pronounced.

In the third scenario, religious stratification is minimal. Religious equality is close at hand. By and large, laws, ideologies, and customs do not favor one group over others, and all groups have equal access to resources. Under these circumstances, whatever destabilizing effects that do remain are also minimal.

If religious stratification was most pronounced in the colonial period and early 1800s (as we predicted earlier), that is when its destabilizing effects should be most muted (scenario 1), and if it has been less pronounced in more recent years (as we also hypothesized), that is when its negative effects should be most disruptive (scenario 2). As we see it, the third scenario expresses the hopes of many Americans, but it is more of a dream than a reality. We test these hypotheses in chapter 6.

CONCLUSION

In chapter 1, we indicated our interest in explaining the origins of religious stratification in America, its persistence and change over time, and its impact on the society. In the present chapter, we have outlined the approach we use to explore these issues. Utilizing a conflict approach, we focus attention on the interaction between religious ingroups and outgroups. We pay particular attention to the roles that religious prejudice, competition, and differential power played in the formation of religious stratification during America's colonial period. To explain the persistence of and changes in religious stratification over time, we examine the power relationships between dominant and minority religions as they deal with the laws, customs, and ideologies that are the structure of religious stratification. The relationship between groups in these arenas affects the extent and nature of religious stratification over time. Finally, we examine the destabilizing effects that religious stratification has on society. We expect to find that it produces social problems that would not exist if it were not for religious groups' differential access to society's resources. We predict that these problems are less pronounced when religious stratification is most severe and most destabilizing when religious stratification is less extreme. It is time to examine these expectations, starting with the question of origins: under what conditions did religious stratification emerge in colonial America?

3

Origins

Although explorers like Columbus had reached the New World in the late 1400s and the 1500s, the Great Migration from Europe to the New World didn't really begin until the early 1600s. For the next 150 years or so, people from all over Europe poured into seaports and settlements like Jamestown, Virginia (1607), Plymouth, Massachusetts (1620), and Savannah, Georgia (1733). Estimates are that by 1776, roughly 2.5 million people lived in the land area covered by the thirteen original colonies (U.S. Department of Commerce 1976, 2005).[1]

Contrary to popular images of the colonists as a very religious people, the fact is that the vast majority of them had no religious ties (Finke and Stark 1992). Those who did have a religion belonged to a variety of religious groups. The largest groups were Congregationalists and Presbyterians. Each group was about 3 percent of the total population and one-fifth of all religious adherents. Next in size were Anglicans and Baptists, each at about 2 percent of the total population and 15 percent of church members. Quakers were about 1.5 percent of all colonists and about 9 percent of all religious adherents. So were members of the Reformed Church (mainly Dutch but increasingly German). In addition to these groups, there were a number of smaller groups, including Lutherans, Methodists, Moravians, other Protestants, Unitarians, Catholics, and Jews.

Congregationalists were concentrated in the New England colonies, but almost nonexistent elsewhere. Presbyterians were a sizable group in both the south and the middle colonies of Pennsylvania, Virginia, and New Jersey, but only a small percentage of the adherents in New England. Baptists were most likely to be in the southern colonies, and accounted for just 8 percent of adherents in the middle colonies. Anglicans were more numerous in the southern and the middle colonies than New England. Quakers tended to be in the middle colonies and were less concentrated in the South and New England. Reformeds, Lutherans, Methodists, and Catholics were small in number but most likely to be found in the middle colonies (Finke and Stark 1992).

Thus, the religious landscape in New England was dominated by Congregationalists. The middle colonies were heavily Presbyterian, but also had sizable numbers of Quakers and Anglicans. In the southern colonies, there were three large groups: Baptists, Anglicans, and Presbyterians.

If these religious groups had been tolerant of one another, cooperated with one another, and had similar resources, the most likely outcome would have been religious pluralism. Under such conditions, the groups would have been on a level playing field. But that was not the case in the colonies. There was a great deal of religious prejudice, lots of competition between religious groups, and significant differences in resources. As we predicted in chapter 2, this combination of circumstances gave rise to religious stratification.

RELIGIOUS PREJUDICE

The fifteenth and sixteenth centuries in Europe had been marred by years of religious warfare (Housley 2003). As the Protestant Reformation spread across Europe, and Protestant denominations became the official state churches in places such as England (Anglicanism), Scotland (Presbyterianism), and the Netherlands (the Dutch Reformed Church), anti-Catholicism became more and more virulent. The Catholic Church, which remained dominant in Italy, Spain, France, and Portugal, became increasingly defensive and hostile toward Protestants and other "heretics." There also were animosities between radical Protestant reformers (such as the Puritans and Anabaptists) and those Protestants who sought more limited reforms (such as Anglicans and Lutherans). Historic tensions between Christians, Jews, and Muslims persisted throughout this period.

Settlers coming to America brought these religious prejudices with them from Europe. With the majority of religious adherents being Protestants, Catholics were the foremost target of derision and persecution. In the colonies, as in England, Catholicism was viewed as heresy and Roman Catholics were perceived as unwelcome interlopers. As a consequence, anti-Catholicism was rampant during the entire colonial period (Curran 1963). Ellis (1956, 19–20) notes that "the transplantation of English religious prejudice to America . . . struck such enduring roots in new soil that it became one of the major traditions in people's religious life." For the Puritan in colonial America, Catholicism was a corruption of the Christian message. A Massachusetts statute of 1647 stated that any Jesuits, priests, and missionaries in the colony should be treated as "an enemy to the true Christian religion" (Hennesey 1981, 57). In a sermon in 1759 Reverend Jonathan Mayhew denounced Catholics as blind and furious zealots out to butcher Protestants (Marty 1986, 141). The nation's most eminent political leaders added fuel to the fire of anti-Catholicism. Patriot Samuel Adams fanned the flames of anti-Catholicism in his declaration that "much more is to be dreaded from the growth of Popery in America than from the Stamp Act" (quoted in Hennesey 1981, 56).

Although there were very few Jews in the colonies, they too were condemned by Christian clerics and government officials. In the 1650s the director general of New Amsterdam (which later became New York) castigated the Jews when he wrote to the Dutch West India Company and advised that "the deceitful race—such hateful enemies and blasphemers of the name of Christ—be not allowed to further infect and trouble this new colony" (quoted in Pratt 1967, 23). Puritan minister Samuel Willard noted in one of his sermons in 1700 that Jews were "a scorn and reproach to the world" (quoted in Hertzberg 1989, 34). Despite this general hostility toward Jews during the colonial period, some Jews did prosper during the colonial era, and they were treated with civility in many localities (Brilliant 1997; Marcus 1970).

Upstart Protestant groups, such as Baptists, also were subject to condemnation. Even though these up and coming faiths were fully part of the Protestant tradition, they were not fully accepted by the established faiths, which regarded them as "dissenters." Religious prejudice bubbled to the surface in the eighteenth century with the proliferation of dissenting sects in the South. Writing in 1760, Parson Reed, an Anglican minister from North Carolina, said:

> The Anabaptists are obstinate, illiterate, and grossly ignorant, the Methodists ignorant, censorious and uncharitable, the Quakers rigid, but the Presbyterians are pretty moderate except here and there [we see] a bigot or rigid Calvinist. As for papists, I cannot learn there are above 9 or 10 in the whole Country. (Quoted in Lefler and Newsome 1973, 106)

Intense animosity existed between Presbyterians and Baptists in the south. One observer noted that Baptists in eighteenth century North Carolina were clearly not up to the social level of more respectable churchgoers when he said, "A Presbyterian would sooner marry ten of his children to members of the Church of England than one to a Baptist" (quoted in Gaustad 1962, 12). Another quipped that he would "rather go to hell than be obliged to hear a Baptist in order to go to heaven" (quoted in Sweet 1965, 304).

Although intergroup relations at times were characterized by tolerance and civility (such as in Maryland prior to 1689), interfaith condemnation was widespread during most of the colonial period. With Anglicans, Congregationalists, and Presbyterians on one side, and Catholics, Jews, and members of Protestant sects on the other, religious bigotry set the stage for religious inequality.

COMPETITION

An additional requirement for stratification is competition over scarce rewards. As we indicated earlier, the competition between groups must be understood in relation to their political resources. More powerful groups used government subsidies and suppression to limit competition with less powerful groups, and less powerful groups resisted. We examine three colonies—Virginia, Pennsylvania, and Massachusetts—with quite different political contexts.

Virginia

As in the other southern colonies, Anglicans in Virginia gained the upper hand quite early on, becoming the established religion. Virginia parishes were organized around a plantation society in which wealthy planters served as Anglican wardens and vestrymen dominating a weak clergy. A pronounced social divide existed between the planter aristocracy and the plain people (Isaac 1982). Anglicans were stubbornly resistant to extending political and religious freedoms to those outside of the Anglican communion, and they attempted to suppress dissenters, who represented a challenge to the hegemony of the ecclesiastical establishment.

In the eighteenth century, authorities tried to limit competition from Protestant sects, which were rapidly growing in Virginia's frontier regions. The crowds who thronged to hear the Great Awakening revivalists in the 1740s were overwhelmingly from the lower strata (Nash 1986), and Virginia's Anglican planter class acted to thwart the sectarian bodies, who were challenging the establishment over power and control over the direction of church and society. Virginia leaders feared that the rapid growth of Presbyterian and Baptist congregations would undermine the authority of the establishment in the western and southern settlements. Baptist preachers mocked the moral and spiritual credentials of Anglican ministers, and they were critical of gentry amusements, such as cock fighting, horse racing, gambling, and drinking. The Baptist denunciation of the gentry style of life resonated with many members of the community (Isaac 1974). The dissenters had made some converts in the Anglican stronghold of the Tidewater, and had even converted some vestrymen. In response, the Virginia legislature in 1759 dissolved several vestries for including non-Anglican vestrymen (Longmore 1996).

After the 1760s, confrontations between Baptists and Anglicans boiled over. The Baptists in 1770 probably outnumbered Anglicans in Virginia (Billings, Selby, and Tate 1986), and they were unwilling to conform to the legal requirements of licensing their ministers to preach only at fixed locations. On discovering their transgressions, angry supporters of the establishment responded with a vengeance, sometimes assaulting itinerant ministers and acting with the full approval of religious and civil authorities. In one instance, the parson of the parish in Caroline County came with his clerk, the sheriff, and others and beat and whipped a Baptist leader (Isaac 1974). Baptists and New Side Presbyterians were mistreated, beaten, and sent to jail for "disturbing the peace." Baptist preachers who were arrested were accused of carrying out a mutiny against the authority of the land. Despite such efforts by the Anglican establishment to curtail the activities of dissenter bodies, sectarian religion in Virginia was rapidly expanding in the late colonial period.

Pennsylvania

Unlike the southern colonies, the middle colonies—with the exception of New York—did not have an official ecclesiastical establishment. Pennsylvania provides an example of a religiously heterogeneous colony in which a variety of faiths competed with one another over scarce resources in an establishment-free context.

Although the majority of Pennsylvania's early settlers were English and Welsh Quakers, within a few years numerous faiths were represented in the colony. In none of the colonies at the end of the colonial period was there so great a variety of religious groups as there was in Pennsylvania (Schwartz 1987).

Despite a high degree of religious diversity in the colony, a Quaker and Anglican minority emerged within Pennsylvania's power structure (Baltzell 1982; Nash 1968, 1986). Quakers ruled the Pennsylvania Assembly during the entire period. During the eighteenth century, Anglicans advanced into the upper ranks of Pennsylvania society (Butler 1978). However, those outside of the Quaker and Anglican traditions, although significantly represented in the larger population, were hard pressed to obtain leadership positions in Pennsylvania politics.

With the swelling of Ulster immigration to Pennsylvania in the eighteenth century, Presbyterians posed a threat to Quaker political control (Bonomi 1986). But Quakers were unwilling to grant the Presbyterians a proportionate share of political power. By 1740 Quakers accounted for no more than one-quarter of Pennsylvania's inhabitants, but they retained political power by weighting representation in the assembly toward those counties where Quakers were most heavily represented. To illustrate, in 1770 Pennsylvania's heavily Quaker eastern counties were able to elect twenty-four assemblymen, whereas the equally populous non-Quaker western counties chose only ten (Ryerson 1986). Thus through manipulating a system of legislative representation in their favor, Quaker lawmakers nullified attempts by Presbyterians to assume the leadership in the Pennsylvania Assembly. The only Pennsylvania legislator to gain great political power who was neither a Quaker nor an Anglican was Benjamin Franklin.

Massachusetts

Congregationalism (Puritanism) became the established religion in all of the New England colonies except Rhode Island, and in no colony was there a closer tie between church and state than Massachusetts. From 1636 to 1686 Puritan magistrates controlled the Massachusetts government. During the initial phase of settlement, voting and office-holding privileges were extended only to orthodox Congregationalists, and settlers who did not conform to the orthodox church were rooted out with dispatch.

However, by the eighteenth century Anglican advances threatened Puritan control. Anglicans, like other dissenters, were initially banned from settlement and denied citizenship rights and religious freedoms. However, English officials put pressure on colonial officials to favor the Church of England, and Anglicans were actively expanding in New England during the 1700s. The Church of England was appointing ministers in areas of New England already served by Puritan clergy, and the Anglican Church used its financial power to lure Puritan ministers to the Anglican communion through the promise of a better salary. To counter these measures, Puritans engaged in a mission to plant new churches in New England to head off Anglican advances. New England Puritans worked together with Presbyterians in the middle colonies in response to the fear that the introduction of an Anglican bishop in North America would restrict their civil and religious liberties. Moreover, Puritans in New England worked closely with their co-religionists in England. Owing in part to these ties between Puritans in America and England, the efforts of Anglicans to send a bishop to North America were continually defeated (Bridenbaugh 1962). Thus, from the late 1600s until the Revolutionary period, Puritans and Anglicans were involved in heated competition in Massachusetts and other New England colonies.

DIFFERENTIAL POWER

Religious prejudice and competition by themselves are no guarantee of religious stratification. Prejudice and competition could lead to "conflict, symbiosis, or a pluralist equilibrium," in which groups have relatively equal control over their destinies (Noel 1968, 163). However, when prejudice and competition are accompanied by differential power, some groups are more able than others to forge a social order that reflects their values and interests. The degree of power is influenced by the size of a group, its level of organization, and its control of resources.

Congregationalists, Presbyterians, Anglicans, and Baptists were the largest groups. Congregationalists had the advantage of size in New England, and for most of the colonial period Anglicans were most numerous in the South. Until 1740 Anglicans and Congregationalists had more congregations than all other groups combined (Gaustad 1962, 3–4). By the time of the Revolution, Presbyterians had more congregations than Anglicans, and Baptists were also experiencing rapid growth (Paullin 1975, 50). Lutherans, Roman Catholics, and Dutch and German Reformed bodies had fewer congregations, especially during the earliest phases of settlement.

During the initial phases of the colonial period, Congregationalists and Anglicans also had the most impressive organizations. The Church of England had ties to the British crown, and its support from the Society for the Propagation of the Gospel in Foreign Parts (SPG) gave it a distinct advantage over other denominations (Bonomi 1986). In the 1600s Congregationalists dominated organized religion in New England. Quakers were well organized in the middle colonies, establishing a centralized institutional structure in the 1680s (Butler 1978). In the eighteenth century Presbyterians had established a strong ministerial organization that monitored clergy activities and contributed to denominational growth (Butler 1990). Baptists also established a ministerial association in the first decade of the 1700s, but they had not penetrated the South very well prior to the Great Awakening. German Reformed and German Lutheran churches established ministerial organizations in the 1740s, but the continued use of the German language limited the denominations' proselytizing activities. Similarly, the Dutch language was used almost exclusively in Dutch Reformed services until the time of the Revolution (DeJong 1978). The first American Methodist conference did not meet until 1773, and Methodists became an independent ecclesiastical body in 1784. Throughout the colonial period Catholics were hampered by discriminatory laws and oaths.

Although a group's size and organization are important, the primary determinant of power is control of resources. The dominant faiths during the colonial period benefited from superior economic and political resources, and they used kinship ties, patronage arrangements, and the intervention of foreign governments to institutionalize their growing advantages. With prejudice as their justification, competition as their incentive, and differential power as their means, they transformed emergent inequality into a more permanent system of stratification.

Kinship networks were entangled in colonial America, as wealthy families formed a coterie of their own and married among themselves generation after generation (Daniels 1986). Family dynasties worked to the benefit of the churches identified with the upper rank of citizens. Kinship ties and revolving appointments were quite common among the Anglican First Families of Virginia (Chickering 1986), the Quaker elite in Pennsylvania (Ryerson 1986), and the Puritan Boston Brahmins (Baltzell 1982; Snell 1986). For the first families in the colonies, religion was an important identity element, and these families were in a strong position to further the interests of the churches to which they belonged.

Patronage arrangements and the power of appointment perpetuated the advantages of the dominant faiths. The English sovereign could influence religion in the royal colonies through gubernatorial appointments and the awarding of colonial charters (Labaree 1967). In most of the colonies the king or proprietor appointed the upper house, and in the case of New Jersey, the upper house was dominated by Anglicans, who controlled the distribution of every civil and military commission in the province (Purvis 1986). Patronage arrangements allowed Quakers to dominate civil authority in Pennsylvania. In eastern Pennsylvania until the middle of the eighteenth century, the whole ladder of public service from township constable to county sheriff to assemblyman remained thoroughly under Quaker control (Ryerson 1986).

Another important source of power is the ability to get a foreign government to intervene on one's behalf. The English crown worked to prop up the Anglican Church in the colonies through gubernatorial appointments and by funding missionary activities designed to propagate the interests of the church in the colonies.

New York serves as a good case to illustrate the degree to which colonial officials and the English crown were active in working to advance the interests of the Anglican Church. Between 1693 and 1708 the Church of England, though it had little support among the populace, was established in New York, and a religious test was prescribed for holders of public office. Roman Catholicism was declared an illegal form of worship, and "increasingly religious affiliation became the measure of a citizen's privileges and standing within the colony, with the Anglican establishment providing the standard" (Pratt 1967, 37). How did Anglicanism come to represent the standard of influence in a colony in which "virtually every religion was represented but the Anglican" (Pratt 1967, 27)?

The crown's interest in promoting Anglicanism was decisive. The governors of New York were ordered by the crown to further the cause of the Anglican Church. In 1693 the New York Assembly passed the Ministry Act for the support of ministers of religion, but the legislation did not mention an establishment of the Church of England. However, the ambiguous wording of the act allowed New York governors to interpret it as establishing the Anglican Church. In 1701 Lord Cornbury, a zealous advocate for the Anglican cause, assumed the governorship, and he used both legal and underhanded measures to establish Anglicanism in the colony. Cornbury was able to force an opposition faction from power in the New York Assembly and steer important religious legislation through the assembly with little difficulty.

Cornbury benefited from the work of the Society for the Propagation of the Gospel in Foreign Parts (SPG), which was chartered by King William in 1701 to strengthen the Anglican Church in the American colonies. Immediately upon its formation, the SPG began soliciting contributions in England from wealthy supporters and from Anglican congregations to supplement the salaries of Anglican ministers in the colonies and to recruit clergy for America. The SPG sent fifty-eight ministers to New York, virtually the only Anglicans who ever served there. Supplied with Anglican ministers, Cornbury filled the parishes. He frequently encountered resistance and resorted to force to overcome it.

In 1704 Rye parish in Westchester County received an Anglican minister, but the town of Bedford lying within the parish had a strong dissenting church opposed to settling the newcomer. Governor Cornbury had to arrest and jail the justice of the peace and pastor of the Bedford church before the local people would submit to having an Anglican minister (Pratt 1967). Other parishes in New York received SPG missionaries. Only with gubernatorial arm twisting and the pressure of influential residents were Anglican ministers able to remain in these parishes, some of which had large Presbyterian populations (Pointer 1988).

Cornbury in 1705 expanded the scope of the Ministry Act and settled Anglican churches in other county parishes. Dissenters lacked the means for effective protest of the governor's actions. In 1707 Cornbury again pitted his will against Presbyterians, who were outspoken critics of the Anglican establishment. Two Presbyterian ministers, Francis Makemie and John Hampton, had come from Virginia and Maryland to build up the Presbyterian Church in New York. Cornbury had them arrested for violating his private instructions against preaching without a license. A grand jury handpicked by Cornbury then returned an indictment to the charge against Makemie. The trial jury, however, acquitted Makemie of the charges.

Actions like these indicate the ability of ascendant groups whose power is not yet institutionalized to draw on political and organizational resources to advance their own interests and suppress others. Royal instruction backed by gubernatorial authority prevailed over popular sentiment for the support of dissenter churches in New York and other colonies. The ability of political appointees to promote the interests of favored churches, even against the will of the people and the legislature, illustrates how superior resources can be used to solidify the power of the dominant faiths.

THE INSTITUTIONALIZATION OF RELIGIOUS INEQUALITY

According to our theory, religious groups that (a) harbor prejudices toward other faiths, (b) struggle with these faiths over access to scarce resources, and (c) have political advantages over their adversaries are able to transform religious inequality into an institutionalized system of religious stratification. The use of religion as a criterion for access to resources becomes embedded in the laws, ideologies, and customs of the society.

Laws

Table 3.1 provides evidence of how much religion was built into the laws of each colony.

The first column shows that religious establishments were maintained in nine of the thirteen colonies. Anglicans were the representatives of the official church in the mother country, and they were established in New York and the five southern colonies (Virginia, South Carolina, North Carolina, Georgia, and Maryland). Puritans (Congregationalists) were established in three New England colonies (Massachusetts, New Hampshire, and Connecticut). These religious establishments endured an average of 117 years (from 19 years in Georgia to 202 years in Massachusetts). Only four colonies— New Jersey, Pennsylvania, Delaware, and Rhode Island—did not maintain religious establishments.

The second and third columns indicate that all of the colonies, including those that lacked religious establishments, imposed legal restrictions on the basis of religious affiliation, and most of the colonies had limits on the toleration of religious dissent. On average, these restrictions were in place for well over one hundred years. Catholics were the chief victims of antitoleration laws, and they were excluded from toleration (denied legal residence) in eleven of the thirteen colonies at some time during the colonial period. Jews

Table 3.1. Legal Status of Religions in Colonial America

Colony	Religious Establishment?	Religious Qualification for Voting or Office-Holding?	Toleration of Religious Dissent?
Virginia	Anglican (1619–1776)	Catholics excluded from office (1641–1699) Catholics disenfranchised (1699–1776) Catholics, atheists, non-Christians, non-Trinitarians excluded from office (1699–1776)	Catholics not tolerated (1609–1679) Nonconformists not tolerated (1642–1654) (1660–1679) Quakers not tolerated (1658–1679) Toleration of all (1679–1690) Toleration of all except Catholics (1690–1776)
South Carolina	Anglican {Carolina Charter} (1663–1669) Anglican {Carolina Constitution} (1669–1704) Anglican (1704–1778)	Assembly members must be Anglican (1704–1706) Voting and office-holding limited to professing Christians (1721–1759) Voting and office-holding limited to Protestants (1759–1778)	Toleration of all {Carolina Charter} (1663–1669) Toleration of all theists {Carolina Constitution} (1669–1697) Toleration of all Christians except Catholics (1697–1778)
North Carolina	Anglican (1715–1776)	Officeholders must take anti-Catholic oaths (1715–1776)	Toleration of all Christians except Catholics (1715–1776)
Georgia	Anglican (1758–1777)	Catholics disenfranchised and excluded from office (1654–1658) Assembly members must be Protestants (1761–1789)	Toleration of all except Catholics (1732–1777)
Maryland	Anglican (1702–1776)	Catholics disenfranchised and excluded from office (1654–1658) Catholics excluded from office (1689–1776) Catholics disenfranchised (1718–1776)	Toleration of all Christians (1637–1649), except those denying Holy Trinity or Christ as son of God (1649–1654) (1658–1687) Toleration of all Christians except Catholics (1654–1658) Toleration of all (1687–1703) Toleration of all except Catholics (1703–1776)

(continued)

Table 3.1.   Continued

Colony	Religious Establishment?	Religious Qualification for Voting or Office-Holding?	Toleration of Religious Dissent?
Delaware	No establishment	Voting and office-holding limited to Christians (1701–1792)	Toleration of all who profess one almighty God (1701–1706)
		Catholics excluded as representatives (1734–1776)	Toleration of all Christians (1706–1776)
Pennsylvania	No establishment	Catholics excluded from office (1689–1776)	Toleration of all who profess one almighty God (1682–1692) (1700–1706)
		Voting and office-holding limited to professing Christians (1701–1776)	Catholics not tolerated (1692–1700)
		Legislators must be Christians (1776–1786)	Toleration of Trinitarian Christians (1706–1776)
New Jersey	No establishment	Officeholders must be Christians (1683–1702, E. Jersey) (1693–1702, W. Jersey)	Toleration of all (1676–1702, W. Jersey)
		Officeholders must take anti-Catholic oaths (1702–1776)	Toleration of all who profess one God (1683–1693, E. Jersey)
			Toleration of all Christians except Catholics (1683–1693, E. Jersey)
			Toleration of all except Catholics (1702–1776)
New York	Dutch Reformed Church {New Amsterdam} (1638–1664)	Officeholders must take anti-Catholic oaths (1689–1777)	Toleration of all Christians (1665–1673) (1683–1686)
	Anglican (1693–1777)	Catholics disenfranchised (1701–1777)	Toleration of all (1674–1683) (1686–1689)
		Jews disenfranchised (1737–1777)	Toleration of all except Catholics (1689–1777)
Rhode Island	No establishment	Voting and office-holding limited to Protestants (original year uncertain, 1789)	Toleration of all (1663–1789)
Massachusetts	Congregational (1631–1833)	Voting and office-holding limited to Congregationalists (1631–1665) or Englishmen with ministerial certification (1665–1691)	Catholics not tolerated (1620–1687)
			Baptists not tolerated (1644–1682)
		Officeholder must take anti-Catholic oaths (1691–1820)	Quakers not tolerated (1656–1665)
			Toleration of all (1687–1689)
			Toleration of all Christians except Catholics (1691–1778)

Table 3.1. Continued

Colony	Religious Establishment?	Religious Qualification for Voting or Office-Holding?	Toleration of Religious Dissent?
Con-necticut	Congregational (1639–1818)	Governor must be Congregationalist (1639, final year undetermined) Officeholders must take anti-Catholic oaths (1662–1818)	Catholics not tolerated (1662–1687) Quakers not tolerated (1656–1675) (1702–1705) Toleration of Protestant dissenters (1668–1687) Toleration of all (1687–1689) Toleration of all except Catholics (1689–1818)
New Hamp-shire	Congregational (1682–1819)	Voting and office-holding limited to Protestants (1680–1682) Officeholders must take anti-Catholic oaths (1682–1777) Officeholders must be Christians (1777–1784)	Toleration of all Protestants (1680–1687) Toleration of all (1687–1689) Toleration of all except Catholics (1689–1784)

Sources: Cobb (1968); Cornelison (1970); Curran (1963); Labaree (1967); Marcus (1970); McKinley (1969); Miller (1900); Stokes (1950); Thorpe (1909).

were excluded from toleration in eight of the colonies, and atheists were denied toleration in seven colonies. Antitoleration laws also applied to Quakers in Massachusetts, Connecticut, and Virginia; non-Trinitarian Christians in Pennsylvania and Maryland; Baptists in Massachusetts; and "nonconformists" in Virginia. Although such restrictive legislation involving religion was no guarantee of its strict enforcement, the sheer number of these legal measures indicates the importance of religious affiliation as a factor affecting civic participation.

Religious affiliation was an important determinant of voting and office-holding privileges (McKinley 1969; Miller 1900). Catholics were denied toleration or otherwise prevented from voting in twelve of the thirteen colonies; atheists could not vote in ten of the colonies, and Jews were denied the franchise in nine. Restrictions on office-holding were even more widespread. Legislation denying Catholics office-holding privileges (usually taking the form of anti-Catholic oaths required of officeholders) was on the books in all of the provinces. Atheists were excluded from office in twelve colonies, and Jews and other non-Christians were prevented from holding office in eleven of the thirteen colonies.

Thus, legislation relating to establishment status, toleration, voting, and office-holding reflected the prevailing beliefs and ideologies of the time. It indicated the high degree to which a structure of religious inequality was normalized and institutionalized during the colonial period.

Colonial laws gave special attention to the role of religion in society. For example, the first legislature assembled in America was the Virginia Assembly, which in 1619 compelled every person to attend Anglican services twice on Sunday or be fined or bodily punished. Other colonies had their own prescriptions regarding church attendance and tax support for clergy. In those colonies with religious establishments, all residents, even those who might prefer going to other churches, were taxed to support the ministers and churches of the established faiths. The ministers who served the established churches enjoyed a monopoly that gave them fees in officiating at baptisms and marriage and death ceremonies. Holding an official religious position in the colonial establishments provided men with a means of earning a living, and some ministers were accused of abusing their offices and pandering to the interests of the well-to-do, who often served on church governing boards.

Ideologies

Ideologies are values and beliefs that justify social arrangements. Several ideologies prevailed in the colonies: racism, ethnocentrism, classism, sexism, and "Anglo-Protestantism" (Feagin and Feagin 2008; Kaufmann 2004). These ideologies emphasized the superiority of being rich, white, Anglo-Saxon, male—and Anglican, Congregationalist, or Presbyterian. They explained why rich, white, male, liberal Protestants were entitled to power, privilege, and prestige and people of more modest means, people of color, people of other ancestries, women, evangelical Protestants, and non-Protestants were not.

The Anglo-Protestant ideology had two components: religious affiliation and religious belief. The affiliation component expressed a clear preference for membership in one of the leading denominations. If one were not a member of these three groups, the next best thing (from the standpoint of elites) was to belong to some other Protestant denomination, preferably Lutheran or Methodist, not Baptist or Anabaptist. People with other religious ties (e.g., Catholics and Jews) or no religious loyalties (e.g., Nones) were viewed as most different and least acceptable.

The belief component gave highest priority to the liberal religious worldview of the three dominant denominations. In this case, "liberal" meant a preference for a type of religiosity that emphasized individualism, voluntarism, rationality, tolerance, and democracy. This type of faith stressed the importance of the individual, the individual's right to choose one's religious outlook, the importance of reason in making religious decisions, respect for others in one's group who may hold different beliefs, and one's right to participate in church-related decisions (Albanese 2007). These values stood over against any other religiosity that emphasized the importance of the group (e.g., as Catholicism and Judaism did), membership based on ancestry or conquest (e.g., Catholicism), emotionalism (e.g., pentecostalism), intolerance of theological differences (e.g., fundamentalism), and autocratic decision making in one's religious group (e.g., cults).

The combination of these two components defined who the religious "insiders" and "outsiders" would be (Moore 1987; Pyle 1996, 33–35). Anglicans, Congregationalists, and Presbyterians who fully embraced liberal Protestant ideals were the insiders. They would have ready access to society's resources. The more similar groups or individuals were to this norm, the more acceptable they would be to the elites. The more different they were, the less acceptable they would be. Individuals and groups that were most different from the norm would be denied access to power, privilege, and prestige.

This pro-Protestant emphasis contained a clear message: religious outsiders should abandon, or at least modify, their own traditions and blend into the dominant culture (Feagin and Feagin 2008; Parrillo 2006). Groups that adopted the policies and practices of the leading Protestant denominations, and individuals who would join one of the elite groups, or, at least, accept their worldview, would be granted more access to resources than those who did not. Marginalized groups would have to decide whether to assimilate and be upwardly mobile, or retain their differences and be excluded from full participation in the society.

Not everyone in Protestant circles embraced this ideology. There were dissenting voices who longed for a more inclusive or pluralistic way of life (Kaufmann 2004). These people knew they were in the minority and would have to take advantage of whatever opportunities they got to shape the society according to their more egalitarian views (more on that later).

Customs

In addition to passing laws and creating ideologies that favored their members in virtually all areas of social life, the dominant faiths developed recurring patterns of behavior—or "customs"—which maximized their access to important resources and restricted other groups' access to them.

With their laws and ideologies firmly in place, elites assumed that they were more entitled to these resources than others were. To make sure that happened, they developed a set of customs that would make power, privilege, and prestige the sole possessions of religious elites. Chief among these customs was the development of private and exclusive social organizations, groups, and social networks in which membership was limited to elites. These entities included family networks, local congregations, privately owned businesses, and church-related colleges and universities (Daniels 1986). In and through these segregated settings, elites were able to enhance their access to resources. With regard to power and politics, they emphasized political issues that contributed to the well-being of their religious groups, nominated candidates who represented their religious groups, voted for their own kind, appointed people to political office who belonged to their religions, and supported lobbies that advocated their values and interests (Chickering 1986). With regard to privilege, elites hired workers who shared their religious affiliation, promoted their own kind over workers with other religious preferences, and left their businesses to members of their own families. With regard to prestige, they staffed their private schools with teachers and administrators who shared their own religious affiliation and gave preference to student applicants who belonged to the same faith traditions (Coe and Davidson 2010).

The effectiveness of these customs has been documented many times. For example, family connections and kinship ties were instrumental in perpetuating the authority of the dominant faith groups in the political sphere. Ryerson's (1986) study of legislators who served in the Pennsylvania Assembly between 1729 and 1776 showed that 100 of the 265 legislators shared their surnames with one or more other members. Snell (1986) in a similar study of Hampshire County in Massachusetts found that the governing class was coextensive with just six interrelated families.

Other religious groups developed customs of their own. Some of their behaviors indicated a desire to assimilate. These customs included a willingness to Anglicize one's name, become Protestant, vote for elite political candidates, work for elite business owners, attend elite schools, join elite clubs, and marry into elite families (Albanese 2007). Charles Carroll retained his Catholicism but demonstrated his willingness to assimilate in other ways. He became the richest person in Maryland and the only Catholic to sign the Declaration of Independence. His cousin, John Carroll, was an outspoken champion of integration into America's religious mainstream (Marty 1986, 143–44).

However, the more common pattern was for nonelites to develop their own communities and retain their distinctive ways of life. Catholics in Maryland are a case in point.

Catholics acted as witnesses for the official transactions of other Catholics. When a Catholic died, other Catholics saw to the disposition of the estate and made sure that the orphans were well cared for. Catholic widows and widowers usually remarried a Catholic spouse. . . . Catholics entered into business partnerships and engaged in commercial activities with other Catholics. Catholics rose in political life together and together supported the church. They frequently knew their priests outside of Church and socialized with them. (Graham as cited in Dolan 1985, 80)

Colonial Ranking

Thus, prejudice, competition, and differential power led to circumstances that gave some religious groups far more access to social resources than other groups had. In chapter 1, we showed that Anglicans and Presbyterians were highly overrepresented among the signers of the Declaration of Independence and the participants in the Constitutional Convention. Additional indications of their political clout are found in Wendel's (1986) study of Speakers of the House, who were the highest elected officers in the colonies (see table 3.2). Wendel examined the religious affiliations of 275 Speakers of the House in the thirteen lower assemblies during 1690–1776. Anglicans and Congregationalists were the most prominent groups at this level of elected office. Together they accounted for 73 percent of the Speakers, whereas these two groups comprised just 36 percent of all religious adherents and only about 6 percent of the total population in 1776 (Finke and Stark 1992). In other words, there were twice as many Anglicans and Congregationalists as one might expect relative to all religious adherents and more than ten times as many relative to the total population. Quakers accounted for about 14 percent of the Speakers, whereas they represented less than 10 percent of all religious adherents and less than 2 percent of the total population. Baptists, Presbyterians, Dutch Reformed, and Free Thought members, on the other hand, were 12 percent of the Speakers, but together these groups accounted for more than one-third of all religious adherents and 6 percent of the total population.

Table 3.2 also shows the degree to which Anglicanism was basically an unofficial requirement for access to Speaker positions in the South. Ninety-four percent of the sixty-five Speakers from the southern colonies claimed Anglican affiliation. Anglicans and Quakers together controlled the assemblies in the middle colonies, along with a small representation of Presbyterians and members of Free Thought and Dutch Reformed bodies. Congregationalists controlled two-thirds of the Speaker positions in New England, with Anglicans and Quakers together accounting for another one-fifth of those positions. Rhode Island was the only colony in which Baptists obtained the Speakership. Thus Baptists, who were highly popular among the people, were hardly represented among national political elites.

Table 3.2. Speakers of the House, 1690–1776, by Religion and Region[a] (N = 225)

Religion	Percent
Anglican	43.6
Congregational	29.8
Quaker	14.2
Baptist	5.3
Presbyterian	4.9
Dutch Reformed	1.3
Free Thought	.9

	Region		
Religion	*Southern Colonies (S.C., N.C, Ga., Md., Va.) (N = 65)*	*Middle Colonies (N.J., Pa., N.Y., Del.) (N = 60)*	*New England Colonies (Mass., N.H., R.I., Conn.) (N = 100)*
Anglican	93.8	43.3	11.0
Congregational	1.5	—	66.0
Quaker	1.5	35.0	10.0
Baptist	—	—	12.0
Presbyterian	3.1	13.3	1.0
Dutch Reformed	—	5.0	—
Free Thought	—	3.3	—

[a]Adapted from Wendel (1986, 192).

Anglicans, Congregationalists, Quakers, and—by the time of the Revolution—Presbyterians also were overrepresented at the highest echelons of economic influence. Congregationalists were the economic elites in New England cities such as Boston. Quakers and Presbyterians were the business tycoons in New Jersey and Pennsylvania. Anglicans had more economic resources than any other religious group in the southern colonies.

Anglicans and Congregationalists were the most highly educated religious groups in the colonies. Many had attended Oxford and Cambridge (both Anglican) and sent their children back to England so they also could graduate from these schools. Among the others, Congregationalists attended Harvard, Yale, and Dartmouth; Anglicans went to William and Mary and Columbia; and Presbyterians matriculated at Dartmouth. Ninety-seven percent of all Ivy League presidents during the colonial period were Anglicans, Congregationalists, and Presbyterians (Coe and Davidson 2010).

Thus, a discernible ranking of religious groups was in place by the time of the American Revolution (see table 3.3). Although they were only about 9 percent of the total colonial population, Anglicans, Congregationalists, and, to a lesser extent, Presbyterians were the Upper stratum in a four-stratum

Table 3.3.   Religious Stratification circa 1776

Upper Stratum*
  Anglicans
  Congregationalists
  Presbyterians

Upper Middle Stratum
  Quakers
  Unitarians

Lower Middle Stratum
  Baptists
  Dutch/German Reformeds
  Lutherans
  Methodists

Lower Stratum
  Catholics
  Jews
  Nones

*Groups are listed alphabetically within strata.

hierarchy of religious groups. Quakers and Unitarians were only about 2 percent of the population but formed an Upper Middle stratum, which had less social, economic, and political influence than the three groups in the Upper stratum. A Lower Middle stratum consisted of a whole collection of Protestant groups, such as Lutherans, Methodists, Reformeds, and Baptists. These groups accounted for only about 5 percent of the population and were clearly outside of the inner circle of Protestant elites, but being Protestant gave them advantages that were not available to the groups in the Lower stratum. Although Catholics, Jews, and nonbelievers were about 84 percent of the population, they had little or no access to power, privilege, and prestige. They were the Lower stratum.

To provide some sense of how dominant Anglicans, Congregationalists, and Presbyterians were, we computed the mean score for the percentage of the signers of the Declaration of Independence (table 1.1), the delegates to the Constitutional Convention (table 1.1), Speakers of the House (table 3.2), and presidents of Ivy League schools (appendix 2) that belonged to these three religious groups. The mean score of 89 means that 89 percent of these leadership positions were held by members of these three groups. Given the fact that these groups were only about 9 percent of the colonial population, there were about ten times as many members of these groups in these leadership positions as there were in the society as a whole. No wonder Baltzell (1964) called them "the Protestant Establishment."

CONCLUSION

In this chapter, we have adapted Noel's (1968) theory of ethnic stratification and combined it with historical data to show how religious prejudice, competition, and differential power gave rise to a clear pattern of religious stratification in the original thirteen colonies. Religious prejudice was pervasive and promoted the maintenance of ingroup and outgroup boundaries, which contributed to competitive relations between the various faiths. Denominations were competing for religious adherents and cultural authority, and they were vying for political power, the freedom to worship without molestation, and exemption from taxes used to support another religion. More powerful religious groups used their connections to colonial governments to protect their own advantages and suppress competing faiths. Laws about voting, office-holding, and religious toleration reflected the prevailing distribution of power at local and regional levels. The advantages of a large membership, superior organization, and abundant resources solidified the power of the dominant faiths.

These conditions led to the institutionalization of religious inequalities. In some colonies, this institutionalization took the form of religious establishments. In others it did not, but in all colonies there were laws and social norms favoring privileged faiths and limiting other religions' access to power, privilege, and prestige. These social arrangements gave Anglicans, Congregationalists, and—to a lesser extent—Presbyterians and Quakers disproportionate access to economic and political power. Outsider groups such as Catholics, Jews, and Protestant sects found themselves at the bottom of the social ladder.

In the next two chapters, we look at what happened to this religious ranking over the course of U.S. history. We begin with an analysis of the late eighteenth and nineteenth centuries, during which America's religious landscape changed dramatically. Our question is: to what extent and in what ways did these changes affect the underlying structure of religious stratification and the ranking of religious groups?

4

Persistence and Change: 1787–1899

This chapter examines the trajectory of religious stratification from the beginning of the new republic through the end of the nineteenth century. Our journey includes three segments: 1787–1829, 1830–1859, and 1860–1899. In each period, we examine the key components of the theory we outlined in chapter 2: the power relationships between elite and nonelite religious groups; the impact these relationships have on the laws, customs, and ideologies affecting people's access to resources; and the prevailing pattern of religious stratification.

1787–1829

As religious groups began life in the new nation, their relationships would be influenced by the size of their memberships, their organizational capacities, and the resources that were at their disposal.

Power Relations

Although estimates of how many newcomers came to America in the late 1700s and early 1800s vary, there is agreement that there was comparatively little immigration (Dinnerstein, Nichols, and Reimers 1990; Kaufmann 2004).[1] Moreover, most of the new arrivals came from the same European nations (England, Scotland, Ireland, and Germany) that had sent immigrants in large numbers to America before the revolutionary period. Most were Protestants, but Catholics and Jews were also represented among the immigrants coming at this time. Their religious representation mirrored the patterns for previous immigrant populations, and the assimilation patterns and acculturation processes for these immigrants were not much different from what had been established earlier. Thus, through the 1820s, immigration did not produce much, if any, shift in the power relations between elite and nonelite religious groups.

Under these conditions, religious group membership gains and losses were largely tied to each group's ability to adapt to conditions on the East Coast and in places out to the west and south (in and around what is now Ohio, Kentucky, Tennessee, and Indiana). Interestingly, the elite religions that dominated the East Coast struggled with these conditions. Their memberships grew in terms of absolute numbers, but their rate of growth paled in comparison to other Protestant bodies.

What was the Anglican Church in the colonial period became the Protestant Episcopal Church in 1789. Mainly because of dependence on support from the mother country and the Society for the Propagation of the Gospel in Foreign Parts, the new church was in disarray. In Virginia only twenty-eight of the ninety-one Episcopal clergy who served before the war were still functioning after the war (Sweet 1952). Many clergy, being English loyalists, left the country. The Episcopal Church also was not committed to frontier evangelism, and as a consequence it experienced little growth during the first half of the nineteenth century. In the southern states, where the Second Great Awakening was getting some traction, defections to other denominations were a problem and the number of Episcopal clergy declined.

In New England, the Congregational Church faced its own set of challenges, especially in relation to its attempts to expand to the newly settled regions of the country. Congregationalists were slow to implement effective church planting efforts on the frontier, and as a consequence, Congregationalism was not effectively transplanted to the western settlements in the nineteenth century. Presbyterians and Congregationalists attempted to extend their reach into the back country by entering into an alliance, which allowed the groups to work together in conducting missionary activities on the Western frontier. Despite this alliance, neither denomination was able to match the impressive membership gains made by Methodists and Baptists.

One reason that the colonial mainline denominations failed to make inroads in the nation's backwater areas was that there was a pronounced social divide between the seminary-trained clergy associated with mainline Protestantism and the unlettered settlers in the newly expanding regions. Unlike the mainline clergy, Baptist lay preachers and local Methodist leaders in newly settled regions were from the same social backgrounds as those they ministered to, and thus their similar stocks of cultural capital enabled them to forge closer bonds with the churchgoers in the back country.

A seminary degree was a requirement for most mainline Protestant clergy at the time, whereas a college degree was the exception for Baptist and Methodist ministers. Between 1780 and 1829, forty colleges and universities were successfully established in the United States, and most of those were developed by the denominations that were prominent during the colonial era. By 1831, Congregationalist, Presbyterian, and Episcopalian seminaries enrolled 530 students, whereas Baptist schools enrolled 107 students (Finke and Stark 1992). Methodists didn't establish their first seminary until 1847. The educated clergy of the mainline denominations were often recruited from the upper orders of society, and they moved comfortably among the social and financial elite of the day. Well educated clergy could expect to earn a comfortable living serving an established congregation, and few were attracted to the prospect of starting a new church in the frontier areas or the South. At the beginning of the nineteenth century the average yearly income of a Congregationalist minister was about four hundred dollars. Methodist ministers, on the other hand, were allowed a maximum annual allowance of sixty-four dollars until 1800, and eighty dollars thereafter (Hatch 1989, 88). Thus the higher educational requirements for Presbyterian, Congregationalist, and Episcopalian clergy led to higher ministerial salaries, which were associated with more comfortable living arrangements and a measure of social respectability—not the more rugged lifestyle of the frontier regions to the west and south.

Other Protestant denominations instituted organizational and liturgical reforms during America's early years. And these changes paid off for them. Dutch and German Reformed churches gradually transitioned to English speaking congregations, although the German Reformed churches were somewhat slower than the Dutch to conduct services in English. The Lutheran Church was organizing to expand in the new nation, with Lutherans passing a resolution in 1818 calling for union among the different synods. But the most rapid growth occurred among Baptists and Methodists. In connection with the Second Great Awakening (McLoughlin 1978), Baptist lay preachers and Methodist circuit riding evangelists were effective at meeting the demands of the faithful in newly settled areas, and their numbers grew so rapidly that by 1850 the Methodists, with 2.7 million members, were the largest religious group in the country. The preachers associated with these upstart faiths were "of the people" and they encouraged an emotional response and high levels of involvement among their flocks (Finke and Stark 1992).[2] Evangelists at outdoor revivals offered salvation in exchange for a commitment to Christ. The meetings could last from four days to four weeks, and ten or twenty ministers of different denominations would preach day and night. A common occurrence at these meetings consisted of congregants being "slain in the spirit," which means that they would fall to the ground and lie there for extended periods of time, only to be revived anew with a heartfelt conviction that they had tasted deliverance. This type of revival-style worship appealed to the plain folk struggling to make their way in the back country (Hatch 1989) but did not have much appeal for the well-to-do in urban settings. Thus, the upsurge in membership for Baptists and Methodists in the first half of the nineteenth century did not markedly shift the established patterns of denominational power.

Just as Baptists and Methodists were more effective than Episcopalians, Presbyterians, and Congregationalists at winning converts on the frontier, they were also more successful in winning converts among slaves and free blacks. Prior to the American Revolution, very few slaves were Christian, except in a nominal sense (Baer 1998). However, by the turn of the nineteenth century there was growing support for converting the slaves to Christianity, and the Second Great Awakening attracted many slaves and free blacks to evangelical Protestantism. During the period from 1790 to 1815, Methodists took the lead in providing religious instruction for African Americans, but the Baptists were also a significant presence in the black community. Early worship patterns found black slaves and whites worshipping together in southern congregations, with blacks usually in the balcony and whites on the main floor. In the South slaves did not form independent congregations because of laws forbidding slave assemblies, but by 1821 two independent African Methodist Episcopal churches had formed in the North.

It was during this time that Unitarianism and Deism gained increasing popularity, primarily among the educated classes (Olmstead 1960). Deists stressed that God was revealed in the creation, but they rejected the orthodoxy and formalism of the recognized Christian religions. Thus, they were viewed as atheists by most clergy associated with the conventional faiths. The growth of Unitarianism among the educated classes signaled a crack in the foundation of the New England Congregational Church. Unitarianism's emphasis on the unity of God challenged Congregationalism's belief in the Trinity: that God is Father, Son, and Holy Ghost. Unitarianism had its greatest appeal for the business and professional classes, which found the doctrines of Calvin disagreeable. According to Lyman Beecher: "All the literary men of Massachusetts were Unitarian. All the trustees and professors of Harvard College were Unitarians. All the elite of wealth and fashion crowded Unitarian churches" (quoted in Olmstead 1960, 297). By 1825, 125 churches had formed the American Unitarian Association (Albanese 2007). Universalism, which was also organized during this period, paralleled the Unitarian movement, but it appealed to a different social segment (Sweet 1952). Like the Unitarians, the Universalists advocated salvation for all, but Universalism was more of a small town and rural movement that was successful in winning converts from Baptist churches.

A number of new religious bodies were formed during this time. The German Reformed Church was organized in 1793, and The United Brethren of Christ (another German body) was formed in 1800. Schisms in the Presbyterian Church in the early 1800s led to the creation of the Cumberland Presbyterian Church in 1810 and the formation of "the Christian Church," which later merged with followers of Thomas Campbell, who were known as "Disciples" (Sweet 1952). Several African American denominations emerged, such as the Baptist Missionary Convention (1814), the African Methodist Episcopal Church (1816), and the African Methodist Episcopal Zion Church (1821). In addition, the Ohio Lutheran Synod (1818) and the General Lutheran Synod (1820) were organized during this period.

Despite the formation of these new religious groups, there was a sense among Christian clerics that irreligion was growing (Ahlstrom 1972). Religious leaders at the time expressed concern that people were indulging in vices previously unknown among them, and they complained that religion generally was in a "low and declining state" Sweet (1952, 53). The period from 1776 to 1812 has often been described as a phase of spiritual deadness in American Christianity. Even the Methodists reported a decline in their numbers during some of these years.

In terms of membership, then, there was no significant change in the membership figures of elite Protestants, Catholics, and Jews, but there was sustained growth for Baptists and Methodists.

In terms of organizational bases, there were several developments. Catholics and Jews continued to lack organizational strength. Roman Catholics faced the challenge of a shortage of priests after the American Revolution, but the election of Bishop John Carroll, a capable administrator, set the stage for the church to be able to respond to the needs of a growing Catholic population in America. Jews also lacked rabbis and struggled to establish strong organizations of their own.

But the biggest factor in the power equation was the fact that elite groups had far more control of resources than other groups did. They were the occupants of the highest political offices in the land, the wealthiest people at the time, and the most educated colonists, all of which helped the three leading Protestant groups maintain their position of dominance over other religious groups. As the religious groups that were associated with power and status in the colonial period, they continued to serve the well-to-do through the first decades of the nineteenth century (Baltzell 1964). After two hundred years of being associated with the upper orders of colonial society, the formerly established faiths continued to be identified with privilege in the new nation.

Laws

In Virginia after the Revolution there was growing support for a bill that would eliminate state assistance for the established church and provide for religious freedoms for minority faiths. Challenges to the establishment were mounted by dissenter bodies like Presbyterians and Baptists, who aligned themselves against the Anglican Church (Stokes 1950). Baptists supported religious freedom because they were poor and had difficulty paying the taxes used to support the established church. Baptists also opposed restrictions on their ability to financially support their own ministers, and they objected to the practice whereby only Anglican clergy could officiate at marriages, baptisms, and funerals. Presbyterians in Virginia opposed the use of their funds to construct Anglican church buildings. Anglicans, as beneficiaries of existing policies, were content to receive public funds for support of their church, but some prominent church members, including James Madison (an Anglican), did support the Virginia bill for religious freedom, which became law in 1786.

The bill was a precursor to the Constitution's First Amendment: "Congress shall make no law respecting the establishment of religion, or the free exercise thereof." The purpose of the amendment was "to prevent any national ecclesiastical establishment which should give to any hierarchy the exclusive patronage of the national government" (Sweet 1952, 88). The First Amendment rejected the principle that particular religious bodies, such as the Episcopal Church, should be favored at the national level, and thus it had the effect of promoting religious pluralism and religious competition in the expanding nation. It was approved by the House and Senate in 1789, and ratified by the states in 1791.

The First Amendment meant that groups like the Anglicans and Congregationalists, who were established in nine of the thirteen colonies, could not count on governmental privileges or tax support at the national level. However, the amendment did not prevent individual states from maintaining religious establishments. The states could address the issue of religious establishments as they saw fit under the provisions of their constitutions. Not all of the states supported the First Amendment provisions. For example, some members of the Massachusetts delegation to the Constitutional Convention wanted to include a religious qualification for membership in Congress (Marnell 1964). Nevertheless, within a few years of the Constitution's ratification, most of the states did eliminate public support for a particular faith, although the Puritan (Congregationalist) establishments were not abolished until 1818 in Connecticut, 1819 in New Hampshire, and 1833 in Massachusetts.[3]

Article Six of the Constitution prohibited the use of religious tests as a qualification for public office. Prior to this time, most of the colonies did prescribe religious tests for officeholders, which prevented Catholics, Jews, and atheists from holding official positions in the provincial governments (Pyle and Davidson 2003). These legal changes meant that minority religions were now in a better position to compete with the dominant faiths for adherents and for cultural legitimacy.

Customs

We also are interested in behavior patterns (customs) that increase or decrease religious groups' access to scarce resources. In chapter 3, we learned that elite religious groups tended to segregate themselves from nonelites. They developed private social organizations and networks in which membership was limited to people with their religious ties. Their churches encouraged members to date and marry "their own kind." Elites started their own businesses, hired workers who shared their religious affiliation, promoted members of the same religion, and, when they grew old or died, bequeathed their businesses to members of their own families (Daniels 1986). In the political arena, they emphasized political issues that contributed to the well-being of their religious groups, nominated elite candidates who represented their religious groups, voted for their own kind, appointed people to political office who belonged to their religions, and lobbied hard for their own values and interests (Chickering 1986). In the cultural sphere, they built a number of church-sponsored colleges and universities, hired teachers and administrators who shared their own religious affiliation, and admitted students of same faith (Butts and Cremin 1953).

Virtually all of these customs survived the birth of the new nation, although some needed modification. The political and family spheres of life are good examples. In politics, for example, members of the elite religions gravitated toward the Federalist Party and made sure that fellow elites became the first six presidents of the new society: George Washington (Episcopalian), John Adams (Unitarian), Thomas Jefferson (raised Anglican, but a Deist in his adult years), James Madison (Episcopalian), James Monroe (Episcopalian), and John Quincy Adams (Unitarian). And, when these elites were in office, they had a habit of appointing co-religionists to their cabinets and the Supreme Court. Between 1789 and 1839, presidents belonging to these elite religions appointed nineteen people to cabinet posts, 58 percent of them also being members of the Protestant Establishment religions. They also nominated eigheen people to the Supreme Court, 56 percent of whom shared their religious connections (Davidson, Kraus, and Morrissey 2005). Interestingly, presidents with other religious ties (the Adamses and Jefferson) also tended to appoint Episcopalians, Congregationalists, and Presbyterians to these posts, thus, helping to reproduce the pattern of religious stratification that emerged in the colonial period.

Also, as in the colonial period, family connections were important in solidifying the dominance of the upper orders of society. Jaher, in a study of urban elites, noted that "from their first appearance as mercantile or agrarian elites . . . commercial needs entailed a reliance upon family connection. . . . Business firms and medical and legal practices were often partnerships with other relatives, employed kin in responsible positions, and frequently were passed on to collateral or direct descendants" (1982, 9). To illustrate the degree to which family ties played a role in the preservation of wealth in the nineteenth century, Jaher (1982) found that 52.5 percent of New York's wealthiest citizens in 1828 were related to each other by blood or marriage. The same pattern applied in other locations. In 1835, 71 percent of the wealthiest Bostonians were interrelated (Jaher 1982, 73, 255). Such a high degree of wealth concentration among a small number of families demonstrates the degree to which economic elites were able to transfer resources to their own kind. To the extent that America's wealthiest families tended to affiliate with the same Protestant denominations, the maintenance of family fortunes perpetuated the status of elite churches.

Ideologies

In chapter 3, we showed that the ideologies of racism, ethnocentrism, classism, and sexism took root in the colonial period. So did an ideology that has often been called "Anglo-Protestantism" (Feagin and Feagin 2008; Kaufmann 2004). Together, these ideologies emphasized the superiority of being rich, white, Anglo-Saxon, male—and Protestant.

But not just any kind of Protestant. Anglo-Protestantism emphasized the importance of being Anglican (later Episcopalian), Congregationalist, or Presbyterian. It also called for an approach to religion that stressed individualism, voluntarism, reason, tolerance of diversity, and democracy. Groups and beliefs that emphasized the collectivity, involuntary membership, emotion, dogmatism, and hierarchical authority were unacceptable.

With members of the three leading Protestant denominations in key roles as the new nation took shape, this pro-Protestant religious ideology became highly institutionalized. Protestant—especially liberal Protestant—values and beliefs became the values and beliefs of the larger culture. The Anglo-Protestantism of the colonial period came to stand as the norm for the population as a whole. It was the standard against which all other groups would be compared and evaluated. The more similar, the better, as far as elites were concerned. Other groups were expected to assimilate and, ultimately, convert

(Albanese 2007; Anderson 1970; Feagin and Feagin 2008; Kaufmann 2004; Parrillo 2006).

Religious Stratification

One way of assessing the degree to which religious groups were differentially represented at the height of power is to analyze the religious connections of those who were appointed to the highest positions in the executive and judicial branches of government. In chapter 1 we looked at the religious backgrounds of American presidents to show how religious groups were differentially represented at the height of political power in America. We also suggested that presidents tended to appoint others to high office whose religious backgrounds were similar to their own. In this section we look at the religious affiliations of cabinet officers and Supreme Court justices, who are nominated by the president and approved by the Senate. An analysis of the religious affiliations of these presidential appointees provides another indication of the differential representation of religious groups among political elites during the early years of the American republic.

Table 4.1 presents the religious affiliations of cabinet appointees and Supreme Court justices during the period from 1789 to 1929. For now, we'll just concentrate on the first two columns, which list the religious affiliations

Table 4.1. Religion of Cabinet Members and Supreme Court Justices (percent)

Religion	1789–1839		1840–1929	
	Cabinet	Supreme Court	Cabinet	Supreme Court
Episcopalian	13	39	14	32
Presbyterian	32	21	25	17
Congregationalist	16	4	7	2
Unitarian	3	7	4	11
Quaker	—	—	8	2
Baptist	13	—	6	4
Methodist	—	4	23	2
Dutch Reformed	3	—	—	—
Disc. of Christ	—	—	3	2
Other Protestant	—	22	—	15
Nones	3	—	2	2
Catholic	16	4	7	6
Jewish	—	—	1	4
N	31	28	132	47

Source: Davidson, Kraus, and Morrissey (2005).

of the appointees during the period from 1789 to 1839. Forty-five percent of cabinet appointees and 60 percent of Supreme Court justices during this fifty-year period were either Episcopalians or Presbyterians. These two groups outdistanced the other religious groups that are listed, with Presbyterians being most likely to serve as cabinet appointees, while Episcopalians were most likely to serve on the Court. But the dominance of these two groups is noteworthy, especially considering the relatively small percentage of the population affiliated with these churches. Congregationalists were also well represented, accounting for 16 percent of cabinet appointees and 4 percent of the justices. Interestingly, Catholics were represented in the cabinet and on the Court at the same level as Congregationalists, suggesting a liberalization of the religious restrictions that hampered Catholics during the colonial period. Baptists accounted for 13 percent of cabinet members, but none of the justices. Those in the Other Protestant category accounted for 22 percent of Supreme Court justices but they were absent from the cabinet. There were a few Unitarians, Methodists, Nones, and Dutch Reformeds represented, but no Jews served on the Court or in the cabinet during this period.

Because of the limited numbers of justices and cabinet members, we should be cautious in interpreting the results. With that precaution in mind, we conclude that the faiths that were overrepresented among political elites during the colonial period continued to be overrepresented at the highest levels of power in the executive and judicial branches of government. Episcopalians and Presbyterians were represented as presidents, Supreme Court justices, and cabinet officials at a level that far exceeded their numbers in the general population. Baptists, Methodists, and Other Protestants were less likely to occupy these high level positions. Based on the small number of cases, it appears that Catholics were beginning to achieve some visibility on the national political stage. Jews and Nones, however, were virtually absent from these high level offices. In other words, the patterns of religious stratification that emerged during the colonial period continued during the early decades of the new nation.

1830–1859

An upsurge in immigration beginning in the 1830s would forever alter the nation's religious landscape. Six hundred thousand newcomers landed on American shores in the 1830s, which represented a fourfold increase over immigration levels in the 1820s. Immigration then surged with 1.7 million arriving in the 1840s, and about 2.5 million for each decade thereafter until 1880. These immigrants were coming to the United States primarily for economic reasons. As the nation expanded territorially and industrially, there was a need for newcomers to clear farmland on the frontier and work in the new industries in expanding urban centers. But the newcomers were not welcomed with open arms. Aside from their large numbers, what was most disconcerting to old stock Americans was that the religious background of many of the immigrants was different from their own Protestant traditions.

Power Relations

One of the most noteworthy developments was the dramatic growth in the size of the Roman Catholic population resulting from a large scale increase in Irish immigration starting in the 1830s. It is difficult to get precise figures on the number of Catholics in America before 1850 because prior to that year the Census Bureau did not collect data on American churches. However, we do know that in the ten years from 1850 to 1860, the Catholic population in America more than doubled from about 1.1 million to 2.4 million (Finke and Stark 1992, 113). Although Roman Catholics occupied the lower rungs in the status hierarchy and were subject to virulent attacks by nativist groups, they were successful in organizing institutions such as schools, hospitals, and charities that enabled them to establish a foothold in the nation.

The Jewish population in America also increased during this period. Estimates suggest that between 1840 and 1860 the number of Jews in America expanded from 15,000 to 150,000 (www.jewishvirtuallibrary.org/jsource/US-Israel/usjewpop1.html) as an influx of Jewish immigrants arrived from central Europe. These German Jews took up occupations as small retailers, and they moved westward with the advancing frontier (Handlin and Handlin 1949). The relative prosperity that they achieved facilitated the assimilation process, and they soon established synagogues and mutual aid associations. B'nai B'rith was established in 1843 as the first national secular Jewish organization, but many charitable and philanthropic societies followed. A high percentage of German Jews who arrived between 1840 and 1860 were prosperous and well educated, and "intermarriage and defection from the Jewish community reached considerable proportions" (Herberg 1960, 175). To prevent the flow of defections, leaders of the German Jewish community adapted Jewish religious patterns to American conditions, and thus Reform Judaism was established in America.

Several new religious organizations were formed during this time. The Mormon Church (the Church of Jesus Christ of Latter-day Saints) was organized in 1830. The Southern Baptist Convention was formed in 1845. Germans who settled in the Midwest established the Lutheran Church Missouri Synod in 1847. The Evangelical Synod of North America was organized in 1849. Dutch Reformeds split into two groups: the Reformed Church in America and the Christian Reformed Church (1857).

Episcopalians, Presbyterians, and Congregationalists built new churches and expanded their membership, but moderate and conservative Protestant groups grew even more rapidly, for two reasons. First, a growing influx of Germans, Scandinavians, and the Dutch after midcentury contributed to growth in the size of the Lutheran and Reformed churches. Second, the middle decades also witnessed continuing growth in the size and the market share of Baptist and Methodist groups, who had adopted effective organizational strategies that allowed them to target newly expanding communities on the nation's frontier. Eventually the Methodists began to achieve middle class respectability, whereas the Baptists continued to serve as a church of small farmers and the working class. As the former upstarts expanded their market share, they attempted to solidify their influence through processes of institution building. All of the major religious groups established institutions of higher education. Newer groups such as the Mormons and Disciples of Christ were busy establishing themselves in the Midwest and western settlements. The issue of slavery led to organizational cleavages for Presbyterians, Baptists, and Methodists, and Black Protestants continued to occupy the lower rungs of the denominational hierarchy.

Although Episcopalians, Congregationalists, and Presbyterians were losing market share to the Baptists and Methodists, there was not as much evidence of a weakening of mainline Protestantism's political, economic, and cultural influence during the middle decades of the nineteenth century. The social and financial elite continued to affiliate with the "respectable denominations," and clergy members of these groups continued to enjoy a comfortable lifestyle and a measure of social honor. Despite some shifts in the power differentials owing to immigration surges, denominational splits, and sectarian growth, mainline Protestant groups had lost little of their cultural, economic, and political leverage during this period of increasing religious diversity.

One indicator of a religious group's relative power is the value of the property that it holds. Table 4.2 lists the value of church property for selected religious bodies in relation to each group's membership. In this case, a church's property refers to the buildings owned and used for worship by the organizations, together with their building sites, furniture, organs, bells, and the like. It does not include the value of parsonages, school buildings, seminaries, or monasteries. Assessing the value of each group's property in relation to the size of its membership gives us a general indicator of the relative wealth for the major denominations.

Table 4.2 shows that Episcopalians, Congregationalists, and Presbyterians had the highest church property values per member.[4] Once the size of the

Table 4.2. Value of Church Property per Member (ratio)

	1850[a]	*1870*[a]	*1890*[b]
Episcopal	40.6	81.5	152.7
Congregationalist	23.2	52.0	84.5
Presbyterian	16.3	45.6	73.9
Lutheran	10.0	33.8	28.7
Roman Catholic	8.5	17.2	16.1
Baptist	7.1	20.5	22.2
Methodist	5.6	19.6	28.7

[a] Church membership figures reported in Finke and Stark (1986, 190); church property figures reported in Bureau of the Census (1894, 526).
[b] Church membership figures reported in Bureau of the Census (1919, 29–30); church property figures reported in Bureau of the Census (1919, 45–46).

membership is factored in, Episcopalians had over seven times the value of church property of Methodists and nearly six times the value of Baptists in 1850. Congregationalists had the next highest property-value-per-member ratio, with Presbyterians ranking third. Lutherans and Roman Catholics had less value per member than the top three groups, but more than Baptists and Methodists. The ratios for 1870 follow a similar pattern. These figures indicate that groups that had the advantages of wealth and property during earlier periods were better able than others to transmit those wealth surpluses to future time periods. As we see in table 4.2, the groups that had the highest property-per-member ratios in 1850 and 1870 were also those that had the highest ratios in 1890.

Despite the increases in growth and organizational capacity for an increasing variety of religious groups during this period, the colonial mainline faiths continued to exert more power than other religious groups. The nation's laws, ideologies, and customs worked to the benefit of the dominant faiths.

Laws

Although the First Amendment prevented an establishment of religion at the national level, it did not abolish religious establishments in states that already had one. The Congregational Church continued to be established in Massachusetts, Connecticut, and New Hampshire until the early decades of the nineteenth century, with the Massachusetts establishment persisting until 1833. By this time, most of the states had eliminated religious restrictions on voting or office-holding. However, it wasn't until 1844 that a Catholic could hold elective office in New Jersey, although there were no restrictions on Catholics as voters in that state. North Carolina's 1776 constitution specified that only Protestants could hold office, but in 1835 the constitution was amended to allow Christians to hold public office. Non-Christians were not eligible for office in North Carolina until 1868, and even then the constitution disqualified "all persons who shall deny the being of Almighty God" (Marnell 1964, 142). During this period the New Hampshire state constitution still limited toleration to Protestants and it continued to require that public officials be Protestants. Even today several states include language in state constitutions or other documents requiring officeholders to believe in God, but in 1961 the Supreme Court ruled that such language violated the First and Fourteenth Amendments to the U.S. Constitution (www.religioustolerance.org/texas.htm).

Ideologies

A pro-Protestant ideology was firmly in place as a cornerstone of American culture. Episcopalians, Congregationalists, and Presbyterians were the insiders; others were outsiders (Albanese 2007; Pyle 1996, 33–35; Moore 1987). Elite groups also viewed these outsider differences as outsider deficiencies. As Merton (1957) so eloquently put it a half century ago, they saw nothing but "in-group virtues and out-group vices."

Nonelites had to decide what to do. Should they maintain their "old ways," or abandon them for the "new ways"? Succumbing to the pressure to assimilate, many of the newcomers looked for ways to adapt. German immigrants to America are a case in point. Most were Lutherans or members of the German Reformed church. They tended to settle in the Midwest in the Ohio, Mississippi, and Missouri river valleys (Parrillo 2006). Many became homesteaders, while others settled in Germantown communities, where German served as the principal spoken language. Although the Germans experienced a measure of hostility from old stock Americans, they were Protestant and adapted to the dominant ideology.

Large numbers of immigrants from Denmark, Sweden, and Norway also assimilated. Most of these immigrants settled in Illinois, Wisconsin, Minnesota, and Iowa, where their Lutheran churches soon dotted the landscape. These Protestant immigrants from north European countries rather easily conformed to Anglo-American cultural patterns, and they embraced the host culture's beliefs about the value of work and industry (Anderson 1970).

Non-Protestant groups faced more obstacles. Irish Catholic newcomers were a good example. The Irish represented the first large scale population of non-Protestants coming to America. During the 1820s 50,000 Irish came to the United States, many of whom were Protestant Scots-Irish coming from Northern Ireland. But in the 1830s the tide shifted, with most Irish immigrants coming from Catholic regions of Ireland. The failure of the potato crop and the subsequent famine during the 1840s forced impoverished Irish peasants to flee to North America. In the 1830s, 200,000 mainly Catholic Irish immigrants came, followed by 780,000 in the 1840s, and 914,000 in the 1850s. Nearly one-fifth of the entire population of Ireland migrated to the United States between 1841 and 1855. This largely peasant population settled in slum areas of the large cities on the East Coast.

The anti-Catholicism that accompanied the pro-Protestant ideology exacerbated the tensions between immigrants and natives and led to discrimination toward the Irish newcomers. Protestant Americans viewed the Irish as a population of poor people prone to alcoholism, brawling, and crime. Most Protestants believed that Catholicism itself was incompatible with American ways. The accepted wisdom was that the Catholic Church was undemocratic and therefore un-American.

For the most part, however, the Irish tried to adapt. Noting Catholics' "passion for democracy," Dolan (2002) says that Catholics in this period sought to run their parishes on democratic principles. Led by Irishman John England, the bishop of South Carolina, they devised a model of church life that was based on lay leadership. While the plan ultimately failed due to a lack of support in the Catholic hierarchy, its evolution was compelling evidence of just how strong the pro-Protestant ideology was at the time, and how much American Catholics were willing to adapt to it.

Customs

Elite and nonelite customs in the area of education were especially important in this period. There was universal agreement among the major religious traditions that they should play an active role in developing schools in the new nation. However, the various faiths competed with each other in an attempt to influence the content and direction of public education. Although public schooling was supposed to be nonsectarian, in fact, during the nineteenth century public schools in America educated children in a type of nondenominational Protestantism. In New York City in 1840, Roman Catholics voiced their opposition to the New York Public School Society, charging that the New York public school system was really a Protestant enterprise. Catholics demanded that part of the school funds should go to Roman Catholic parochial education. However, the state responded by asserting that state funds should not be used for sectarian purposes and during the next two decades, nine other states banned public aid to sectarian education (Olmstead 1960, 325). Although they were not allowed to provide sectarian instruction, public schools did give instructions in basic Christian principles without sectarian emphasis. Nevertheless, Roman Catholics and Lutherans were not happy with the religious content of public education, and they developed successful parochial school systems on a wide scale. The Roman Catholic system was by far the largest system. By 1840, there were approximately two hundred Catholic parish schools in America, with many of them west of the Allegheny Mountains. By the year 1900 there were approximately four thousand Catholic parochial schools. Sectarian education also took the form of a national Sunday school movement, which was organized in 1824 and supported by all of the major Protestant denominations. This made it possible to establish Sunday schools in communities where no single denomination was strong enough to maintain its own school.

During the 1800s religious groups were actively involved in the expansion of centers for higher learning throughout America. Denominations viewed the planting of colleges as one of the most important means of solidifying their influence in newly settled regions of the country. Most of the colleges established in America during the first eighty years after the colonial period were operated by religious groups. Churches planted colleges not just because of their reverence for the value of higher learning, but because they felt the need to compete with other denominations that had done the same. Baptists and Methodists organized colleges in part because of their resentment over the planting of Congregational and Presbyterian schools on the frontier (Olmstead 1960). During the eighty years between 1780 and 1860, the number of colleges in the United States increased from 9 to 173. While a few were public institutions, most were operated by religious groups. The Presbyterians controlled 49 of the colleges, which extended from Princeton in the East to Pacific University in the West. Congregationalists controlled 21 colleges in New England and the Midwest. Roman Catholics founded 14 institutions, Episcopalians 11, German Reformed and Universalists 4 each, Friends and Unitarians 2 each, with Dutch Reformed and United Brethren establishing 1 each. By 1860 Baptists had 25 colleges and Methodists had 34 (Olmstead 1960, 287). Thus the establishment of religiously based institutions of higher learning was in part fueled by a sense of one-upmanship on the part of denominations mobilizing in response to the efforts at college planting by rival denominations. But it was also a means by which sectarian values and ideals would be transmitted to the next generation of leaders.

Religious Stratification

To provide some sense of religious stratification in this period, we looked at the religious affiliations of the thirty-two men who were presidents, vice presidents, and either chief justices or associate justices of the Supreme Court between 1830 and 1859.[5] Of these thirty-two men, eleven (34 percent) were Episcopalians, including John Tyler who was vice president for one month in 1841 before succeeding William Henry Harrison as president, and John Marshall, Chief Justice of the Supreme Court from 1801 to 1835.

Eight men (25 percent) were Presbyterians, including President Andrew Jackson, who nominated the only Catholic on this list, Roger Taney, who served as Chief Justice from 1836 to 1864. Four men (12 percent) were Unitarians, including Millard Fillmore, who was vice president in 1849 and 1850, then president from 1859 to 1853. Thus, three religious groups that represented less than 10 percent of the population at the time accounted for 61 percent of these key officeholders. No other religious group had more than one member on the list. In short, the same groups that had disproportionate access to public office in the colonial period continued to be overrepresented in the mid-1800s.

1860–1899

In the next four decades the immigrant population in America expanded quite dramatically. As American industrialism flexed its muscles in the late 1800s, the nation attracted massive numbers of European immigrants seeking opportunities in a new land. What was special about this wave of European immigration was that the national origins of immigrants began to shift toward the end of the nineteenth century. For the first time in American history, large numbers of immigrants were coming from southern and eastern European countries with large populations of Catholics and Jews.[6] Many old stock Americans were convinced that this new wave of immigrants represented an inferior racial strain, and religious prejudice bubbled to the surface as more and more Catholic and Jewish immigrants disembarked at immigrant processing centers. The presence of so many aliens in the nation's urban centers caused alarm among those who feared that the newcomers posed a threat to America's cultural unity. These developments had consequences for the evolution of a system of religious inequality.

Power Relations

From 1860 to 1880, most European immigrants came from Great Britain, Germany, and Ireland. The substantial German and Scandinavian immigration resulted in the Lutheran church becoming the third largest Protestant denomination in America. The majority of immigrants prior to 1880 were Protestants from northern Europe, although a significant population of Irish Catholics settled during this period. However, during the twenty-year period after 1880, southern and eastern Europeans represented an increasingly large segment of the immigrant population. This new strain of immigration signaled not just a shift in the national origins of newcomers but a change in the religious makeup of the nation as a whole. For the first time America encountered a large population of Jews coming from eastern Europe, along with a large number of Catholics arriving from Italy. Prior to the 1880s, there was virtually no Italian presence in the United States; however, during the 1880–1900 period Italians were one of the major immigrant groups represented at the processing center of Ellis Island. Toward the end of the century, Slavs represented another new population of immigrants, and they added to the numbers of Roman Catholic (and Orthodox) parishioners in America (Dinnerstein, Nichols, and Reimers 1990). By 1896, immigrants from southern and eastern Europe for the first time outnumbered those from northern and western Europe (Parrillo 2006).

This shift in the national origins of immigrants and the expansion of religious diversity led to an intensification of interfaith hostilities in the nation, and immigrant groups increasingly turned to fraternal organizations and mutual aid societies to help them adjust to the harsh conditions of urban living (Metress 1985). Mutual aid societies supporting German immigrants began to appear in the United States as early as the 1830s. They provided information, employment, and direct relief to immigrants. Jewish benevolent societies began to appear in the 1840s and 1850s. Jewish immigrants would join together in America to form *landsmanshaftn*, Jewish immigrant aid societies, where membership was granted according to the town of origin in Europe (Handlin and Handlin 1949). Irish immigrants founded mutual aid associations and benevolent societies by the 1850s, which were started as neighborhood associations by saloonkeepers, priests, and grocers. Irish mutual aid societies such as St. Patrick's Beneficial Society Aid and the St. Vincent de Paul Society were operating by the 1850s, but they were often criticized by WASP charities for being overly generous and nondiscriminatory in determining who would receive the aid (Metress 1985). The ancient order of Hibernians, incorporated in 1853, was an Irish organization that had some mutual aid functions. The Knights of Columbus was a national Catholic fraternal order established in 1882 and dominated by the Irish during the early years. Later, the Italians developed the Sons of Italy in 1905. These organizations attempted to relieve some of the destitution experienced by the immigrant poor, and they were an important force in contributing to mobility for the nation's growing population of Catholics and Jews.

During this period a number of new religious groups were organized, and many of these were associated with the evangelical tradition. The Seventh-day Adventists (1863) and Jehovah's Witnesses (1870) were sectarian bodies that grew out of the nineteenth century Bible prophecy movement associated with William Miller. The Salvation Army was introduced to America in 1865, and the Church of Christ Scientists, which promoted Bible-based Christian healing, was founded by Mary Baker Eddy in 1879. The Church of God (Anderson, Indiana) was founded in 1881, followed by the Church of God (Cleveland, Tennessee) in 1886. A number of African American religious bodies were formed at this time, including the National Baptist Convention, USA (1895), the Cumberland Presbyterian Church (1874), and the Church of God in Christ (1897), a black pentecostal denomination.[7] After emancipation, there was a mass withdrawal of blacks from racially mixed congregations in the South as blacks began to form their own churches. In addition, many black churches formed mutual aid or beneficial societies to help members survive financial crises that accompanied the death or illness of family members (Johnstone 2007).

The most dramatic growth in organized religion took place in the Roman Catholic Church, which increased its membership from 2.4 million in 1860 to 7.3 million in 1890. The Lutheran and Baptist churches also saw healthy growth during the thirty years after 1860, as their memberships increased by 88 percent (see table 4.3). Although it is difficult to obtain precise estimates of the number of Jews in America during the period, it appears that the Jewish population expanded by about 150 percent between 1860 and 1890 (www.jewishvirtuallibrary.org/jsource/US-Israel/usjewpop1.html).

The expansion of immigration and the growth of organized religion at the end of the nineteenth century signaled changes in the power relations between religious groups. Despite growth in the membership for elite faiths, these religious traditions represented a declining share of the religious market, and the dramatic expansion in the size of the Catholic and Jewish population in America signaled that Anglo-Protestants were increasingly forced to compete with

Table 4.3. Reported Church Membership for Select U.S. Religious Groups

	1860[a]	1890[b]	Percent Change
Episcopal	396,000	532,048	+34.4
Presbyterian	1,136,000	1,260,984	+11.0
Congregational	427,000	512,771	+20.1
Lutheran	808,000	1,518,817	+88.0
Roman Catholic	2,439,000	7,343,186	+201.1
Baptist	1,955,000	3,679,682	+88.2
Methodist	3,759,000	4,571,492	+21.6

[a] Membership figures reported in Finke and Stark (1986, 190).
[b] Membership figures reported in Bureau of the Census (1919, 45–46).

those from other religious traditions for valued resources. Despite changes in the power relations between religious groups, Anglo-Protestants still had advantages in terms of wealth, political power, and cultural influence.

Laws

As we have indicated, the First Amendment did not prevent religious establishments at the state level; it merely prohibited the establishment of religion at the national level. Thus individual states could maintain an established church, and it wasn't until 1833, which was forty-two years after the ratification of the First Amendment, that the Congregational Church was finally disestablished in Massachusetts. Although that event would seem to mark the end of the era of established religion in America, it was still possible under existing law for states to designate an established church. That possibility ended, however, in 1868, when the Fourteenth Amendment was ratified. This amendment extended the limitations imposed by the federal government in the Bill of Rights to the states (Marnell 1964). Thus the Fourteenth Amendment represented an extension and solidification of First Amendment principles.

One piece of legislation that had the potential to affect the organization of religion in America was the Chinese Exclusion Act, passed in 1882. Prior to the passage of this legislation, there was never an attempt at the federal level to prevent an ethnic or racial subpopulation from entering America. Chinese immigration to the United States began during the California Gold Rush of the late 1840s, and in the 1860s the Chinese helped build the western end of the transcontinental railroad. However, after the Depression of 1873, the supply of laborers exceeded the demand, and there were increasing calls for restrictions on Chinese immigration. Although liberal Protestant clergy and clergy-led organizations opposed such restrictions, rank and file members of these elite denominations—including members of Congress—were in favor of them (Kaufmann 2004, 65–66). The 1882 Chinese Exclusion Act barred Chinese laborers for a ten-year period. Congress extended the act for another ten years in 1892 and then extended it indefinitely in 1902 (Parrillo 2006). The exclusion of the Chinese (and later restrictions on other Asian populations in 1907, 1917, and 1924) meant that Eastern religious traditions such as Buddhism or Confucianism would not be a visible part of America's religious mosaic until the 1960s, when the national origin quotas were eliminated.

Customs

Members of elite religions developed a number of ways of separating themselves from the largely Catholic and Jewish immigrants who were filling the lower strata, while also trying to assimilate these seemingly unassimilable groups into the American way of life. Among other methods, they tried to privatize education, employment, and community life.

Upper Class Anglo-Saxonism

The presence of a growing population of southern and eastern Europeans led upper class white Anglo-Saxon Protestants (WASPs) to begin to draw their wagons in a circle in an attempt to isolate themselves from the ethnic brew percolating in urban America. A sense of caste-like exclusion in the upper class intensified in the late 1800s in response to the growing numbers of Irish and Italian Catholics and eastern European Jews in America. Increasingly Jews were barred from attending exclusive hotels, clubs, and schools, and these policies of exclusion illustrate how customs are part of the institutionalization of a system of stratification. Policies of Jewish exclusion represented a defensive response on the part of WASPs fearful of losing status in the face of increasing competition from a successful ethnic subpopulation. Most often the restrictive practices were aimed at excluding Jews from the elevated social spheres associated with affluent white Protestants.

This rejection of Jews represents a shift in earlier patterns of Protestant-Jewish relations among the privileged classes. By the 1870s, a stable German Jewish upper middle class had emerged in America, and at this time prominent Jews were accepted socially at the highest levels of society (Baltzell 1964). However, the newer eastern European Jews arriving after the 1880s were subject to negative stereotyping because of their "alien ways" and their status as low wage workers. The presence of so many eastern European Jews was seen to have lowered the status of the more assimilated German Jews who had earned a degree of security and respectability in America. In this context, negative stereotyping was transplanted to the larger Jewish community, and it was increasingly common for Jews to be restricted from the domains of genteel society.

One of the watershed moments of gentlemanly anti-Semitism took place in 1877 when New York banker Joseph Seligman was, without warning, excluded from the Grand Union Hotel in Saratoga Springs, a hotel that he had frequented in the past. In 1877, Seligman had chartered a train to transport his family, furnishings, and servants for a summer stay at the Grand Union, only to be told that the hotel had approved a new policy of accepting Gentiles only. Soon, other prominent Jews were turned down at leading hotels in other resort locations. It wasn't long until resort establishments began to advertise their discriminatory admissions policies in newspapers. Private schools and clubs also began to enact restrictive admissions practices that discriminated against

Jews. Pioneer American sociologist E. A. Ross defended these policies of Jewish exclusion when he said that "the line drawn against the Jews in hotels, resorts, clubs, and private schools" was not because of bigotry or dislike of their religion; rather it was justified by their manners, which were those of "vulgar upstart parvenus" (quoted in Baltzell 1964, 107). Such policies of exclusion were first enacted on a wide scale in the 1880s, during a time when Jews were advancing in to educational and economic realms formerly seen as the province of well-heeled WASPs. WASPs chastised the Jews for their supposed tribalism or clannishness, not seeing the obvious irony that their WASP-only hotels, clubs, and social associations promoted tribalism to an even higher level.

Another step in the direction of ethnic exclusion was taken with the emergence of ancestor societies. These organizations were established in response to the ethnic diversity brought on by the new European immigration. Taking pride in one's Nordic (northern European) ancestry was a way of affirming one's social pedigree during a time of rapid ethnic change. Ancestral associations such as the Daughters of the American Revolution, the Colonial Dames, the Society of Mayflower Descendants, and the Sons of the Revolution were all formed between 1880 and 1900. Baltzell observes that "this whole movement was, of course, intimately bound up with anti-immigrant and anti-Semitic sentiments" (1964, 115). Newly built suburban country clubs and country day schools also served to reinforce a kind of tribalism among upper class WASPs who preferred to remain with their own kind. Golf clubs, yacht clubs, and cricket clubs promoted social intermingling among "people like us" and embraced formal and informal policies of admitting Gentiles only.

New England boarding schools and Ivy League colleges were also important in the maintenance of a Protestant upper class in America. The schools played a key role in socializing the children of newer wealth into the values of the more established old money families. The boarding school movement experienced its greatest period of growth in America during the fifty years after 1880 (Baltzell 1964). Very few Catholics and even fewer Jews applied to these schools at this time. Many of the graduates of the eastern boarding schools would then go on to Harvard, Yale, Princeton, or other prestigious colleges, where a "gentleman's C" represented an acceptable level of academic achievement. By the 1900s the use of purchased papers by wealthy students at schools like Yale was widespread. It was left to the "greasy grinds" (Jews and hard-working public school students) to demonstrate excellence in academic matters, and their high scholastic achievement only served to reinforce the social boundaries between themselves and their more privileged, but less studious, classmates (Synnott 1979). The students earning gentleman's Cs were the chief players in the college fraternities and the eating clubs, which were for Gentiles only. Membership in a high ranking fraternity or university social club was expected for those who aspired to leadership positions in the nation's most powerful banks, corporations, and law firms.

After college, many of these Ivy League graduates would join a prestigious city club, which offered them the opportunity to cultivate business connections and social ties with influential older members. Thus the club was important in the making of gentlemen. It was a place where well placed men could fraternize with other "good fellows" who moved effortlessly in circles of power and privilege. According to Baltzell, "almost without exception, every club in America developed a caste-like policy toward Jews" (1964, 138). In the late nineteenth century in cities across America, prominent Jews were expected to resign from clubs that they had been affiliated with. The exclusion of Jews by WASPs was a response to the perception that a growing class of affluent Jews posed a threat to a long-standing tradition of institutional and economic control by Anglo-Protestants. This provides another illustration of how the dominant groups developed customs that maximized their access to scarce resources while at the same time restricting other groups' access to them.

Just as club membership policies reinforced insider-outsider distinctions between WASPs and non-WASPs in circles of privilege, society blue books also served to reinforce social boundary distinctions between those born into privilege and those who were not. America's most highly regarded society directory has always been the *Social Register*. Starting in the late 1880s the *Social Register* began publishing a listing of the names and addresses of members of "proper" families residing in the nation's major metropolitan areas. Separate *Social Registers* were published for New York, Philadelphia, Chicago, Boston, and eight other metropolitan areas. From its inception, the *Social Register* was regarded as the most reliable index of who was in and who was out of "high society" (Higley 1995). One's inclusion in this directory signaled a person's eligibility for social intercourse with old money families, and a *Social Register* listing was expected for those seeking high level employment with socially prestigious law firms, known as "white shoe" firms. A listing in the *Social Register* also signaled that a person had the social pedigree required for entry into a top-drawer gentleman's club. Exclusion from the *Social Register* was a death sentence of sorts for those who aspired to free movement among the blue blooded families whose members directed affairs in the power centers of American life.

The *Social Register* has always been a Gentile directory. Although socially prominent Roman Catholic families have been listed in the *Register* since its inception, most of the families listed have been affiliated with the same Protestant denominations that have been associated with old stock Americans since the nation's founding (Baltzell 1964). The Social Register Association has always maintained a tightly guarded policy regarding its procedures for selecting family units (Sargent 1997). It has denied any suggestion that it restricts its listings to Gentile families, but observers have noted that few, if any, families with Jewish surnames have been listed over the years (Higley 1995). To the degree that Jews and other non-Christians have been excluded from social directories like the *Social Register*, then their religious affiliation limited their access to important spheres of social interplay that were crucial for advancement into the upper ranks of society.[8]

Ethnic Identity and Assimilation

Nonelite religions looked for ways to maintain their own identities and traditions, while also adapting to the Protestant-American way of life. We learn of some of these methods by focusing on the experiences of Irish Catholics in the late 1800s.

Although there was considerable social distance between Irish Catholics and the dominant group of Anglo-Protestants, there was also a significant social boundary between the Irish and the newer immigrants from southern and eastern Europe. According to Shannon (1989, 132), at the beginning of the twentieth century the Irish were the ethnic subpopulation closest to being "in" while still being "out." How did Irish Catholics begin to move up in American society? A number of factors can account for Irish Catholic mobility during this period.

For one thing, they took the lead in developing an elaborate parochial school system, which "[by] the end of the nineteenth century . . . had become a distinctive trademark of American Catholicism" (Dolan 2002, 60). Given that the Irish were disproportionately overrepresented among American bishops, they played the key role in the development and expansion of parochial education. At a national meeting of Catholic bishops (the Third Plenary Council of Baltimore in 1884) a resolution was adopted that emphasized the "absolute necessity" for pastors to establish Catholic parochial schools in their parishes. Thus all Catholic parishes were expected to develop parochial schools to educate the largely Irish population of Catholic school children.

This well-known system had two effects. On the one hand, it allowed Catholics to preserve their own cultural traditions in the face of pressures to "Protestantize" them. At the same time, however, these parochial schools became settings within which succeeding generations of Catholics were "Americanized" (i.e., assimilated in the democratic values of American public life). Thus Catholic parochial schools protected students from the Protestantization efforts associated with public schooling, and at the same time, they provided students with skills and knowledge that promoted economic advancement.

Politics was another setting where segregation and assimilation seemed to go hand in hand. Having coped with British control for two centuries in their homeland, the Irish knew how to organize politically. During the early years of migration, the Irish, like other migrant populations, would help one another, creating a mutual welfare system through trade associations and self-help organizations (Shannon 1989). Starting in the mid-nineteenth century, Irish residents of American cities took control of local political organizations and began to shape government programs to help their constituents. Irish-dominated political machines awarded government contracts to Irish companies that would be involved in the construction of major public infrastructure projects (streets, sewers, and subways). Favors were exchanged for votes, and in essence, the political machine served as an effective tool by which the Irish could gain power. Patronage arrangements were used to reward supporters with jobs and government contracts (Clark 1975). Civil service employment was influenced by machine politics, with the result that the Irish were soon overrepresented as big city police officers, firefighters, and municipal engineers. By the 1890s, the Irish controlled city governments in the largest urban centers in America: New York, Philadelphia, Chicago, Boston, St. Louis, and San Francisco (O'Grady 1973). Irish ward and precinct captains effectively organized Irish voters in a bid to limit the influence of the Protestant dominated political structures. As a result, Irish Catholics gained local political power at the expense of the dominant group by controlling a patronage system that provided economic and political opportunities for the Irish community. Although the Irish were quite successful at using machine politics to benefit themselves economically and politically in large urban centers, they still did not have much political influence at the national level before the twentieth century.

Ideologies

The dominant pro-Protestant ideology was very much intact during the last half of the 1800s. It was championed, quite predictably, by the elite religions, but also, less predictably, by some nonelite Protestants. Both groups saw the influx of Catholics, Jews, and other non-Protestants as a threat to their concept of America as a Protestant-Christian society. The combination of the two factions had important consequences because "whenever the northeastern 'WASP' elite make common cause with their less prestigious but more numerous provincial kin, Anglo-Protestant ethnic nationalism revives" (Kaufmann 2004, 26).

The result was a widespread reaffirmation of the dominant ideology and an equally widespread animosity toward groups that seemed unwilling to adapt.

And, among some leaders of the elite denominations, there was an increasing sense that the newcomers from eastern and southern Europe and Asia were just that—unassimilable. This situation led to an increase in hostilities aimed at these groups, but it also worked to the advantage of some others.

Compared to Italian Catholics, for example, Irish Catholics were seen as being more like Anglo-Protestants. This similarity and Irish Catholics' willingness to embrace dominant cultural values facilitated their assimilation and upward mobility toward the end of the nineteenth century. As an English speaking white population, the Irish could blend in with the host culture and fill low level clerical positions as store clerks and bookkeepers. America's rapid industrial expansion after the Civil War was associated with a demand for new clerical and sales positions, and the Irish were available to fill these vacancies. Irish females had a high rate of labor force participation, finding employment as domestic servants in the homes of middle class Protestant families and as operatives in the textile industry. Many daughters of Irish maids became school teachers or white collar workers, thus contributing to social mobility for the Irish population (Feagin and Feagin 2008).

Irish Catholic mobility also benefited from the growing presence of groups that were seen as more socially different from the dominant group. In other words, Irish Catholics were pushed up by the later waves of southern and eastern European immigrants, whose cultural orientations (languages, dress, demeanor, education, and type of Catholicism) were even more distinct from that of the Protestant core. As Herberg (1960, 6) said some years later, "Each new group, as it came, pushed upward the level of its predecessors, and in turn was pushed upward by its successors." Irish Catholics were a visible presence in America for more than a half century before the arrival of Italians and eastern European Jews, and Irish mobility was facilitated by the arrival of these newer groups who in effect displaced the Irish at the bottom levels of the socioeconomic hierarchy. Although early Irish immigrants were the targets of vicious prejudice and occupational discrimination, by the late 1880s the Irish were viewed more favorably by old stock Americans than the Italians and Jews who were beginning to arrive in massive numbers. These newer immigrant groups took jobs at the lower levels of the wage scale and they replaced the Irish as residents of the least desirable urban neighborhoods. As the Italians and Jews moved in, the Irish moved up and out. Although such a process of ethnic succession is most often discussed in the context of the ethnic transformation of neighborhoods, this same process is associated with occupational mobility and the replacement of ethnic groups in other spheres, such as athletics, entertainment, and organized crime.

Religious Stratification

In chapter 1 we presented data on the religious makeup of industrial elites in the 1870s (see table 1.3). These data indicate that Episcopalians, Congregationalists, and Presbyterians, who represented less than 10 percent of the U.S. population, accounted for 61 percent of the leaders in the textile, steel, and railroad industries. Unitarians and Quakers, who represented about 1 percent of the general population accounted for 18 percent of industrial leaders. Other Protestants were decidedly underrepresented among these nineteenth century economic elites, suggesting the degree to which WASPs dominated the economy during a period of dramatic industrial growth.

We also presented data on the religious characteristics of U.S. presidents (table 1.2) during the period 1850–1899. We found that Episcopalians and Presbyterians accounted for 46 percent of U.S. presidents during this time, with Methodists accounting for 23 percent of the presidents. We also looked at the religious affiliation of Ivy League presidents (table 1.4) to assess the religious character of America's cultural elites. We found that 60 percent of the presidents of Ivy League colleges during 1850–1899 were Episcopalians, Presbyterians, or Congregationalists. It is true that most of the eight Ivy League schools had a historical connection with one of these denominations, but we showed that when Ivy League schools hired presidents who were not affiliated with the churches that founded the institution, they tended to hire presidents who were members of one of the other elite faiths.

Earlier in this chapter we analyzed the religious affiliation of cabinet appointees and justices of the Supreme Court during the period 1789–1839 (table 4.1). We saw that Episcopalians and Presbyterians were most likely to occupy these high level positions. The last two columns of table 4.1 indicate the religious affiliations of Supreme Court justices and cabinet appointees during the period 1840–1929. Again, Episcopalians and Presbyterians were most likely to fill these positions. Thirty-nine percent of cabinet appointees were members of these two faiths, as were 49 percent of the Supreme Court justices. We also see that Methodists were now represented in the president's cabinet, accounting for 23 percent of the appointees. There was some decline in the proportion of cabinet members and Supreme Court justices with Congregationalist affiliations. Jews first made their appearance in the cabinet and Supreme Court at this time.

All in all, these data indicate that Episcopalians, Presbyterians, and Congregationalists were the dominant force among the nation's political, cultural, and economic elites at the end of the nineteenth century. However, compared to the colonial period and the early 1800s, their control of the nation's resources had diminished.

TRENDS

How, then, does religious stratification at the end of the 1800s compare with religious stratification at the end of the colonial period? One way to answer that question is to compare the overall rankings of religious groups at both times (see table 4.4). At the end of the nineteenth century, the Upper stratum included Anglicans/Episcopalians, Congregationalists, and Presbyterians—the same groups that comprised the Upper stratum more than one hundred years earlier. Quakers and Unitarians were in the Upper Middle stratum at both points. Lutherans, Methodists, and Reformeds were still in the Lower Middle stratum. In other words, there was remarkable consistency in most rankings.

But there also were signs of change. Catholics (especially Irish Catholics), Jews (especially German Jews), and Nones had moved into the Lower Middle stratum. Although there were some socioeconomic differences among the various Baptist bodies that existed at this point, Baptists as a group had lost some ground. Meanwhile, Black Protestants, East European Jews, Italian Catholics, and Mormons were newcomers to the Lower stratum.

Table 4.4.   Religious Stratification circa 1776 and 1899

Stratum	1776	1899
Upper	Anglicans Congregationalists Presbyterians	Congregationalists Episcopalians Presbyterians
Upper Middle	Quakers Unitarians	Quakers Unitarians
Lower Middle	Baptists Dutch/German Reformeds Lutherans Methodists	Dutch/German Reformeds German Jews Irish Catholics Lutherans Methodists Nones
Lower	Catholics Jews Nones	Baptists, Fundamentalists Black Protestants East European Jews Italian Catholics Mormons

Note: Groups are listed alphabetically within strata.

Finally, in chapter 3, we saw that the groups in the Upper stratum occupied 89 percent of the leadership posts in our data set (see appendix 2). Relative to their percentage in the total population, they were overrepresented among elites at a rate of about 10 to 1. By the end of the nineteenth century, their dominance had declined. Averaging their percentages among presidents of the United States (table 1.2), presidents of Ivy League schools (table 1.4), and industrial leaders (table 1.3), we find that they now held 56 percent of these leadership positions (as compared to 89 percent earlier). Assuming they were about 7 percent of the total population (Davidson, Kraus, and Morrissey 2005), that means they were overrepresented among elites at a rate of about 8 to 1 (versus 10 to 1 in the colonial period).

CONCLUSION

Our account indicates that, with increased immigration and other changes in the nation's religious landscape, the power differential between elite Protestant denominations and other religious groups narrowed considerably. That led to changes in federal and state laws relating to religious stratification. However, it also led to the invention of new customs to protect elites' economic, political, and cultural dominance. It also reinforced the dominant pro-Protestant ideology and its bias against outsiders. The net effect was that the rank order of groups had not changed much from the end of the colonial period to the end of the nineteenth century. Episcopalians, Presbyterians, and Congregationalists were still most likely to be associated with the upper orders of society, but they did not have quite the stranglehold on social resources that they had a hundred years earlier. In the next chapter, we examine how these patterns of religious stratification would evolve in the twentieth century.

5

Persistence and Change: 1900–2010

So far our historical account has shown that the structure of religious inequality established during the colonial era remained largely intact through the mid-1800s, with some narrowing of the differences in the last half of the nineteenth century. Three religious groups associated with power, privilege, and prestige during the colonial era (Episcopalians, Congregationalists, and Presbyterians) continued to be overrepresented among those in the upper segments of society, but Methodists, Jews, and Irish Catholics made modest improvements in their socioeconomic position. In this chapter, we look at the evolution of American religious stratification by focusing on the period from the turn of the twentieth century until the present. We subdivide this lengthy era into three periods: 1900–1929, 1930–1959, and 1960 to the present. Within each period, we examine the power relations between elite and nonelite religions and their implications for laws, ideologies, and customs related to groups' access to resources. The chapter concludes with the current ranking of religious groups.

1900–1929

Since immigration was the dominant factor in ethnic change in America at the turn of the twentieth century, we start our discussion by examining the effect of immigration on America's religious landscape and, especially, the power relationships between elite and nonelite religions.

Power Relations

The era of cheap steamship fares (with rates as low as $10 for an ocean crossing) provided opportunities for Europeans to start a new life in what they believed was a land of boundless opportunity. This great wave of European immigration signaled an expansion of religious diversity in America as immigration from traditionally Catholic and Jewish areas in southern and eastern Europe began to match or surpass immigration from Protestant regions of northern and western Europe. As a result, Protestants were increasingly forced to share land and resources with an expanding population of non-Protestants.

Roman Catholics, who accounted for almost 10 percent of the total U.S. population in 1865, had grown to 16 percent of the population in 1900, and nearly 19 percent by 1930. In 1900, there were 12 million American Catholics. By 1930, there were 20 million. As the Catholic population grew, so did the Catholic Church's organizational capacity. New dioceses and parishes were added. New seminaries were built to accommodate the increasing number of males who wanted to become priests. New parochial schools, colleges, and universities were founded, as were new orphanages for children, new asylums for the mentally ill, and new homes for the elderly. In 1912, for example, the church reported 17,491 priests, 9,256 parishes, 88 seminaries, 229 colleges for boys, 701 colleges and academies for girls, and 393 facilities for orphans, the disabled, and the elderly (*Official Catholic Directory* 1912). With their limited material resources and outsider status, Catholics formed alliances with Jews and other outsiders as they opposed nativists' efforts to curtail immigration from eastern and southern Europe, but they had few allies in Protestant circles.

The population of Jews, which was estimated to be about 400,000 in 1880, grew to 1 million by 1900 and 3.4 million by 1917. Predictably, many new Jewish organizations were founded, including the Anti-Defamation League (1913), the American Jewish Congress (1922), the first Hillel Foundation (1923 at the University of Illinois), and the Synagogue Council (1925). Numerous Hebrew schools were established to promote religious education for children raised in the Reform and Conservative Jewish traditions. The founding of the National Council of Christians and Jews (1928) signaled a growing alliance between Jews and some Gentiles, but Jews were more likely to be isolated from the larger society than to be integrated into it.

The early twentieth century was a period of spiritual awakening among evangelical Protestants. A large number of new fundamentalist and pentecostal churches came into being in this period. A sampling of some well-known groups includes the Church of the Nazarene (1908), Pentecostal Holiness Church (1911), Assemblies of God (1914), the Northern Baptist Convention

(1918), American Baptist Association (1924), and the International Church of the Foursquare Gospel (1927). Southern Baptists increased their membership by 75 percent between 1906 and 1926 (see table 5.1). Seventh-day Adventists grew by 78 percent during the same twenty-year period. Twelve years after its formation, the Assemblies of God had nearly fifty thousand members. Although fundamentalist and pentecostal groups were part of the conservative Protestant family, there were deep theological differences between these groups and even deeper social and spiritual divisions between these evangelical groups and mainline Protestant denominations. Thus, the lack of allies on the part of conservative Protestants limited their power and influence. So did the isolation that followed the Scopes trial in 1925 (more on that later).

Meanwhile, membership in elite Protestant denominations continued to grow. Between 1906 and 1926 the Episcopal Church increased its membership by 110 percent, the Presbyterian Church in the United States of America grew by 61 percent, and the Congregationalists grew by 26 percent. New denominations were formed, mainly as a result of schisms within existing mainline traditions. These included the founding of the United Lutheran Church in America (1918), the Wisconsin Evangelical Lutheran Synod (1917), and Protestant Reformed Churches of America (1926). To create unity amidst the various mainline denominations, an umbrella organization, the Federal Council of Churches (FCC), was founded in 1908. The FCC was formed by twenty-nine mainline Protestant and Eastern Orthodox bodies that wanted to promote interfaith cooperation in sparsely populated areas of the country. The FCC was also engaged in social advocacy and its member denominations were encouraged to address social justice concerns.

In 1907, the Episcopal Church began construction on a magnificent symbol of Episcopalians' extraordinary access to the nation's social, financial, and political resources—the Washington National Cathedral. President Theodore Roosevelt (Dutch Reformed Church) and the Episcopal Bishop

Table 5.1. Reported Church Membership for Select U.S. Religious Groups

	1906[a]	1926[b]	Percent Change
Episcopalian	886,942	1,859,086	+109.6
Presbyterian	1,179,566	1,894,030	+60.5
Congregationalist	700,840	881,696	+25.8
Roman Catholic	12,070,142	18,605,003	+54.1
Southern Baptist	2,009,471	3,524,378	+75.4
Seventh-day Adventist	62,211	110,998	+78.4
Churches of God, N.A.	24,356	31,596	+29.7

[a] 1906 membership figures reported in Bureau of the Census (1910).
[b] 1926 membership figures reported in Bureau of the Census (1930).

of London spoke at the laying of the cornerstone. Episcopal church leaders view the cathedral as "a church for national purposes, . . . an indispensable ministry for people of all faiths and perspectives, and a sacred place for our country in times of celebration, crisis, and sorrow," and "a grand spiritual center where Americans unite to worship and pray, mourn the passing of world leaders, and confront the pressing moral and social issues of the day" (www.nationalcathedral.org). In 1918, President Woodrow Wilson attended an official Thanksgiving service at the cathedral marking the end of World War I.

Overall, the power gap between elite and nonelite religious groups persisted into the early decades of the twentieth century, although it was smaller than it had been in the colonial period and the first half of the 1800s. Despite their relatively small size, groups in the Upper stratum continued to grow organizationally and still had more access to resources, including allies, but nonelites (including conservative Protestants, Catholics, and Jews) also grew in size, organizational complexity, and solidarity. These trends had consequences for laws relating to elite and nonelite religions.

Laws

Nativists—who were a mixture of elite and other Protestants—demanded that legislators take action to stem the tide of "undesirables" landing on American shores. In 1907 Congress established the Dillingham Commission to investigate immigration, and in 1911 the commission issued a forty-one-volume report that concluded that, unlike the old immigrants who dispersed on arrival, southern and eastern European immigrants tended to congregate together, thus slowing the assimilation process (Parrillo 2006). To curb the new immigration, the commission recommended tighter immigration restrictions or a mandatory literacy test for immigrants. After repeatedly passing literacy bills, only to have the legislation die because of a lack of presidential support, in 1917 Congress overrode President Wilson's second veto of such a bill. This literacy act denied admission to immigrants over sixteen who couldn't read a short passage in English or another language. However, because the literacy rate in Europe had risen since 1900, the literacy test was not an obstacle for most immigrants, and immigration from southern and eastern Europe remained high after the law's passage (Dinnerstein, Nichols, and Reimers 1990).

World War I brought about a renewal of hostility toward the new immigrants. Jews, often portrayed as crafty and clannish, were increasingly identified in the public mind with political radicalism. Immigrant Jews were not welcomed during a time when "one hundred percent Americanism" was a rallying cry uniting Americans in the midst of a world war. The loyalties of Catholic immigrants were also widely scrutinized during the period (Olmstead 1960). This was the period of the Red Scare, a time when Attorney General A. Mitchell Palmer received widespread public approval after deporting hundreds of aliens suspected of political radicalism. During the 1920s a revived Ku Klux Klan emphasized patriotic themes in its declaration that blacks, Catholics, and Jews were the agents responsible for the social and moral decay of urban America.

The belief that America's moral and social fabric was under assault was reflected in the passage of prohibition legislation, as a revived Temperance Movement in America maintained a strong religious undercurrent. Although some Catholics were affiliated with temperance societies, the movement was largely supported by Protestants trying to reassert rural Protestant values in the face of urban ethnic pluralism (Kaufmann 2004). Baptist and Methodist churches were instrumental in providing support for the Eighteenth Amendment, which in 1919 outlawed the sale, manufacture, and transportation of alcoholic beverages. However, the widespread breach of prohibition laws indicated that a wide cross-section of the public, native born Protestants included, were willing to break the law in order to satisfy their urge for alcoholic beverages, and Prohibition was overturned in 1933.

In the 1920s, anti-immigrant sentiment contributed to a successful effort to postpone congressional reapportionment (Eagles 1990). Every ten years, seats in the U.S. House of Representatives are reallocated on the basis of population shifts reported in the decennial census. The 1920 Census revealed that the urban population surpassed the rural population for the first time in American history. Catholics and Jews were a major population force in America's urban centers, and the rural Protestants who controlled the House of Representatives refused to allow reapportionment because members feared that the increasing representation of urban based ethnic groups in Congress would signify a diminished role for Anglo-Protestants in the national legislature (Kaufmann 2004). Legislators justified inaction on the reapportionment issue by suggesting that immigrant masses in the cities did not represent the backbone of American democracy. Representative Cyrenus Cole of Iowa (a member of the Dutch Reformed Church) expressed the view of many in Congress when he stated that "a home on the farm stands for something more than a tenement in the city" (quoted in Kaufmann 2004, 33). Thus, no reapportionment of the House of Representatives occurred between 1911 and the 1930 Census. As a result, throughout the 1920s, the 1911 congressional distribution was in effect, which facilitated the passage of legislative measures favored by the rural Protestant majority. The refusal of Congress to give the cities more seats in the House revolved in no small degree around

Protestant fears of increasing Catholic control in government. This episode of congressional inaction on reapportionment was unprecedented. "Never before or since the 1920s has the United States Congress failed to reapportion the House of Representatives after a decennial census" (Eagles 1990, 116).

In this climate of hostility to immigrants, sweeping immigration restrictions were enacted in the 1920s. As a result of pressure from nativists and eugenicists, Congress, by a vote of 296–42, agreed in 1920 to suspend all immigration for one year. The House Committee on Immigration claimed that "unassimilable" Jews were coming to America in unprecedented numbers, and at least one prominent scholar has suggested that the chief purpose of the immigration restrictions of the twentieth century was to limit the number of Jews coming to America (Higham 1988, 310).

In 1921 Congress passed the National Origins Quota Act, which limited immigration to just 3 percent of foreign born persons of each nationality living in the United States in 1910. Republicans Albert Johnson of Washington, a Mason and "energetic nativist," and David Reed of Pennsylvania, an Episcopalian and a Mason, drafted a bill to halt immigration (Baltzell 1964, 201–02). Over opposition from colleagues representing states and districts with large numbers of Catholics and Jews—such as Democrat Emanuel Cellar of New York, a Jew—Congress passed the National Origins Act in 1924 (Davidson 2008). This law, referred to as the Johnson-Reed Act, limited immigration to 2 percent of the number of foreign born residents of each nationality residing in the United States as of 1890. In accord with the intent of its sponsors, the law severely curtailed immigration from southern and eastern Europe. Senators and House members passed the legislation even though it was opposed by their own denominational leaders (yet another case where progressive clergy from high status denominations advocate egalitarian policies, but the lay members of their churches are less likely than the church leaders to support values and policies that promote equality). While mainstream Protestant publications expressed mixed reaction to the immigration restrictions, Princeton University awarded Reed an honorary degree (Marty 1986, 391–92).

These immigration acts represented the closing of the door of European immigration for the first time in American history, and religious prejudice was certainly one of the factors leading to the passage of such legislation. This is not to suggest that religious hostility toward the growing population of Catholics and Jews was the only force in the decision to limit immigration from southern and eastern European countries. Other issues such as fears of crime and political radicalism were contributing factors. But Anglo-Saxon ethnocentrism and religious bigotry played a key role in the passage of the immigration restrictions.

Ideologies

As the immigration legislation indicates, white Protestant Americans did not joyously embrace the sharing of territory and resources with other religious groups. There was substantial resistance to the new immigrants, who were increasingly viewed as a threat to the American way of life. Much of the hostility to the newcomers could be traced to problems in urban areas where the immigrants were concentrated. Urban poverty, disease, crime, and political radicalism were associated with the masses of southern and eastern Europeans streaming to America's congested industrial centers in the early decades of the twentieth century (Gaustad 1966).

In response to the perception that the new wave of immigration was associated with urban social problems and cultural decay, new nativist publications appeared (Nordstrom 2006). One such publication was *The Menace*, which was the brainchild of Congregationalist Rev. D. Theodore Walker in Aurora, Missouri. Published weekly, *The Menace* reached 1.5 million readers. The anti-Catholic articles in *The Menace* prompted Bishop Noll of Indiana to launch a Catholic newspaper, *Our Sunday Visitor*, in an attempt to defend and explain Catholicism.

Many native born Protestants embraced the idea that the newer immigrants were genetically inferior to the older American stock. As southern and eastern European immigration increased in the early decades of the twentieth century, statements regarding Anglo-Saxon supremacy were more widely disseminated. Such assertions about the superiority of "the Anglo-Saxon race" were trumpeted by supporters of the eugenics movement, which was launched in the United States during the first decade of the twentieth century, reaching its zenith in the 1920s. Eugenicists advocated a program of restricting the number of offspring from what they termed "inferior racial stocks." They claimed that the English, Germans, and other northern Europeans of the old immigration were racially superior to the expanding population of Catholics and Jews, whose presence threatened the traditional American stock.

Eugenicist views were forcefully expressed in Madison Grant's highly influential 1918 book entitled *The Passing of the Great Race*. Grant's book was important because it gave intellectual support to the claim that there were superior and inferior European racial strains, and this brand of scientific racist logic was instrumental in generating support for the passage of immigration restrictions (Higham 1988). Grant suggested that there was a three-tiered hierarchy of European races, with Nordics (northern Europeans) at the top, followed by Alpines (central Europeans) in the middle, and Mediterraneans (southern Europeans) positioned at the bottom. Grant argued that the U.S. stock, which consisted primarily of Nordics, was disappearing because Nordic fertility rates were lower than those of the Slav, the Italian, and the Jew (Parrillo 2006). Grant reasoned that old stock Americans were thus being crowded out of their communities by southern and eastern European immigrants, and he referred to this passing of the Nordic element in America as "race suicide." Grant regarded any Nordic mixture with the other two Europeans races as mongrelization. Jews were not even part of the three-tiered hierarchy, and Grant suggested that a cross between any of the three European "races" and a Jew was a Jew.

Customs

The early decades of the twentieth century saw a continuation of the WASP tribalism that surfaced in private schools and prestigious social clubs at the end of the nineteenth century (Baltzell 1964). Policies of religious exclusion were designed to ensure the social homogeneity of America's elite schools and clubs, and the policies illustrate how discriminatory cultural practices were rooted in prejudicial attitudes. The customs were a reflection of an ideology embraced by eugenicists such as Madison Grant (1918) who were worried about social and racial pollution as a result of the intermixing of different European "racial" strains. The discriminatory customs served to limit religious outsiders' access to spheres of social interplay that were important for career mobility. For instance, if an individual was unable to join an exclusive social club because of the club's religious bars, and if membership in such a club was expected for those holding top positions in the nation's leading corporations and law firms (Baltzell 1958), then religious outsiders would not be nominated for such high level positions because of their limited access to other elites. Religious stratification thus played a role in the reproduction of power and privilege.

Restrictive educational admission policies at the nation's most prestigious private prep schools and colleges also perpetuated white Protestant privilege. During the early twentieth century, it was customary for America's first families to send their sons to one of the nation's socially elite prep schools, which served as feeder schools for Ivy League colleges. The nation's six most socially exclusive private boarding schools were all Episcopal schools, collectively known as "St. Grottlesex" (Groton, St. Mark's, St. Paul's, St. George's, Middlesex, and Kent). These boarding schools were places where boys from old and new money families would be turned into "Christian Gentleman." The schools taught students the manners and social skills associated with breeding and privilege. Few, if any, Catholic or Jewish students were admitted to these schools before World War II (Levine 1980).

Graduates from socially elite boarding schools were given preferential admissions to Ivy League colleges. Episcopalians, Congregationalists, and

Presbyterians were the dominant religious groups at America's elite colleges, especially the Big Three of Harvard, Princeton, and Yale (Karabel 2005; Baltzell 1964). In 1901 Presbyterians represented about one-half of all students at Princeton, and by the mid-1920s Episcopalians and Presbyterians together accounted for two-thirds of Princeton undergraduates (Synnott 1979, 176–77). Nevertheless, Jews were increasingly represented at Ivy League colleges. The proportion of Jews admitted as freshmen to Harvard had risen from 7 percent in 1900 to 21.5 percent by 1922. At Yale, Jews increased from 2 percent of students at the turn of the century to 13.4 percent by 1925 (Synnott 1979). The Jewish presence at Columbia was even larger.

Starting in the 1920s, Harvard, Yale, Princeton, and other elite schools imposed admissions quotas on Jews (Synnott 1979). The quotas were imposed largely because Jews were so successful academically. Academically oriented Jews were often disparaged as "curve raisers" and "greasy grinds" by their WASP peers (Baltzell 1964). By studying hard, Jews made non-Jewish students uncomfortable (Howe 1976). Feeling pressure from alumni who threatened to close their pocketbooks unless something was done to limit the number of Jews in attendance, administrators imposed anti-Jewish quotas at Harvard, Yale, Princeton, and other prestigious colleges (Levine 1986). In the 1920s Princeton decided to limit the number of Jews in the student body to the percentage of Jews in the national population—about 3 percent. Other Ivy League schools adopted similar, if less severe, restrictions on the number of Jewish undergraduates.[1]

Ivy League colleges developed other strategies to limit the Jewish presence on campus. The schools increasingly recruited students on the basis of geographical diversity, which served to suppress the representation of Jews, who were clustered in the urban Northeast. Schools also increased the admission of legacy students (Coe and Davidson forthcoming). At Yale between 1930 and 1940, the proportion of students who were children of alumni increased from 11.3 percent to 22.7 percent (Karabel 1984). Some observers have suggested that the legacy system itself was devised to keep Jews out of prestigious universities (Larew 1991; Lind 1995; Coe and Davidson forthcoming). The schools also instituted "character tests" that were used as social screening devices to limit the numbers of Catholics and Jews in attendance (Levine 1980).

Elite schools served as a springboard to elite professional status. Recruiters for the nation's top business and legal firms tended to select graduates from a limited range of prestigious schools, and those schools adopted formal or informal policies of restricting the admission of Jews or other non-Protestants. Thus, these restrictive admissions practices contributed to the overrepresentation of the historically dominant religious groups in the nation's most powerful corporations and law firms. These same firms also found it beneficial to sponsor the club memberships for senior officials, so religious restrictions in club membership limited the selection of religious outsiders to these high level posts. Because executive recruitment or senior partnership standing was also influenced by one's eligibility for a listing in the *Social Register*, which itself practiced religious discrimination in the form of restricting listings to Gentiles, all three spheres (college admissions, club memberships, and society blue book listings) were self-reinforcing mechanisms that worked to limit opportunities for religious outsiders who sought admission into spheres of power and privilege.

Such exclusionary customs are typically adopted by elite groups who feel that their status is threatened by outsiders who are vying for a larger share of the pie. According to Massey (2009, 392):

> Elites takes steps to restrict social ties to other members of the elite. Marriage outside the group is discouraged; friendships are turned inward through exclusive organizations such as clubs, fraternities, and lodges; and rules of inheritance conserve elite status along family lines. To the extent that group members are successful in confining social ties to other group members, they achieve *social closure*. Outsiders trying to break into elite circles are labeled bounders or interlopers, and they are derided for acting "uppity" or "above their station."

In the 1920s, Jews were seen as the interlopers whose rapid mobility was viewed with alarm by old line WASPs, who then adopted policies of exclusion as a way of preserving their own privileges. The insider-outsider divisions were facilitated by customs and practices that perpetuate differential access to various forms of capital: social, economic, and cultural. The policies of exclusion were undergirded by prejudicial attitudes about the social, if not biological, inferiority of religious outsiders.

In the political arena, Protestants tended to vote for Protestants, especially those who were Republican. When they had opportunities to do otherwise—for example, when Al Smith became the first Catholic candidate for the presidency in 1928—they continued to vote for their own kind (in this case, Herbert Hoover). Catholics tended to support Protestants who were Democrats, but when they had a chance to vote for one of their own, they did (the vast majority voted for Al Smith [Menendez 1977, 214]). The Jewish community also voted for Protestants who were Democrats. For example, 55 percent of Jews voted for Woodrow Wilson in 1916, and 51 percent voted for John Davis in 1924. But, in 1928, they voted for the Catholic Democrat Al Smith in even larger numbers, giving him 72 percent of their vote. The only time they departed from this pattern was in 1920, when 43 percent of Jews voted for Republican Warren Harding, 38 percent went to Socialist Eugene Debs, and 18 percent went to Democrat James Cox (www.jewishvirtuallibrary.org/jsource/US-Israel/jewvote.html).

As we saw in chapter 4, when Episcopalians, Presbyterians, and Congregationalists were in the White House between 1840 and 1929, they tended to appoint other members of these same religious groups to cabinet posts and the Supreme Court (Davidson, Kraus, and Morrissey 2005). When they did not appoint their own kind, they were most likely to appoint members of other Protestant denominations, such as Methodists or Lutherans. They were least likely to appoint Catholics, Jews, Others, and Nones. Notably, their tendency to appoint their own kind to these offices was less pronounced after 1840 than it had been in the late 1700s and early 1800s, and during the 1840–1929 period their appointment of members of nonelite Protestant groups increased. They were less likely to appoint members of nonelite religious groups to their cabinets, but they were somewhat more likely to appoint them to seats on the Supreme Court. When Quakers and Unitarians occupied the Oval Office, they were even more likely to appoint elite religious groups, and they did so more often after 1840 than they had done earlier. When presidents were affiliated with nonelite Protestant groups, they still tended to appoint members of elite religions. However, they were more likely than presidents affiliated with elite faiths to appoint non-Protestants to high level posts. There were no Nones in the White House between 1900 and 1930.

As we indicated earlier, religious conflict did not just take the form of Protestant-Catholic and Protestant-Jewish hostilities. Theological and social divisions between liberal and fundamentalist branches within Protestantism intensified during the early decades of the twentieth century. In the nineteenth century liberal Protestants began challenging a literal interpretation of the Bible, and many liberals believed that churches should be actively involved in efforts to pursue social justice. Liberalism was given voice in the Unitarian and Congregational churches, and it also thrived in the Episcopal Church and the northern branches of Methodism and Presbyterianism (Ahlstrom 1972). Liberalism engendered a fundamentalist countermovement supported by churchgoers who were troubled by a decline in old-time religion. Fundamentalists were concerned with what they viewed as the increasing secularism in society. During the late nineteenth and early twentieth centuries the conservative/fundamentalist wing within American Protestantism (composed of holiness, pentecostal, and fundamentalist groups) took the position that Christianity was being betrayed from within (Johnstone 2007). Fundamentalist Protestants believed that an increasing emphasis on social service and the social gospel among liberals meant that a traditional emphasis on redemption and salvation was being neglected. Fundamentalists opposed the teaching of evolution in schools, and liberal-fundamentalist cleavages were given a national spotlight during the Scopes trial of 1925.

In short, the continuing power gap between elite and nonelite religions contributed to laws, ideologies, and customs perpetuating religion's utility as a means for allocating social resources. To be sure, elites encountered opposition, but they were still able to get their way when it came to the legal, cultural, and social foundations of religious stratification. Studies of religious stratification during the period indicate the degree to which religious groups had differential access to economic and political resources.

Religious Stratification in the General Population

The Congressional Commission that prepared the forty-one-volume report on immigration and acculturation organized several large scale research projects, including a report on the earnings of foreign born and native born workers. Although the commission was not primarily concerned with the issue of religious stratification, its report provides a glimpse of the relative economic standing of the major ethnic and religious categories in America near the beginning of the twentieth century.

One of the interesting findings was that as early as 1908 Irish male immigrants and Jewish immigrants from Russia earned nearly as much as whites born in America, but southern Italian immigrants earned far less than U.S. born whites, and their earnings were also less than those of native born blacks (U.S. Senate Commission on Immigration 1911). Thus, as early as 1908, Irish Catholic immigrants were in a more favorable socioeconomic position than Italian Catholics, and the total population of Jewish immigrants was earning nearly as much as native born whites. We can assume that most English immigrants were Protestant and their earnings were slightly higher than those of whites born in America.

Religious Stratification among America's Elite

Despite America's increasing religious diversity in the early twentieth century, the social power of traditionally elite Protestant denominations had not diminished, at least not according to scholarly tallies of the religious affiliations of American business and political leaders. William Miller (1962) conducted a study of the social backgrounds of presidents and board chairmen from the largest companies in manufacturing, railroads, utilities, banking, and insurance during the 1901–1910 period, and he also examined the social backgrounds of political leaders at that time. He was able to determine the religious affiliation for 174 of the 190 business leaders and 165 of the 188 political leaders, and his findings are reported in table 5.2. This table provides a snapshot of the religious representation of the power elite at the turn of the twentieth century.

Table 5.2 illustrates the disproportionate influence of just two denominations at the height of economic and political influence. Forty-six percent of America's top business officials and 29 percent of its political leaders during the first decade of the twentieth century were Episcopalians or Presbyterians. Thus, these two groups were 2.8 times as likely as all other groups were to be business leaders and 1.1 times as likely to hold public offices.[2] The differences between elites and nonelites are even more impressive given the fact that these elites accounted for a diminishing share of all religious adherents during a time of expanding religious diversity in the nation.[3] Table 5.2 also illustrates the degree to which Methodists had begun to move up in the ranks of power and privilege, with 9 percent of business leaders and 13 percent of political leaders being Methodist adherents. Catholics were underrepresented among business and political leaders, although they were more prominently positioned in business circles than among national political leaders. Jews accounted for 3 percent of top business leaders and 2 percent of the political leaders.

Luther Fry (1933b) studied the religious affiliations of all of individuals listed in the 1910 *Who's Who* whose last names began with the letters A–M. His findings are presented in table 5.3. Again, we see that Episcopalians and Presbyterians are disproportionately represented in this social index of American leaders. These two groups together accounted for about 40 percent of all *Who's Who* entries. Fourteen percent of the entries indicated a Methodist affiliation, and Congregationalists accounted for about 8 percent of listings. Unitarians represented about 5 percent of the listings, which is noteworthy since Unitarians accounted for less than 1 percent of all religious adherents

Table 5.2. Religion of American Business and Political Leaders, 1901–1910 (percent)

	Business Leaders	Political Leaders
Episcopalian	25	12
Presbyterian	21	17
Methodist	9	13
Baptist	5	7
Unitarian	6	—
Other Protestant	8	20
Protestant, unspecified	16	25
Catholic	7	4
Jewish	3	2
Total cases	174	165

Source: Miller (1962, 324, 334).

Table 5.3.   Religious Affiliations of Individuals Listed in the 1910 edition of *Who's Who in America* (percent)

Episcopalian	19.7
Presbyterian	19.5
Methodist	14.3
Congregationalist	7.8
Baptist	7.8
Roman Catholic	7.8
Unitarian	5.7
Lutheran	2.3
Disciples of Christ	1.2
Jewish	1.1
Quaker	1.1
All Others	5.1
Listees reporting an affiliation (n = 2,884)	25.0

Source: Fry (1933b).

in the general population. Quakers were also overrepresented in *Who's Who*, although just 1 percent of entries indicated a Quaker affiliation. Roman Catholics, Jews, and other Protestant groups were represented in *Who's Who* in smaller numbers than might be expected, given the size of these groups in the general population. All in all, the three liberal Protestant groups that Baltzell called the Protestant Establishment were three times more likely to be leaders than members of other groups. They also were well overrepresented among leaders relative to their numbers in the total population.[4]

1930–1959

Now we turn to the era stretching from the end of the first great wave of immigration and the stock market crash of 1929 on one end to the beginning of the social and cultural turbulence of the 1960s on the other end. In between, there was more consolidation and retrenchment than expansion and growth in America's religious landscape.

Power Relations

Mergers between mainline Protestant denominations gave rise to the United Church of Christ (1957) and the United Presbyterian Church, U.S.A. (1958).[5] Mainline Protestant churches also grew in size and cultural influence in this period. For example, membership in the Episcopal, Congregational, and Presbyterian churches increased, as did membership in Lutheran and Methodist churches (Hoge and Roozen 1979). The organizational base of mainline Protestantism also expanded as these denominations built new congregations in the suburbs and expanded existing congregations to accommodate new and larger families during the post–World War II baby boom. Ties among mainline groups also increased as the spirit of ecumenism, interfaith dialogues, and efforts toward church unity increased. With roots in the 1950s, the Consultation on Church Union (COCU) spent the 1960s exploring the possibility of uniting several of the largest mainline denominations (before that goal was declared unattainable). In 1950, the primary organizational representative of mainline Protestantism changed its name from the Federal Council of Churches of Christ in America (FCC) to the National Council of the Churches of Christ in the USA (NCC). As a symbol of its position at the center of mainstream Protestantism in America, the NCC headquarters were housed in a nineteen-story building in the heart of New York City's central business district, erected with a generous contribution from John D. Rockefeller (a Baptist). The building's cornerstone was laid in 1958 by President Eisenhower. Over the years, the FCC and NCC enjoyed special relationships with the nation's major radio and television networks, which resulted in the networks donating free blocks of time for the broadcast of religious programming produced by FCC and NCC affiliated ministries. But the close relations between the Federal and National Council of Churches and the networks would soon come to an end as evangelicals began to mobilize in defense of their common interests.

The Nation of Islam (a.k.a. Black Muslims) was formed in this period, as were the General Association of Regular Baptist Churches (1932), the Evangelical United Brethren Church (1946), American Baptist Convention (1950), the Billy Graham crusades (in the late 1940s and 1950s), and Oral Roberts' healing ministries (in the 1950s). Evangelicals also built organizational ties within their own ranks. The National Association of Evangelicals (NAE) was formed in 1942 to counter the influence of the Federal Council of Churches. The exclusion of evangelicals from free network broadcast time was an important issue that caused evangelicals to form the NAE. The Federal Council of Churches had earlier persuaded the CBS and NBC radio networks to donate free broadcast time to recognized faith communities like the Federal Council, instead of selling airtime to religious groups. Since evangelicals at that time had not developed nationally representative organizations like the Federal Council, they were not granted free air time by CBS and NBC. However, in 1944 the NAE formed the National Religious Broadcasters, which then persuaded the Mutual Radio Network to resume its earlier practice of allowing paid-time religious broadcasting (Hadden and Swann 1981).

Since their formation, the NAE and the NCC have tried to maximize the power and influence of their respective constituencies. After the formation of the NCC in 1950, the NAE denounced it as an ominous super church threatening the freedoms of American Christians (www.nae.net/about-us/history/62). The NAE did not allow its members to be affiliated with the NCC.[6]

Other interfaith alliances surfaced during the middle decades of the twentieth century. African American churches in the 1950s began to draw together to fight racial oppression (Morris 1984). Civil rights activism witnessed the development of alliances among blacks, Catholics, and Jews who were attempting to challenge Jim Crow relations in the South and North. Black evangelicals would eventually form a separate National Black Evangelical Association in 1963.

Despite the slowdown in immigration during midcentury, the Catholic population continued to increase, mainly due to the fact that Catholics had relatively high fertility rates. The total Catholic population more than doubled, from 20 million in 1930 to 42 million in 1960 (D'Antonio et al. 2001, 12). Church leaders sought ways to meet Catholics' social and spiritual needs. As they saw it at the time, that task meant defending the church against the anti-Catholicism in society, strengthening social ties among Catholics, providing the laity with health and social services, and passing the Catholic faith on to succeeding generations of laypeople. With increasing numbers of priests, sisters, and brothers to call upon, Catholic bishops greatly expanded the church's organizational capacity. Between 1930 and the mid-1960s, the number of Catholic parishes rose from 12,484 to 19,723. The number of priests nearly doubled, going from 28,297 to 54,682, the number of sisters rose to 179,954, and there were 12,271 brothers. The number of elementary schools rose to 10,372, and the number of high schools increased from 937 to 2,433. The number of Catholic hospitals climbed from 645 to 808. The number of colleges and universities increased to 265 (Davidson 2005). This clearly was an institution-building period for Catholics.

Although Jewish immigration and the growth of the Jewish population in the United States slowed down, the organizational capacity of the Jewish community continued to grow. New Jewish organizations included the Council of Jewish Federations (1932), the Jewish Labor Council (1934), the United Jewish Appeal (1934), Brandeis University (1948), and the Conference of Presidents of Major Jewish Organizations (1955).

Overall, the power gap between elite and nonelite religions persisted more than it changed. Elite Protestants were able to retain their cultural influence. Both elite and nonelite religious groups grew in size and in organizational strength during this period, and they found that they had more allies than they had in the previous period.

Laws

Congress passed a major piece of legislation in the 1940s that contributed to the expansion of the middle class in America, and it also contributed to upward social mobility for Catholics and Jews. The 1944 Serviceman's Readjustment Act, better known as the G.I. Bill of Rights, was a massive government assistance program that helped many white Catholics and Jews move out of the working class and into the middle class (Brodkin 1998). The G.I. Bill led to the greatest expansion of college admissions in American history. Returning servicemen with an honorable discharge were granted one free year of college education (tuition and expenses included) for each ninety days of military service. In 1947 veterans accounted for about half of the nation's college students. G.I.s were also given loans to start their own businesses and low interest home loans to allow them to move out into the expanding suburban districts. Such legislation disproportionately helped European origin servicemen and thus it contributed to social mobility for Catholics and Jews, many of whom were the first in their families to attend college and own their own homes. Although G.I. Bill benefits were supposed to be available to all veterans, in fact, African Americans had a more difficult time securing the benefits (Katznelson 2005). The Veterans Administration's mortgage guarantee programs enabled whites to move out of the cities and into suburbs, but because of restrictive covenants and redlining policies, nonwhites could not take advantage of these provisions. Thus, the G.I. Bill not only promoted mobility for white ethnics but it also contributed to black-white residential segregation in America's metropolitan zones.

In the 1950s, Congress considered a revised immigration policy. President Truman saw this as an opportunity to abolish the national origins quotas that were instituted in the 1920s. The State Department was also hopeful that the quota system would be eliminated. Diplomats believed that the current policy of immigration restrictions was at odds with a spirit of international cooperation that characterized diplomatic relations in the aftermath of World War II. However, there was not enough support in Congress during the 1950s to repeal the immigration quotas, and the revised immigration legislation, the 1952 McCarran-Walter Act, retained the national origin restrictions implemented three decades earlier. Truman subsequently vetoed the McCarran-Walter Act, and in speaking about his position on the issue, he challenged the principle of giving admission preferences to immigrants from northern and western Europe. Referring to the 1952 bill, Truman said, "The idea behind this discriminatory policy was, to put it baldly, that Americans with English or Irish names were better people and better citizens than Americans with Italian or Polish names" (quoted in Kaufmann 2004, 183). Despite Truman's veto, Congress had the votes to override the veto and the McCarran-Walter Act became law. Senator John F. Kennedy attempted to amend certain provisions of the immigration law in 1957, but Southern supporters of immigration restrictions prevented a liberalizing of immigration policy (Kaufmann 2004).

Ideologies

Religious outsiders felt a special need to express their identification with and support of Anglo Protestantism during this period. For example, many Jews endorsed the concept of America being a "Judeo-Christian" society as the United States stood up against fascism and godless communism in the 1930s and 1940s (Silk 1984). Catholics took a leadership role in putting the phrase "under God" in the Pledge of Allegiance (Davidson 2005).

And yet anti-Catholicism and anti-Semitism were palpable in the middle decades of the twentieth century. Before World War II it was relatively common for employers to discriminate on the basis of religion. In the 1930s employers would often use the acronym "WPX" in advertisements and in job orders for employment agencies to indicate that they sought employees who were white Protestant Christians (Dinnerstein, Nichols, and Reimers 1990). One study of employment discrimination in the 1930s showed that in Minneapolis, more than 60 percent of the city's retail and manufacturing employers refused to hire Jews (Dinnerstein, Nichols, and Reimers 1990, 250). Also in the 1930s, Detroit's Father Charles Coughlin presented anti-Semitic diatribes in his regular radio broadcasts (Ribuffo 1997). One poll conducted during World War II showed that over half of Jewish soldiers had changed their names to generic American surnames to avoid anti-Semitic remarks from other soldiers (Koppelman and Goodhart 2008, 152). Another study found that in the early 1950s, 17 to 20 percent of all job openings in Los Angeles and Chicago requested non-Jewish applicants (Waldman 1955). Jews were also systematically excluded from political office in Los Angeles at the time.

Despite the high levels of anti-Semitism in the military, observers have noted that World War II represented a watershed of sorts in that the bravery demonstrated on the battlefield by white ethnic Americans went a long way toward reducing religious hostilities between Protestants, Catholics, and Jews in America (Baltzell 1976). After World War II, studies suggest a decline in levels of anti-Catholicism and anti-Semitism. Since 1937, the Gallup Organization has periodically asked American adults about their willingness to vote for a well-qualified presidential candidate from different faith traditions. Although less than half of Americans indicated a willingness to vote for a qualified Jewish presidential candidate in 1937, more than four-fifths of the public stated that they would support a Jewish candidate in 1967 (Jones

2007). Levels of support for a Catholic candidate also increased during the period. Sixty percent of Americans in 1937 said they would vote for a qualified Catholic for president, but this figure had risen to 90 percent by 1967.

Other surveys indicated a decline in levels of religious prejudice. In 1945, 19 percent of respondents in a national survey claimed that Jews were "a threat to America." Five years later, just 5 percent of respondents made the same claim, and by 1955 only 1 percent of respondents stated that Jews threatened America (Erskine 1965). A 1945 National Opinion Research Corporation survey found that 13 percent of respondents felt that Jews had too much power in this country, whereas just 9 percent felt that Catholics had too much power, with 1 percent agreeing that Protestants had too much power (Erskine 1965). These studies indicate the degree to which anti-Semitism and anti-Catholicism had decreased in intensity around the time of World War II.

Customs

According to Weber (1968, 316), at all social levels, and especially at the upper level, people express and protect their lifestyles by restricting potential marriage partners to social equals. Homogamous marriages allow for the intergenerational transfer of wealth and privilege and they serve to promote class unity among families that make up the social elite. During the middle of the twentieth century, religion was still an important factor influencing mate selection decisions, especially among those in the upper ranks of society.

Over the years there have been several studies of marital homogamy in the upper class. Hatch and Hatch (1947) analyzed 413 marriage announcements reported in the *New York Times* society section.[7] They found that 188 of the announcements listed one or both parties in the *Social Register*. Fifty-eight percent of the marriages took place in an Episcopal church. However, no announcements acknowledged marriage in a Jewish synagogue. Thus, in New York City, which had the largest concentration of Jews outside of the Middle East, Jews were hesitant to publicly announce their marriage in the city's major newspaper. This suggests that although Jews were well positioned on the basis of their income, educational attainment, and occupational standing, they had not penetrated the exclusive domains of old society. During the 1940s and 1950s scholarly discussions of a triple melting pot in American society emphasized the degree to which social cleavages in America were increasingly drawn along religious lines, rather than along nationality lines, leading to a division into the three major categories of Protestant, Catholic, and Jew (Herberg 1960). Researchers looked at patterns of mate selection to illustrate the importance of this tripartite faith division. Studies of intermarriage trends indicated that religious affiliation continued to be an important factor in mate selection, with Catholics tending to marry other Catholics, Protestants marrying Protestants, and Jews marrying Jews (Kennedy 1944). Thus, social boundaries based on religious identification continued to play an important role in channeling lines of social intercourse.

Religious boundaries were also evident in residential housing patterns. From the 1930s to the 1960s, Jews were not welcome in many traditionally WASP neighborhoods, some of which maintained "gentleman's agreements" among property owners not to sell or rent their properties to Jews. These gentleman's agreements and other restrictive measures were evident in affluent suburban districts, such as Detroit's Grosse Pointe and Philadelphia's Main Line. In Grosse Pointe, prospective residents were asked to fill out a three page questionnaire that rated the applicants on the basis of skin tone, dress, accent, and other qualities. Applicants were then assigned a rating based on a 100 point scale, with Jews needing to score a minimum of 85 points to qualify for home ownership in this wealthy community. For comparison purposes, Italians had to score a minimum of 75 points, and Greeks could qualify with a score of 65. Blacks and Asians could not qualify for home ownership in Grosse Pointe ("Grosse Pointe's Gross Points" 1960). Philadelphia's Main Line was another upper income community that discouraged Jewish homeownership before World War II (Varady 1979). Baltzell's (1958) study of leading Philadelphia Jewish families in 1940 found that not one Jewish family listed a residence on the Main Line.

Another custom perpetuating the privilege of white Anglo-Saxon Protestants during midcentury was the practice of preferential hiring and appointment. Several studies indicated the importance of religion in recruitment to high level positions in business and law during the period in question. One study found that although Jews made up between 12 and 15 percent of graduates of the Harvard Business School, they accounted for only 1 percent of the graduates who ended up in banking (Kiester 1968). Religion was also shown to influence recruitment in the legal profession. Smigel (1969) found that Irish, Jewish, and Anglo-Saxon law firms were clearly distinguishable, and he reported that the leading Wall Street law firms preferred lawyers who were "Nordic." A study of Jewish and Gentile graduates of an Ivy League law school in the 1950s found that Jews were significantly less likely than Gentile graduates to obtain one of their first three job choices (Goldberg 1970). Religion has also been shown to influence career promotion. A study of religion and executive promotion found that executives believed that being a member of the Jewish faith negatively influenced career success (Powell 1969).

Religious groups also differed in terms of their political preferences. During this period, Catholics and Jews were strong Democrats (Davidson 2005; Maisel and Forman 2001). Jews gave FDR (an Episcopalian) 80–90 percent of their votes; Catholics gave him two-thirds to three-quarters of theirs. Both groups voted for Truman (a Baptist) in 1948 (Catholics 70 percent, Jews 75 percent) and Stevenson (a Unitarian) in 1952 (Catholics 52 percent, Jews 64 percent). Catholics went for Eisenhower in 1956 (54 percent) while Jews went for Stevenson again (60 percent). Protestants, on the other hand, voted for the Republican candidate in every one of these elections.

In short, with the slowdown in immigration and the increased nationalism that accompanied World War II and the Cold War, elite Protestants were able to consolidate their control and count on nonelites to support the American way of life, including laws, ideologies, and customs that perpetuated elite hegemony. Nonelites were not powerless and did challenge some policies and practices, but they did not attempt to overturn the legal, cultural, and social foundations of religious stratification.

Religious Stratification

Despite claims by some analysts that the social power of mainline Protestantism was in sharp decline by the middle of the twentieth century, research indicated that the historically dominant Protestant denominations were still well represented in the upper ranks of the status hierarchy, but also that Jews had advanced into the upper socioeconomic levels. By the middle of the twentieth century, researchers had conducted the first comprehensive studies of denominational socioeconomic rankings (Cantril 1943; Pope 1948). Pope's (1948) analysis of data collected in the late 1930s by the American Institute of Public Opinion showed that Episcopalians, Congregationalists, Presbyterians, and Jews occupied the upper socioeconomic ranks based on their income and educational attainment. Methodists, Lutherans, Catholics, and Baptists ranked lower on socioeconomic indicators. Lazerwitz (1964), analyzing data from the Census Bureau's 1957 survey of religion in America, formulated a three-tiered hierarchy of religious groups based on their socioeconomic position. Episcopalians, Jews, and Presbyterians were positioned at the top; Methodists, Lutherans, and Catholics occupied the middle ranks; and white and black Baptists were at the bottom. Community studies of the 1930s and 1940s, such as the Lynds' *Middletown in Transition* (1937), Warner and Hunt's *Social Life of a Modern Community* (1941), and Elin Anderson's *We Americans* (1937), demonstrated that Protestants of British heritage were overwhelmingly represented in lucrative managerial and professional occupations. Beverly Davis (1953) sampled listings in *Who's Who in the East* for 1942–1943 and found that the listees came disproportionately from high status denominations: Unitarian, Congregational, Episcopalian, and Presbyterian. The 1957 Census of Religion found that over 55 percent of Jews employed in the United States were in the "Professionals and Technical" or "Managers, Officials, and Proprietors" category, as compared with about 23 percent of the general population (Howe 1976).

These studies indicated that colonial mainline Protestants (Episcopalians, Presbyterians, and Congregationalists [UCCs starting in 1957]) were still positioned atop the status hierarchy. However, it was increasingly evident that Jews had begun to penetrate the upper tier on the basis of their socioeconomic standing. Catholics also were making some progress up the social ladder. This upward mobility suggests that older religious hierarchies were undergoing some revision, but not to the extent claimed by disestablishment and modernization theorists. While Protestants no longer had the nearly exclusive access to valued social, political, and economic resources that they once had, they continued to be well represented in spheres of power, privilege, and prestige.

1960–2010

Finally, we turn to the most recent period in the history of religious stratification. And, a very transformative period it has been.

Power Relations

Conservative Growth, Mainline Decline

In the 1960s, important changes were taking place in Americans' religious affiliation patterns. Mainline Protestant denominations began to experience membership declines, while conservative Protestant churches continued to grow at a consistent rate. Observers like Martin Marty referred to the contrasting growth patterns of mainline and conservative churches as a "seismic shift" in American religion (Hoge and Roozen 1979). For the first time in American history, denominations like the Episcopal or Presbyterian churches experienced a decline in their membership.[8] The publication of *Why Conservative Churches Are Growing* by Dean Kelley in 1972 stimulated a good deal of discussion about the reasons for denominational growth and decline. Kelley argued that strict churches, those that made significant demands of their members, were the ones that were thriving, whereas low-demand churches provided fewer benefits to their members and elicited lower levels of commitment. Although scholars debated the merits of "the Kelley thesis," they acknowledged that denominational growth trends suggested a historic shift that signaled the potential for a reconfiguration of long-standing associations between religion and power in American life. In short, as the mainline denominations were losing members, it was assumed that they were also losing a corresponding measure of power and cultural influence, while evangelical and fundamentalist groups, which had traditionally been seen as representing the cultural periphery, were gaining members and cultural clout at the expense of the mainline groups.

These two trends—mainline membership decline and conservative Protestant growth—have continued to the present day. (See table 5.4.) Between 1965 and 2008, the Episcopal Church, long recognized as the church of America's upper class, lost 40 percent of its total membership. During the same period, the United Church of Christ lost 46 percent of its members, with the Presbyterians losing 17 percent. Facing membership challenges, mainline churches entered a period of reorganization and merger. Mergers after 1960 gave rise to the Unitarian-Universalist Association (1961), and the Lutheran Church in America (1962). The Methodist Church and the United Brethren merged into the United Methodist Church (1968), the American Lutheran Church and Lutheran Church in American morphed into the Evangelical Lutheran Church of America (1988), and northern and southern divisions of Presbyterianism evolved into the Presbyterian Church, USA (1983).

While the mainline denominations were losing a significant part of their membership base, evangelical Protestant denominations were experiencing growth. The Southern Baptists increased their membership by 50 percent after 1965, and the Assemblies of God and the Church of God (Cleveland) saw a fourfold increase in their membership. By the start of the twenty-first century, about 26 percent of Americans identified themselves as evangelical (Green 2004). In 2003 religious historian Martin Marty, in a speech presented to the National Association of Evangelicals, declared, "You won!" Marty was suggesting that evangelicalism was now the major force in American Christianity, and he affirmed that the open struggle between the National Council of Churches and the National Association of Evangelicals was over.

However, evangelicals do not speak with one voice on social and political issues, and there are current signs of political discord among members of the NAE. Recently the organization has adopted moderate positions on issues like immigration reform and aggressive interrogation tactics (torture), and this has generated criticism among the more traditionalist supporters of evangelicalism, who claim that the NAE has accommodated to secular politics and has given increasing emphasis to civic engagement activities. Some evangelicals decry what they term the "leftist tilt" of the NAE (Hartford 2009). Thus we may be witnessing an incipient political schism within the confines of the nation's largest evangelical organization. In recent years, the NAE's Governmental Affairs unit, headed by Richard Cizik, began to articulate a framework for evangelical civic engagement, which included taking action on climate change. This alienated some, such as Focus on the Family's James

Dobson, who in 2007 sent a letter to the NAE asking that Cizik limit his speech on "creation care" (environmentalism) or be asked to resign (National Association of Evangelicals 2009).[9] In 2009 the NAE issued a statement on immigration that focused on treating immigrants with justice and compassion. Furthermore it has encouraged the government to establish a process to allow undocumented immigrants to earn legal status. This new focus on civic engagement has alienated many in the organization, and today we see a split between younger evangelicals, who are concerned over hunger, poverty, and the environment, and older evangelicals whose political concerns are rooted in life and marriage issues.

Changes in Catholicism

As seen in table 5.4, the number of Catholics has jumped from 46 million to about 68 million. Most of this increase is the result of Catholics' overrepresentation in the last wave of immigrants. Since President Johnson signed the Immigration and Nationality Act of 1965, Catholics coming from Central America (e.g., Mexico, Puerto Rico, Cuba), South America (e.g., Colombia, Venezuela, Chile), and the Pacific Rim (e.g., the Philippines, Vietnam, Indonesia) have accounted for about 40 percent of these newcomers (Jasso et al. 2003).

Although the total number of Catholics is increasing, the Catholic infrastructure that grew so rapidly in the 1930s–1950s has declined since the mid-1960s. The number of parishes peaked at 19,723 in 1995 and has declined

Table 5.4. Reported Church Membership for Select U.S. Religious Groups

	1965[a]	2008[b]	Percent Change
Episcopalian	3,429,153	2,057,292	−40.0
Presbyterian	3,984,460	2,844,952	−17.2
United Church of Christ	2,070,413	1,111,691	−46.3
United Methodist	11,067,497	7,853,987	−29.0
Jewish[c]	5,725,000	6,489,000	+13.3
Roman Catholic	46,246,175	68,115,001	+47.3
Southern Baptist	10,770,573	16,228,438	+50.6
Assemblies of God	572,123	2,899,702	+406.8
Church of God (Cleveland)	205,465	1,072,169	+421.8
Jehovah's Witnesses	330,358	1,114,009	+237.2

[a] 1965 membership figures reported in Jacquet (1976).
[b] 2008 membership figures reported in Lindner (2010).
[c] Membership figures reported in American Jewish Yearbook (1968, 2009).

ever since. The numbers of priests, sisters, and brothers is declining (e.g., there are now just 41,489 priests [one for every 1,600 Catholics]). The number of elementary schools has plunged from 10,372 to 6,133, and the number of high schools is down to 1,341. The number of Catholic hospitals has fallen to 562, and there are now only 234 Catholic colleges and universities. It is fair to say that the Catholic Church does not have the organizational capacity it had in the mid-1960s (Davidson 2005).

Jewish Membership

Estimates of the size of the Jewish population vary widely (ranging from about 4 million to 7.5 million). The *American Jewish Yearbook* reports that the Jewish population as of 2008 was 6.5 million. However, this figure includes cultural Jews in addition to those who are members of synagogues. When asked which branch of Judaism they identify with, 34 percent consider themselves Reform, 26 percent say they are Conservative, 13 percent identify themselves as Orthodox, about 2 percent say they are Reconstructionists, and 25 percent are "just Jews" (Ament 2005). By most accounts, Jews as substantially assimilated into American culture and highly intermarried with non-Jews (about half of recent marriages involve a non-Jewish partner). Moreover, only about one-third of intermarried couples raise their children as Jewish. In addition, Jews have fewer children than other religious groups. This combination of factors means that the Jewish population is getting smaller and less distinctively Jewish (Dershowitz 1998).

By now, the organizational base of the Jewish community has been established. It already includes a wide variety of organizations dedicated to charity, social services, youth, and environmental issues. It also has a network of organizations that are concerned with American-Israeli relations and other global issues affecting American Jews. The Conference of Presidents of Major Jewish Organizations, which describes itself as the "central coordinating body of American Jewry," claims fifty-two member organizations (www.conferenceofpresidents.org). Few new organizations were begun after 1960, but long-standing groups continued to recruit volunteers and remained active.

The Jewish community does not have a network of specifically religious colleges and universities like the Catholics. Jewish students are most likely to attend a mixture of private schools (e.g., New York University, Boston University, Cornell, University of Miami, George Washington, Penn, and Yeshiva) and public schools (e.g., the University of Maryland, the University of Central Florida, Rutgers University, University of Central Florida, the University of Michigan, Penn State, Indiana University, and the University of Wisconsin-Madison) (www.hillel.org/about/news/2006/feb/20060216_top

.htm). Judaism has 759 day schools, which are heavily attended by Orthodox children, but few others (Schick 2005).

Other Religions

The size and influence of other religious are often disputed. It is difficult to get exact figures on the size of the newer religious groups (Bureau of the Census 2010, Wuthnow 2005). Muslims are estimated to range from less than 2 million to 6 or 7 million. Estimates of the number of Buddhists in America range from 1 million to 4 million. Hindu estimates range from 500,000 to over 1 million. The Pew Forum's 2008 U.S. Religious Landscape Survey showed that .7 percent of Americans were Buddhists, .6 percent were Muslims, and .4 percent were Hindus (religions.pewforum.org/reports). The 2008 American Religious Identification Survey (ARIS) indicated that Buddhists were .5 percent of the adult population, Muslims were .6 percent, and Hindus .3 percent (Kosmin and Keysar 2009).

The organizational capacity of these groups varies, but is growing. The Muslim community includes a sizable number of organizations devoted to spiritual, cultural, and political matters. There are about 1,200 mosques in the United States. Among the largest and most influential Islamic groups are the Islamic Society of North America, the Islamic Circle of North America, the Islamic Assembly of North America, the Muslim Student Association, the American-Muslim Alliance, the American-Muslim Council, the Council on American-Islamic Relations, and Islam Information Center (en.wikipedia .org/wiki/Islam_in_the_United-States).

Buddhism has experienced rapid growth in America in recent decades. According to the 2008 ARIS study, from 1990 to 2008 the number of Buddhists in America increased by 194 percent (www.americanreligionsurvey-aris .org/). Buddhism's growth is mainly the result of the conversion of native born Americans. One author (Lewis 2008) estimates that just 30 percent of American Buddhists are of Asian ancestry (www.bffct.net/id65.html). The World Buddhist Directory currently lists 2,154 Buddhist organizations in America, including temples and meditation centers (www.buddhanet.info/ wbd/). The three major branches of Buddhism (Theravada, Mahayana, and Vajrayana) are represented in American Buddhist centers. Buddhists have established several colleges in America, such as Naropa University in Colorado, the Institute of Buddhist Studies in California, and the University of the West, also in California.

Hindus have also experienced growth, but not to the extent of Buddhists. The ARIS survey indicates that in 2008 there were fewer Hindus in America than during 2001 (www.americanreligionsurvey-aris.org). Nevertheless, during the period from 1990 to 2008, the number of Hindus in America increased by 156 percent. Currently, there are 243 Hindu temples located throughout the United States (www.hindumandir.us/). American Hindus have established the Hindu America Foundation, which serves as a human rights group educating the public about Hinduism. This organization has also worked with the American Jewish Committee to address issues of bias against Hindus and Jews on American college campuses.

In short, although there is much discussion of the declining power of mainline Protestantism (largely due to declining membership), this discussion often overlooks the fact that its power relative to Catholics and Jews has not declined very much. Although the number of Catholics continues to grow, the organizational base of the Catholic Church is shrinking, and alliances with various Protestant groups have faltered. And, although Jews have been upwardly mobile in recent decades, the Jewish percentage of the total population is declining, the Jewish community's organizational base is not growing, and its alliances with other groups are more fragile than firm. Other faith traditions such as Buddhism and Islam are expanding their membership and organizational bases, but these religious traditions do not wield the power and influence of Protestants, Catholics, and Jews. Now let's turn to the implications these developments have had on the legal, cultural, and ideological foundations of religious stratification.

Laws

Since the 1960s, a number of laws have been passed that favor religious equality. An important piece of legislation that benefited religious minorities was the 1964 Civil Rights Act, which prohibited discrimination based on race, color, religion, or national origin in voting, education, employment, and the use of public facilities. Although the legislation's primary intent was to provide greater opportunities for African Americans and to eliminate the worst of the discriminatory practices associated with the Jim Crow era, it did address the issue of religious discrimination in American life and it provided the federal government with the tools necessary to enforce the various anti-discriminatory provisions. Thus this legislation signaled movement toward a new era when the most overt forms of public discrimination would no longer be tolerated.

A legal challenge to Protestant hegemony took the form of Supreme Court rulings in 1962 and 1963 stating that prayer and Bible reading in public schools were violations of the Establishment Clause of the First Amendment. Although the Supreme Court did not rule against any particular religious group in *Engel v. Vitale* (1962) and *Abington Township School District v.*

Schempp (1963), the rulings challenged long-standing practices established by nineteenth century Protestant educators who wanted public schools to be places where Christian principles were taught as part of the educational curriculum (Butts and Cremin 1953). In the late 1800s Catholics had developed a parallel system of parochial education because of the perception that public schooling in America was actually Protestant schooling under the guise of religious neutrality. Catholics had criticized the reading of the Protestant King James version of the Bible in public schools. The practice of requiring students to read Bible passages in American public schools was based on the belief of nineteenth century educators that a Protestant Christianity as taught by the Bible was the basis for good citizenship. It was believed that society had an obligation to teach its young people to be good citizens and to expose them to Christian precepts in the schools. The Supreme Court's decisions on school prayer and Bible reading challenged the notion that public schools should sponsor religious activities, thus validating the principle that no one religious tradition should be favored by state institutions.

Revised religious broadcasting policies adopted by the Federal Communications Commission (FCC) in 1960 helped shift the balance of power in religious broadcasting away from mainline religious broadcasters toward evangelical Protestant broadcasters, who vastly expanded their presence on the airwaves after this time. Historically, mainline religious groups had benefited from government regulations regarding the broadcast of religious programming on radio and television (Finke and Stark 1992). Since the 1920s, the FCC regarded religious programming as public service broadcasting, and the presentation of religious programs on local stations was one means by which stations could fulfill their obligations to devote a portion of their broadcast schedules to public service programming. Local stations provided free airtime to mainstream religious organizations (usually affiliated with the Federal Council of Churches or the National Council of Churches) in order to fulfill their public service requirements, but in 1960, the FCC ruled that paid religious programming could be given public service credit. Thus instead of meeting those public service requirements by offering free airtime to mainstream religious organizations, local stations found it much more profitable to meet those requirements by selling the airtime to religious groups that could pay for it. This worked to the advantage of evangelical broadcasters, who were much more willing than NCC affiliated broadcast ministries to use direct on-air appeals to raise funds to pay for broadcast time. Soon, evangelical broadcasters came to dominate religious broadcasting, with an especially heavy representation of pentecostal broadcast ministries (Schultze 1991). By dominating paid time religious broadcasting, evangelicals in effect displaced mainline religious groups from the airwaves.

The year 1965 marks a watershed period in American history because of the introduction of a new immigration policy that abolished the national origin quotas that were enacted in the 1920s. With the blessing of elite denominations (Kaufmann 2004, 142), the Immigration and Nationality Act of 1965 was passed in the spirit of reforms growing out of the civil rights movement of the 1960s. It eliminated race and national origins as selection criteria for immigration, and it prepared the way for increasing religious diversity in America. As noted above, the legislation opened the door to a large scale increase in the numbers of non-European immigrants allowed to enter the United States. Since 1965, more than 75 percent of immigrants to America have come from Asia, Africa, or Latin America (Chin 1996).

Two other pieces of legislation growing out of the civil rights movement of the 1960s signaled that the U.S. government had expanded its commitment to greater equality for all groups. Congress passed the Voting Rights Act in 1965, which outlawed discrimination in voting on the basis of race or color. The 1968 Civil Rights Act was enacted as a follow-up to the 1964 Civil Rights Act, and it prohibited discrimination in housing based on race, religion, color, and national origin. This act is commonly known as the Fair Housing Act and prohibited practices such as redlining and racial steering.

In 1993 Congress passed the Religious Freedom Restoration Act (RFRA), which was designed to protect a person's free exercise of his or her religion despite other laws that might restrict particular behaviors performed during the course of religious activities. The RFRA was passed in the wake of a 1990 Supreme Court ruling (*Employment Division v. Smith*) that asserted that religious beliefs do not relieve someone of the duty of following general laws. The Smith case affirmed Oregon's right to deny unemployment benefits to two Native Americans fired from their jobs after testing positive for the drug mescaline, with they used in a religious ceremony. Thus the RFRA was passed to protect a person's free exercise of religious practices. Adamczyk, Wybraniec, and Finke (2004) found that minority religious groups were more likely than mainline groups to go to the courts to fight for religious freedoms. At the same time, minority religious groups were less likely than mainline Protestant groups to receive a favorable decision on religious freedom protections. Nevertheless, the RFRA's intent was to protect the rights and privileges of minority faiths, which was consistent with other legislation supportive of greater religious diversity.

Ideologies

Numerous books and articles have been written about the demise of a pro-Protestant or Anglo Protestant ideology in America (Brookhiser 1991; Christopher 1989; Hutchison 1989; Hammond 1992; Kaufmann 2004; Schrag 1971). These publications differ on exactly when the decline began, why it began, and the pace at which it has occurred, but they affirm the theme that the values and ideals associated with Anglo-Protestantism no longer stand as the point of reference for the nation as a whole. The argument is that "the cultural center of the American nation is fragmenting" (Kaufmann 2004, 1). The consensus among these writers is that the expansion of racial, ethnic, and religious diversity during the twentieth century has been accompanied by a broadening of the nation's ideological vision, with the result that a pro-Protestant or liberal Protestant ideology has been replaced by one that increasingly values difference, diversity, and egalitarianism. Some scholars speak of our having entered a post-Protestant phase in American life (Berger 1986).

But are these observers right? If their account is accurate, then religious groups that value the collectivity more than the individual should be just as acceptable as those that value the individual more than the collectivity. Faiths that stress membership by ascription should be just as acceptable as those that emphasize commitment-based personal choice. Reason and affect should be equally acceptable approaches to faith. Insistence on compliance with group norms should be just as acceptable as tolerance of diversity. Top-down decision making should be as acceptable as bottom-up decision making. We don't believe any of these assertions are correct.

There is no denying that the ideals of multiculturalism have gained some traction in academic circles and among nonelite groups who want that ideology to succeed. However, it has not made as much headway in the general population and certainly not in the economic and political spheres of American life. Consider the data related to the persistence and/or demise of religious prejudice. Although survey research has documented a reduction in levels of anti-Semitism and anti-Catholicism after World War II, Americans have not fully embraced those whose religion is outside of the Judeo-Christian tradition. Public opinion polls indicate a substantial degree of prejudice against Muslims, Buddhists, and Hindus.

As indicated earlier, Gallup surveys have shown a steady decline in the percentage of Americans who refused to vote for a Catholic or Jewish presidential candidate. In 1965, 15 percent of Americans said they would not vote for a well-qualified Jewish candidate, but by 2003 just 8 percent said they would refuse to vote for a Jewish candidate. Ten percent of Americans said they would not vote for a Catholic presidential candidate in 1965, but just 5 percent would not vote for a Catholic in 2003 (Moore 2003). A 2008 Gallup Poll showed that just 4 percent of Americans maintained a negative view of Jews, with 13 percent holding negative views of Catholics. However, the percentage of Americans harboring negative views of Catholics and Jews is relatively small in comparison to hostility demonstrated toward those outside of the Judeo-Christian tradition. A 2008 Gallup Poll showed that 34 percent of Americans had negative views of Muslims, and 45 percent had negative views of atheists (Jones 2008). According to a 2010 Gallup survey, 43 percent of Americans admitted feeling some prejudice toward Muslims (Gallup Organization 2010).

Religious prejudice provides the foundation for religious discrimination. According to a national survey of religion and diversity, 20 percent of respondents favored making it illegal for Buddhist and Hindu groups to meet in the United States, and 23 percent said this about Muslim groups (Wuthnow 2005, 89). In the same survey, 60 percent of Americans said they favored the government collecting information about Muslim religious groups in the United States, with 51 percent supporting the collection of information about Hindu groups, and 48 percent supporting the collection of information about Buddhist groups. Because of the increase in the number of immigrants from Middle Eastern and Asian countries after the 1965 Immigration Act was passed, and because of public fears about Islamic terrorists after the 9/11 attacks, we see that a significant portion of the larger public supports the denial of basic rights of privacy and assembly to Buddhists, Hindus, and Muslims in America. Moreover, there is some evidence to suggest that fear of Islamic terrorism has been generalized to the point that many Americans also feel threatened by other non-Western religions that have never been connected with terrorist activities. So although the specific nature of religious ethnocentrism has changed over the years, religion continues to serve as an important factor in the maintenance of group boundary distinctions, and despite a general societal commitment to the support of egalitarian principles, a significant proportion of Americans would deny basic civil rights to other Americans who are outside of the Judeo-Christian fold.

Customs

Ethnic groups continue to settle near each other in culturally homogenous neighborhoods, and some of these areas are segregated on the basis of religion. For instance, Islamic neighborhoods are evident in some metropolitan areas, such as Dearborn, Michigan, and Jewish neighborhoods persist in various regions of the country. Ten percent of American Jews live in a neighborhood that they would describe as "very Jewish." According to Sheskin (2000), 17.6 percent of Jews in Florida would describe their neighborhood as "very Jewish," as would 16.5 percent of Jews in New York State.

Many private clubs continue to limit membership to Gentiles. One study in the 1960s found that 67 percent of a national sample of private clubs practiced religious discrimination (Braverman and Krapin 1967). The Anti-Defamation League of the B'nai B'rith reported in 1967 that a nationwide survey of 1,152 city and country clubs showed that most of them (665) discriminated against Jews, with 513 of the clubs banning Jews completely and another 152 using a quota system to limit the number of Jewish members (Howe 1976, 612). Although religious restrictions on club membership have declined over the years, many clubs continue to discriminate against Jews. Jeffreys (1999) has reported that the top five country clubs in the Dallas-Fort Worth area have no Jewish members, and he indicated that clubs like the Baltimore Country Club continue to place restrictions on the numbers of Jews who are admitted. The Bath and Tennis and the Sailfish clubs in Palm Beach have had a reputation of denying membership to Jews, and there are few Jewish members present at the Merion Cricket Club on Philadelphia's Main Line (Pyle 1996). Such a policy of "No Jews" is not always formalized or publicly acknowledged by the clubs, but it is adhered to nevertheless. Like most exclusive clubs, the Baltimore Country Club requires that a prospective member be recommended by current members, but in this case, an applicant must be recommended by twelve current members, a policy that surely would deter any but the most dogged of applicants. Rather than trying to enter such clubs, Jews have developed their own social clubs. However, there is evidence to suggest that religious restrictions on club membership have been relaxed. Friedman (1986) notes that starting in the mid-1960s prominent Philadelphia Jews were invited to become members of the Union League, a WASP club with a past pattern of Jewish exclusion. Friedman notes that even the Rittenhouse and the Philadelphia Club took in a small number of leading Philadelphia Jews after the 1960s.

Since the 1960s we have also witnessed an increase in the number of interfaith marriages. Kalmijn (1991, 1998) found that in recent decades traditional religious boundaries have lost their impact on mate selection decisions, and education has replaced religion as a key factor in spouse selection. Thus the triple melting pot of Protestant, Catholic, and Jewish endogamy described by Kennedy (1944) has largely disappeared. Kalmijn (1998) reported that Jewish-Gentile marriages increased considerably after the 1970s. Baltzell (1976, 513) noted that in Philadelphia in the 1960s, an unprecedented number of the daughters of WASP elites were marrying Jews. Zweigenhaft and Domhoff (2006, 23) suggest that about 50 percent of Jews today marry outside their faith.

Inheritance is another custom that plays an important role in the intergenerational transfer of wealth (Keister 2005). It is one way families are able to pass money along to children and grandchildren, but its use varies with religious affiliation. Mainline Protestants and Catholics are similar in their use of inheritance. Compared to these groups, people "who [are] raised in Jewish families [are] significantly more likely to ever receive an inheritance. Likewise, affiliation with a conservative Protestant faith in childhood [is] negatively associated with receiving an inheritance" (Keister 2005, 168).

There is some evidence to suggest that religion plays less of a role in hiring and promotion practices today than it did during previous decades. This is especially true when it comes to the hiring and promotion of Jews. Friedman (1986) suggests that after the 1960s Jews made substantial progress in gaining admission to large Philadelphia law firms. Klausner (1989) studied religion and mobility into executive management positions in corporate America. He concluded that as of the late 1980s there was still a Gentile/Jew divide in big business, although it was not as sharply delineated as it was before World War II. Jews were especially prominent in investment banking firms, and they were less well represented in manufacturing. Nevertheless, Klausner concludes that Jews are being absorbed into the establishment.

Silberman (1985) says that American society has broken open to Jews and that religion has little effect today on people's decisions about where to work or go to school. He says that it was not until the 1960s or 1970s that large corporations began to employ Jewish college and business school graduates in significant numbers. Zweigenhaft and Domhoff (2006) suggest that Jews today are full-fledged members of the nation's power elite. They are overrepresented in the Senate and the House of Representatives, in the president's cabinet, and in the executive suites of America's largest corporations. Although subtle patterns of WASP favoritism may still operate in corporate America, the blatant anti-Semitism of an earlier era has largely gone by the wayside. Whether or not these organizations are hiring Buddhists, Hindus, and Muslims is another issue, and we'll have to wait for future studies of religion and executive recruitment before commenting on this issue.

Religion continues to be a factor in election outcomes. The election of John F. Kennedy, a Roman Catholic, to the presidency in 1960, signified that Catholicism was part of the America mainstream, and it suggested the willingness of a large segment of the population to distance itself from the religious bigotry that had characterized earlier election cycles, such as the 1928 presidential election. Yet the results also indicated the persistence of traditional voting habits. In the 1960 election Catholics strongly supported Kennedy's candidacy, while American Protestants overwhelmingly supported the Republican candidate, Richard Nixon. Kennedy received the support of 82 percent of Catholics in 1960, whereas just 36 percent of Protestants voted for Kennedy (Brewer 2003). In both the 1960 and 1964 presidential elections, Catholics and Jews gave 80–90 percent of their votes to Democratic candidates.

Although Catholics in recent decades have continued to side with the Democrats, the political orientations of Catholics have changed a bit since the 1960s, but not as much as some observers suggest. Some people (e.g., Prendergast 1999) have suggested that the Catholic-Democrat connection that was an important force in U.S. politics before World War II has largely vanished. They contend that Catholics' support of Republican candidates has increased to the point that Catholics are now equally divided between the two parties. There are tendencies to cite Catholics' support for Ronald Reagan in 1980 and 1984 and their lack of support for John Kerry—a Catholic—in 2004. This shift has been attributed to the Church's opposition to abortion (corresponding to the Republican Party's pro-life stance), Catholics' upward social mobility (resulting in their support for Republican tax cut proposals), and the influx of Latino Catholics (who are seen as politically conservative).

However, the weight of the evidence does not support these claims (Brewer 2003; Brooks and Manza 2004; Davidson 2005). While there has been some decline in Catholics' identification with the Democratic Party in recent years, it is due to the fact that Catholics—especially younger Catholics—have increasingly thought of themselves as independents, not because they have embraced the Republican Party. Also, while Catholics no longer support any Democratic candidates as much as they supported FDR, John Kennedy, and Lyndon Johnson, they still vote for Democrats over Republicans by about a 55–45 margin. Catholics voted for Michael Dukakis over George H. W. Bush in 1988 (52 percent–47 percent), Clinton over George H. W. Bush in 1992 (50 percent–30 percent, with the rest going to Ross Perot), Clinton over Robert Dole in 1996 (55 percent–37 percent), Albert Gore over George W. Bush in 2000 (50 percent–47 percent), George W. Bush over John Kerry in 2004 (52 percent–47 percent), and Barack Obama over John McCain in 2008 (54 percent–45 percent).

Like Catholics, Jews also have become a bit more politically independent over the years, but they are still predictably Democratic in both their political identity and their voting habits. They have voted for every Democratic presidential candidate since 1924, by about an 80 percent–20 percent margin. That has not changed much in recent years, with 64 percent voting for Dukakis, 80 percent for Clinton in 1992, 78 percent for Clinton in 1996, 79 percent for Gore, 76 percent for Kerry, and 78 percent for Obama (Maisel and Forman 2001; www. Jewishvirtuallibrary.org/jsource/US-Israel/jewvote.html).

A study of political appointments has shown that when Episcopalians, Presbyterians, and UCC/Congregationalists were in the White House between 1930 and 2003 they appointed other members of these same religious groups to cabinet posts and the Supreme Court more often than they appointed members of other religious groups (Davidson, Kraus, and Morrissey 2005). Their tendency to appoint their own kind to these offices was no less than it had been between 1840 and 1929, but their willingness to appoint other Protestants declined as their tendency to appoint Catholics and Jews increased. When Quakers and Unitarians have been president, they too appointed members of elite religious groups, although less often than they used to. They were increasingly willing to appoint Catholics and Jews to their cabinets and other Protestants to the Supreme Court. When other Protestants have been president, they have been less inclined to appoint religious elites and more likely to appoint their own kind or Catholics and Jews.[10] When Kennedy was president, he appointed almost as many Catholics and Jews as Protestants to his cabinet. He made two appointments to the Supreme Court, Byron White (an Episcopalian) and Arthur Goldberg (a Jew).

To summarize, the fact that the power differential between elite and non-elite religions has declined somewhat in recent years has led to a number of new laws limiting the use of religion as a criterion in the allocation of social resources. These laws have imposed constraints on elite religions, but violations occur. Nonelites also have challenged long-standing ideologies relating to WASP superiority, but multiculturalism has penetrated the margins more than it has the center of U.S. culture. Meanwhile, a variety of customs relating to religious affiliation continue to affect people's access to power, privilege, and prestige.

Religious Group Socioeconomic Disparities

Changes in the nation's laws, customs, and ideologies suggest a general leveling of religious group socioeconomic divisions after the 1960s. But that is not always what researchers have found. Research on religion and socioeconomic status conducted in the 1960s and 1970s generally reinforced the findings of earlier studies (Davidson 1977; Demerath 1965; Glenn and Hyland 1967; Goldstein 1969; Roof 1979; Greeley 1981). Researchers emphasized that there were noteworthy socioeconomic differences among the major Protestant religious categories (Liberal, Moderate, Conservative, and Black Protestants). The consensus was that Liberal Protestants (Episcopalians, Presbyterians, Congregationalists/UCCs) and Jews ranked highest in income, educational attainment, and occupational prestige. Ranked just below these groups were those with no religious preference (Nones). Catholics and Moderate Protestants (e.g., Lutherans, Methodists, Disciples of Christ) occupied the middle ranks of the status hierarchy, with Black and Conservative Protestants (e.g., Southern Baptists, Nazarenes, Churches of God, Assemblies of God) positioned at the bottom.

However, after the 1970s some analysts argued that the social bases of denominationalism were no longer as important as they once were in separating America's faith traditions (Christopher 1989; Park and Reimer 2002; Stark 2003; Wuthnow 1988). Christopher (1989, 237) pointed to "the declining importance of religion as a divisive factor in American life." He cited the rapid increase in interethnic marriages as a factor in the reduction of cultural differences between European ethnic groups. He also suggested that the civil rights movement of the 1960s and the blunders of Vietnam policy served to erode WASP hegemony. Christopher argued that the adoption of need-blind admissions policies by private universities and the use of guaranteed student loans served to open the doors of college opportunity to a wider cross section of the public. Wuthnow (1988) agreed that the boundaries separating the major religious traditions were recast after World War II. Rising levels of education contributed to a decline in interdenominational status differences, resulting in a pattern of convergence among the various denominations in terms of their demographic characteristics. The implication was that the status ordering of religious groups was not as clearly defined as it once was.

Others studies suggested a decline in religious group socioeconomic differences over the years. Park and Reimer (2002) claimed that denominational socioeconomic boundaries had blurred in recent decades, and they disagreed with the status theories of Pope (1942) and Glock (1964), which focused on social or economic deprivation as a basis for sectarian affiliation. Park and Reimer suggested that "class has a weak effect on religious affiliation, since both the rich and poor are attracted to sects" (2002, 741–42). Stark (2003) agreed that social class was an unreliable predictor of religious adherence. According to Stark, members of evangelical and fundamentalist Protestant groups "are as likely to have gone to college and to earn high incomes as are members of more liberal denominations as well as Roman Catholics" (2003, 6). Lindsay (2007, 2008) has indicated that evangelicals are well positioned among America's power elite, and he has emphasized that evangelical social ties to others who are highly placed leads them to have more institutional influence than has previously been acknowledged. Lindsay has argued that evangelicals wield influence through "convening power." By this, he means that evangelical elites have the ability to convene groups and join with other evangelical leaders in common cause.

Despite these claims about a decline in religious group socioeconomic differences, other researchers have emphasized that America's major faith traditions continue to be distinguished on the basis of the social standing of their members (Coreno 2002; Darnell and Sherkat 1997; Davidson 1994, 2008; Davidson, Pyle, and Reyes 1995; Keister 2003). Several studies have emphasized the persistence of socioeconomic distinctions between mainline and Conservative Protestants. Davidson, Pyle, and Reyes (1995) and Pyle (1996) studied the religious characteristics of individuals listed in *Who's Who in America* and found that Liberal Protestants were disproportionately over-represented among the nation's business, political, and cultural elites from the 1930s to the 1990s. Baptists and sectarians were substantially underrepresented among *Who's Who* listees during the same period. Darnell and Sherkat (1997), in a study of education and religious adherence, found a negative link between fundamentalism and educational attainment, which partly explained the persisting socioeconomic deficits for Conservative Protestants.

Coreno (2002) and Smith and Faris (2005) found significant differences between mainline and Conservative Protestants on the basis of socioeconomic indicators. Keister (2003) looking at religious affiliation and the accumulation of wealth found that Conservative Protestants had significantly less wealth than Jews, Catholics, and mainline Protestants. Keister (2007) also reported that white non-Hispanic Catholics have been upwardly mobile in recent decades. She has suggested that Catholic values related to work and money contributed to high saving behavior that facilitated mobility. On the other hand, the unique economic values of Conservative Protestants serve to reduce their wealth relative to other religious groups (Keister 2008). Massengill (2008) examined how a conservative Protestant background reduces educational attainment. She found that those who self-identify as evangelical tend to be of higher socioeconomic status than those affiliated with denominations classified as evangelical. McCloud (2007) emphasized the importance of cultural resources and situational factors in accounting for the persistence of socioeconomic differences between religious groups. Incorporating Bourdieu's concept of habitus, McCloud suggested that cultural resources are associated with class codes that predispose individuals from similar social locations to join particular religious groups.

Thus researchers disagree about the degree to which we have witnessed a blurring of religious group socioeconomic distinctions in recent decades. Some claim that the older religious hierarchies have given way to greater socioeconomic equality among religious groups. Others maintain that socioeconomic boundaries between the major faith traditions have been quite persistent over the years.

To analyze the degree to which religious group socioeconomic differences declined in recent decades, Pyle (2006) conducted an analysis of the 1972–2000 General Social Surveys. The large number of cases (over 40,000) included in this data file permitted an analysis of denominational socioeconomic scores for three time periods (1972–1980, 1982–1990, and 1991–2000).

Respondents were classified into twenty-five categories, in accord with the classification method presented in Roof and McKinney (1987, 253–56). Members of Protestant denominations were assigned to four major categories (Liberal, Moderate, Conservative, and Black Protestant) following Roof and McKinney's classification scheme.

Socioeconomic Index

Table 5.5 indicates the relative position of the major religious categories on the socioeconomic index. (The vertical scale indicates the number of standard deviation units above or below the national mean for each religious group on the socioeconomic measure.) Table 5.5 suggests a pattern of persisting differences between the major faith traditions on socioeconomic indicators. Jews are distinguished from the other faith groups by having the highest socioeconomic scores. The scores for Jews indicate a curvilinear pattern, with the highest score (.93) observed during the 1980s. Liberal Protestants ranked second below Jews, with standard scores of .48 in the 1970s and 1980s and .40 in the 1990s.

Moderate Protestants, Catholics, Nones, and All Others were positioned closer to the national average on the socioeconomic index. Moderate Protestants consistently occupied the middle ranks of the socioeconomic hierarchy, with scores of .00, 02, and −.01 during the three periods. Groups in the All Others category were positioned above Catholics and Moderate Protestants, with scores of .11, .23, and .18. Catholic scores ranged from .01 in the 1970s to .07 in the 1990s. Conservative Protestants and Black Protestants had the lowest socioeconomic scores. The scores for Conservative Protestants from the 1970s to the 1990s were −.30, −.35, and −.25. Black Protestants had the lowest scores, but the socioeconomic deficits for Black Protestants moderated over the years (rising from −.56 in the 1970s to −.43 in the 1990s), indicating some improvement in the socioeconomic positioning of Black Protestants.

Table 5.5 indicates some narrowing of differences between Liberal Protestants and the other Protestant traditions since the 1970s. At the same time, the overall socioeconomic ranking of the major Protestant traditions did not change from the 1970s to the 1990s. These socioeconomic differences among the major religious categories remained after the introduction of controls for a wide range of demographic factors, including gender, region, father's occupation, and other variables. One noteworthy change in the rankings was the decline in the scores for Nones (falling from .29 in the 1970s to .05 in the 1990s). Previously, religious Nones ranked close to Liberal Protestants on socioeconomic indicators (Roof and McKinney 1987), but by the 1990s those with no religious preference were positioned near the center of the rankings.

Table 5.5.　Religious Group Rankings on the Socioeconomic Index

Standard Score	1972–1980	1982–1990	1991–2000
.95		Jews	
.90			
.85			Jews
.80			
.75			
.70	Jews		
.65			
.60			
.55			
.50	Liberal Protestant	Liberal Protestant	
.45			
.40			Liberal Protestant
.35			
.30	Nones		
.25		All Others	
.20		Nones	All Others
.15			
.10	All Others*		
.05		Catholics	Nones, Catholics
.00	Moderate Protestant, Catholics	Moderate Protestant	Moderate Protestant
−.05			
−.10			
−.15			
−.20			
−.25			Conservative Protestant
−.30	Conservative Protestant		
−.35		Conservative Protestant	
−.40		Black Protestant	
−.45			Black Protestant
−.50			
−.55	Black Protestant		

*Includes Mormons, Jehovah's Witnesses, Unitarians, Christian Scientists, and Others.

Despite some narrowing of differences among the religious categories on socioeconomic indicators, religious groups continue to be distinguished on the basis of their socioeconomic positioning, and the overall religious group status ranking remains largely unchanged from the rankings of fifty years ago. Jews and Liberal Protestants remain at the top, Catholics and Moderate Protestants continue to occupy the middle ranks of the socioeconomic hierarchy, and Black and Conservative Protestants remain at the bottom. Although the deficits for Black Protestants have lessened during the period, Black Protestants continue to rank near the bottom of the socioeconomic scale.

Unfortunately, the General Social Surveys do not include a large enough sample of Muslims, Buddhists, and Hindus to allow comparisons of their socioeconomic position with that of the other religious groups. However, in 2008, the Pew Research Center released the results of a national survey of over 35,000 American adults, and because of the large size of this sample, there were enough cases to permit a comparative analysis of the income and educational characteristics of the major religious groups, including Buddhists, Hindus, and Muslims. The results are presented in table 5.6.

The Pew survey shows that Jews and Hindus rank higher than other groups on the basis of their educational attainment and income. Members of the Orthodox, Buddhist, and Mainline Protestant traditions are positioned below Jews and Hindus. It must be noted that the Mainline Protestants category includes both moderate and liberal Protestants, not just the colonial mainline denominations. Pew data not reported here show that, if we distinguish between Liberal and Moderate Protestants, Liberal Protestants rank above Orthodox and Buddhists, and Moderate Protestants are positioned in the Lower Middle

Table 5.6.　Income and Educational Characteristics of Major Religious Categories (percent)

	Earning >$100,000	Bachelor's Degree
Jews	46	59
Hindus	43	74
Orthodox	28	46
Buddhists	22	48
Mainline Protestants	21	34
Unaffiliated	19	29
Roman Catholics	19	26
Mormons	16	24
Evangelicals	13	20
Black Protestants	13	16
National average	18	27

Source: Pew Forum on Religion and Public Life (2008).

stratum. Nones, Catholics, Mormons, and Muslims are placed in the Lower Middle stratum, with Evangelicals and Black Protestants occupying the Lower stratum. The Pew findings suggest that there are important socioeconomic differences between Hindus, Buddhists, and Muslims. Hindus clearly outrank the other two groups in income and educational attainment. Buddhists have moderate incomes and relatively high educational attainment, whereas Muslims score below the other two groups on the basis of income and education.

The current status rankings of religious groups are presented in table 5.7. The rankings are based on our assessment of each group's relative standing on the dimensions of power, privilege, and prestige. Several factors are considered. A group's relative socioeconomic standing is important, but it is not the only factor determining its position in the status hierarchy. For instance, there is evidence that Hindus today outrank most other religious groups on the basis of their income and educational attainment, but because Hindus are a relatively recent population that has yet to establish itself as a major force in the power centers of American life, and because a large segment of the American population remains somewhat hostile toward faith traditions identified with Asian and Middle Eastern immigrants, the elevated income and educational attainment of Hindus would not justify placing them in the upper tier of the status rankings, irrespective of other factors. Thus in addition to considering a group's socioeconomic position in the general population, we look at a group's standing among political and economic elites. We also consider a group's cultural influence—its location and influence over American culture. Religious groups that are more closely aligned with the center of the nation's core culture and those that are more closely identified with the American national character exert more influence over major spheres of American life (politics, family, education, the media, etc.) than groups that are associated with the cultural periphery. Admittedly, an assessment of a religious group's cultural influence is at least partly based on subjective considerations, but any discussion of religious stratification has to take into account a group's standing in the nation's economic, political, and cultural hierarchies.

The status rankings for 2010 are based on information culled from a variety of studies of religion and socioeconomic status, such as the Kosmin and Keysar analysis (Davidson 2008), the Pew Forum study (2008), the analysis of General Social Survey data (Pyle 2006), and the studies of religion in *Who's Who in America* (Davidson, Pyle, and Reyes 1995).

The latest ranking puts Episcopalians, Jews, Presbyterians, and Unitarians in the Upper stratum. Catholics, Hindus, Methodists, Mormons, Quakers, and UCCs form the Upper Middle stratum. Buddhists, Reformeds, Lutherans, and Nones make up the Lower Middle stratum. The Lower stratum consists of the Assemblies of God and other pentecostal groups, Baptists and other

Table 5.7.   Religious Stratification circa 1776, 1899, and 2010

Stratum	1776	1899	2010
Upper	Congregationalists Anglicans Presbyterians	Congregationalists Episcopalians Presbyterians	Episcopalians Jews Presbyterians Unitarian Universalists
Upper Middle	Quakers Unitarians	Quakers Unitarians	Catholics Hindus Methodists Mormons Quakers United Church of Christ
Lower Middle	Baptists Dutch/German Reformed Lutherans Methodists	Dutch/German Reformed German Jews Irish Catholics Lutherans Methodists Nones	Buddhists Dutch/German Reformed Lutherans Nones
Lower	Catholics Jews Nones	Baptists, Fundamentalists Black Protestants East European Jews Italian Catholics Mormons	Assemblies of God, Pentecostals Baptists, Fundamentalists Black Baptists, Black Methodists Muslims

Note: Groups are listed alphabetically within strata.

Fundamentalist bodies, Black Baptist and Black Methodist denominations, and Muslims.

How severe are religious inequalities these days? To answer that question, we used eight data points for the four groups at the top of today's society (the

New Upper stratum). The data points indicate how these groups fare in terms of being president of the United States since 1960, president of Ivy League schools since 1960,[11] in the *Who's Who* in 1970–1971, in the *Who's Who* in 1992–1993, a member of the economic elite in 1976–1977, a member of the political elite in 1976–1977, a member of the intellectual elite in 1976–1977, and a college graduate in 2001. The results show that, on average, these groups account for 46 percent of the people in these elite situations. Although they are less than 10 percent of the total population, they are 34 percent of the power elite (U.S. president, business elites, and political elites) and 56 percent of the cultural elite (Ivy League presidents, intellectual elites, and college graduates).

TRENDS

These findings invite us to take an even more refined look at the trends in religious stratification from the colonial period to the present. Table 5.7 also lets us compare the rankings of religious groups over time. Five groups have been in the same stratum all along: Anglicans/Episcopalians and Presbyterians in the Upper stratum; Quakers in the Upper Middle stratum; and Lutherans and Reformeds in the Lower Middle stratum. Five others are within one stratum of where they started out: UCC/Congregationalists, Unitarian-Universalists, Baptists, Methodists, and Nones. Two groups have moved up two or more strata: Jews and Catholics. One of the two groups that were founded in the 1800s, one has remained in the same stratum (Black Protestants) and one has moved up two strata (Mormons). In other words, these rankings point to remarkable continuity and considerable change.

To get a sense of how severe religious inequalities have been over time, we have estimated the percentage of the Old Upper stratum (Episcopalians, UCC/Congregationalists, and Presbyterians) at each of thirty data points located in five time periods: the colonial years, 1787–1859, 1860–1929, 1930–1959, and 1960–2010. In addition, we have calculated scores for the New Upper stratum (Episcopalians, Jews, Presbyterians, and Unitarians) at eight data points since 1960 (for details see appendix 1 and appendix 2).

Our findings (see figure 5.1) suggest that it is useful to distinguish between an early period in which religious stratification was highly institutionalized and highly pronounced (the colonial period through the mid-1800s) and a later period in which it was less institutionalized and less pronounced (the mid-1800s to the present). There also are fluctuations within each period. The Old Upper stratum's dominance declined from 89 percent in the colonial period to 65 percent in the 1787–1859 period. In the more recent period, the pattern has been curvilinear, with the Old Upper stratum's dominance declining

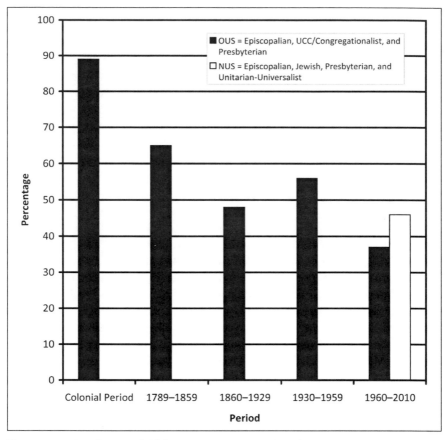

Figure 5.1. Dominance of Old Upper Stratum (OUS) and New Upper Stratum (NUS) by Period (mean percentages)

to 48 percent between 1860 and 1929 and rising to 56 percent between 1930 and 1959, before the New Upper stratum's dominance dipped to 46 percent between 1960 and 2010.

CONCLUSION

The evidence presented in chapters 4 and 5 supports several conclusions. First, religious stratification was more pronounced and more highly institutionalized in the colonial period and the early-1800s than it has been in the past 150 years or so. The social, economic, and political gaps between elite and nonelite groups are narrower now than they were 200 to 250 years ago, but religious stratification is still an important part of the American way of life.

Second, there has been both persistence and change in religious stratification within the more recent of these two major time periods. Episcopalians, Presbyterians, and Congregationalist/UCCs, who had substantial power, privilege, and prestige in the mid-1800s and at the beginning of the twentieth century, are still well positioned socioeconomically. The same is true for Quakers and Unitarians, although not quite to the same degree. Meanwhile, evangelical and Black Protestants, who were in the bottom half of the social hierarchy in the early 1900s are in much the same situation in the early 2000s. However, elite Protestant groups do not control the nation's resources as much as they used to. Jews were penetrating the Upper and Upper Middle strata by the 1950s and 1960s and now outrank colonial mainline Protestants on socioeconomic indicators. Catholics have reached the Upper Middle stratum, although Irish and other Catholics in the largely European wave of immigration rank higher than Latino Catholics in the most recent wave of immigrants from other continents. With changes in American immigration policies after 1965, we also have seen an increase in the numbers of Buddhists, Hindus, and Muslims in America, and we have enough evidence from survey and ethnographic data to know that Hindus ranker higher than Buddhists who, in turn, rank higher than Muslims. In this sense, older patterns of religious stratification have shifted somewhat as newer groups have entered the society and as others have moved up or down in the rankings.

The main explanation for these changes is that laws relating to the allocation of resources have become more inclusive. Old laws allowing religion to affect access to resources have largely been replaced by ones that prohibit religious favoritism and discrimination. The main reason there is so much continuity is that religious ideologies and customs still give liberal Protestants and groups that embrace liberal Protestant culture advantages over other religious groups. The persistence of these supports contributes to the tenacity of religious stratification.

Lying behind both of these explanations are two other facts: (a) elite religions continue to have more power than nonelites, but (b) the power differential between elite and nonelite religions has declined in recent decades. Elite groups have always been comparatively small in membership, but they have been getting even smaller since the mid-1960s relative to the growth of nonelites. Elites' organizational advantages and alliances also have shrunk a bit, as nonelites have strengthened themselves in both areas. Despite these changes, the power differential still tilts toward elites.

In light of these findings, we turn to our last question: what effects has religious stratification had on our society?

6

Consequences

Our final question is: So what? Does religious stratification really matter? Does it have any impact on society? If so, what kinds of effects does it have?

In chapter 2, we described two competing views of how social stratification affects society. According to functionalists Kingsley Davis and Wilbert Moore (1945) and other scholars working in the functionalist tradition, stratification contributes to social integration and stability. Conflict theorist Melvin Tumin (1953) and colleagues working in the conflict tradition believe that stratification creates disorder and destabilizes the society.

The literature on stratification related to race, ethnicity, class, and gender supports the conflict view more than it does the functionalist view (e.g., Beeghley 2005; Hurst 2007; Kerbo 2006; Rothman 2005). It shows that these forms of stratification adversely affect society. Instead of contributing to the well-being of the society, they create social problems that otherwise might not exist.

We contend that religious stratification also is likely to have negative consequences. It, too, should create social problems and produce social instability. In chapter 2, we pointed to several indicators of social instability: the absence of unifying behaviors such as ecumenical activities and interfaith partnerships, and the existence of nativist groups, hate groups, and self-defense organizations; marches, strikes, and boycotts; hate speech and the publication of hate literature; killing, kidnapping, and/or raping members of other groups; vandalism, rioting, and other ways to destroy other groups' property; the number of people killed or maimed in interfaith conflicts; the dollar value of destroyed property; the number of police and fire personnel who are called upon to restore order; and the cost of the investigations and the prosecutions that follow. We are only interested in these behaviors to the extent that they are related to—rooted in—religious stratification. In other words, the only ones that matter to us are those that involve relationships between elite and nonelite religions. For the most part, that means problems involving groups in the Old Upper stratum (Episcopalians, UCC/Congrega-tionalists, and Presbyterians) and historical minorities, especially evangelical Protestants, Catholics, and Jews. In more recent years, it points to problems between groups in the New Upper stratum (Episcopalians, Presbyterians, Jews, and Unitarian-Universalists) and a mixture of older and newer minori-ties, such as evangelical Protestants and Muslims.

We also suggest that the severity of these problems varies with the amount of religious stratification at the time. Based on our reading of the literature on other types of stratification, we offer three scenarios depicting the most likely relationships between the amount of religious stratification at any given time and amount of social instability. In the first scenario, religious stratification is so pronounced (high) that its destabilizing effects are muted (medium). In the second scenario, religious stratification is less pronounced (medium) and its destabilizing effects are more severe (high). In the third scenario, religious stratification is minimal (low) and so are its harmful effects (low).

Now, based on the history reported in chapters 1, 3, 4, and 5, we can be even more specific. First, we have seen that the United States has always had medium to high levels of religious stratification, and that there has never been a period in which religious equality has prevailed. Thus, there is no empirical foundation for scenario 3. Although it remains a dream for many Americans—including the coauthors—and may be attained at some future time, it never has been and is not yet an empirical reality.

Second, we have found that religious stratification was more pronounced from the colonial period through the mid-1800s than it was after the mid-1800s. Thus, if our theory is right, we should find that religious stratifica-tion had fewer destabilizing effects when liberal Protestant hegemony was at its zenith in the colonial period and first half of the 1800s than it has had in the past 150 years, when the Protestant Establishment's grip on social resources has been loosened. Put differently, we should find that religious stratification has produced more disruptive social problems in the past 150 years than it did in the first 150 years of American history. Scenario 1 should describe the first period, and scenario 2 should describe the second (see figure 6.1 for an illustration).

We also have observed changes in the amount of stratification within each of the two main periods of time. The gap between elites and nonelites nar-rowed in the mid-1800s, closed even more in the late 1800s and early 1900s, widened again in the mid-1900s, and has narrowed again in recent decades.

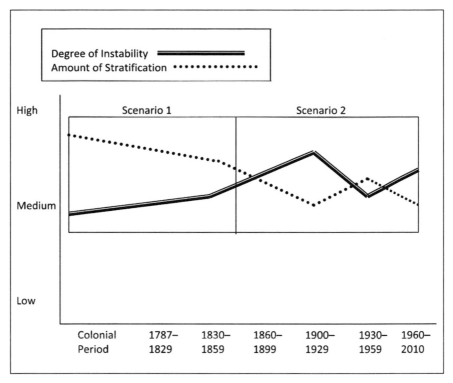

Figure 6.1. Trends in Religious Stratification and Its Consequences

As a result, we also expect to find fluctuations in stratification's destabilizing effects within each period. Reductions in inequality should be accompanied by more instability, and any increase in inequality should result in less instability (see figure 6.1).

COLONIAL PERIOD THROUGH THE MID-1800s

This period encompasses the seventeenth and eighteenth centuries and the first half of the nineteenth century.

The Colonial Years

Although the New World was explored by French and Spanish Catholic explorers and missionaries in the 1500s, it was European—and, especially, English—Protestants who came here in the 1600s with the intention of establishing colonies. Almost from the beginning, they thought of the New World as a Christian and Protestant land. Despite denominational and class differences, Protestants shared a common identity as people who had come into their own during the Protestant Reformation and, because of these historical circumstances, became the founders—and, in their minds at least, the rightful owners—of the emergent society.

But denominational and class differences also mattered. Over time, a clear ranking of religious groups emerged. Episcopalians, Congregationalists, and Presbyterians dominated the upper ranks of society. Quakers and Unitarians formed a second tier. They were followed by a cluster of other Protestant groups, most notably Baptists and Reformed. At the bottom, there were Catholics, Jews, and people with no religious ties.

The social, economic, and political differences between elite religions and all others were dramatic. These differences also were highly institutionalized in the form of laws, ideologies, and customs that favored the elite groups and worked against the nonelite groups. These supports were most evident in the nine colonies that had established churches. In these colonies, there were laws requiring the support of the established religions; laws that made it illegal for nonelite groups to be citizens, own property, or hold public office; and laws requiring public officials to take oaths to uphold all of these laws. Customs favoring elite religious groups included private church-related colleges and universities, at which it was legal to limit student admissions and employment opportunities to members of elite religions; the creation of privately owned businesses that could be passed down to succeeding generations of family members; social networks made up almost exclusively of members of elite denominations and congregations; and habits of voting for political candidates belonging to elite religions. Ideological supports included beliefs about the superiority of elite religious doctrines and rituals and the lifestyles of Anglicans, Congregationalists, and Presbyterians.

These conditions led to considerable religious segregation and some disruption of daily life. The Puritans drove Roger Williams and Anne Hutchinson out of Massachusetts in 1636 and 1638 respectively. Four Quakers (known as the Boston Martyrs)—most notably Mary Dwyer—were executed between 1659 and 1661. The wave of religious fervor that bubbled up among lower status Protestants in the 1730s and 1740s (aka the First Great Awakening) magnified the tensions between elite and nonelite Protestants. As the emotional style of preachers like George Whitefield attracted large crowds of common folks in parks and churches, elites such as Charles Chauncy responded with both private and public disdain (Griffin 1980). Privately, they wrote letters mocking the emotionalism that appealed to lower ranking Protestants. Publicly, they expressed these criticisms in worship services, other gatherings with their congregants, and heated debates over the organizational implications of their differences. Ultimately, denominational divisions increased as "Old Lights" aligned themselves with elite groups such as the Anglicans and "New Lights" joined nonelite groups such as the Baptists. Within denominations, there also were realignments of congregations along theological and class lines, and new colleges and universities (e.g., Princeton and Brown) also were founded. Yet, these Protestant divisions did not lead to violence and social problems that disrupted daily life in the colonies.

As we showed in chapter 3, liberal Protestants and their allies seemed obsessed with the few Catholics who were in the colonies. Laws were passed restricting Catholics' ownership of land and presence in public offices. The Catholic Church was maligned with claims that it was not really Christian. Catholic priests and sisters were excluded from some colonies and threatened with death if they violated these laws. Colonial Jews also knew they were on the outside looking in. Peter Stuyvesant, the governor of New Amsterdam, tried to expel them from the colony of New York, and laws in several colonies limited their participation in public life. There were many more Nones, but they also were treated as outsiders.

With religious inequalities being so highly institutionalized, elites had little or no need to attack nonelites in ways that would disrupt daily life. And, with so few resources of their own, nonelites had little or no chance of attacking elites in ways that would improve their lot in life.

1787–1829

This was a period of growth among Catholics. Here's how Billington (1938, 37) described the Catholic situation at the time:

> In 1807 the entire hierarchical establishment consisted of one see [diocese], with seventy priests and eighty churches caring for the needs of the 70,000 Catholics in the entire country. By 1830 there were 14,000 Catholics and sixteen churches in New England alone. In Ohio, where not a single church had existed fourteen years before, there were twenty-four priests and twenty-two churches, a newspaper, a college, and a seminary. By this time there were ten sees in the United States, together with six seminaries, nine colleges, thirty-three monasteries and houses of religious women, and many schools and hospitals.

Protestants responded by creating new interdenominational groups such as the American Bible Society (1816), the American Sunday School Union (1824), the American Tract Society (1825), and the American Home Missionary Society (1826). These groups warned of the dangers of Catholicism's growing presence (Billington 1938, 42–43). New Protestant-sponsored news-papers such as the Boston *Recorder* (1816), the *Christian Watchman* (1819), and the New York *Observer* (1823) were

> distinctly anti-Catholic in tendency, with regular sections or weekly articles devoted to attacks on Popery. These ran the gamut of attack; singling out the idolatry, moral weakness, blasphemy, cruelty, and anti-Christian nature of Romanism and warning that Protestant vigilance was required to protect America from subjugation by the papal power. (Billington 1938, 44)

Catholic leaders responded by forming self-defense organizations and publications of their own, such as the *United States Catholic Miscellany* (1822), *The Truth Teller* (1825), and the Catholic Tract Society (1827). These groups and publications tried to counteract anti-Catholic myths and explain Catholic teachings, but "[in] all probability . . . [they] did more harm than good" (Billington 1938, 47).

Jews were also entering a phase of growth and readjustment. With the ratification of the First Amendment and the protections it offered, Jews adapted to their largely Christian surroundings. In 1824, the first Reform temple was formed in Charleston, South Carolina, which had the largest Jewish population in the colonies at the time. With its shorter worship services (conducted in the vernacular, not Hebrew) and regular homilies, it expressed Jews' willingness to assimilate. The beginnings of immigration from Germany in the 1820s (lasting through the 1880s) included mostly middle class people who were willing to assimilate. Apart from Christian attempts to proselytize these religious outsiders, Jewish-Gentile relations during this period did not destabilize daily life in Savannah, Charleston, New York, Philadelphia, Newport, or other communities with Jewish residents.

A combination of religious and class differences contributed to growing hostilities between elite Protestant denominations, which were concentrated on the East Coast, and nonelite Protestant groups, which were expanding out to the Western frontier. For one thing, membership in the elite Protestant denominations continued to grow, but the spiritual energy of and growth rates among lower ranking Protestant groups—especially Baptists and Methodists—were even greater (Finke and Stark 1992). A great deal of this energy and growth was associated with what has been called the Second Great Awakening, a revival movement that stretched from the 1790s through the 1840s. Learned representatives of elite groups continued to disparage the more evangelical style of nonelites. For example, Congregationalist Lyman Beecher accused revivalist Charles Finney of conducting highly emotional camp meetings that would set back "civilization, science, and religion, at least a whole century" (as quoted in Finke and Stark 1992, 98). Several new

Protestant denominations—such the Christian Churches (Disciples of Christ), and the Seventh-day Adventists—also were founded during this period. In the late 1820s, conversations between Joseph Smith and the angel Moroni also led to the founding of another group with even more distinctive teachings: the Church of Jesus Christ of Latter-day Saints (the Mormons).

According to Finke and Stark (1992), the vast majority of early nineteenth century Americans were still Nones. They also remained at the bottom of the socioeconomic ladder. They were no more likely than Catholics and Jews to be either the victims or perpetrators of violence related to their minority status.

In short, the conflict between the high and low status religious groups was largely limited to verbal and written attacks. There was not much in the way of overt or violent disruption of daily life.

1830–1859

As we said in chapter 4, this period saw a marked increase in the immigration of Irish Catholics, both laity and clergy. Their numbers began increasing in the 1830s, and it wasn't long before Yankee nativists were producing a torrent of anti-Catholic propaganda. A lot of it centered on the idea that Catholics would soon overrun Protestants. In 1834, for example, Samuel F. B. Morse, inventor of the telegraph, began to publish anti-Catholic tracts, and esteemed Reverend Lyman Beecher claimed that the pope was plotting to overrun the American West by sending Catholic settlers there (Dinnerstein, Nichols, and Reimers 1990). Nativists gained the support of people in lower strata with books, such as Samuel B. Smith's *The Flight of Popery from Rome to the West* (1836), advancing the idea that the Catholic Church intended to take over American society.[1] They mobilized the middle classes by enlisting the support of Protestant newspapers such as the Boston *Recorder*, the *Christian Watchman*, and the New York *Observer* in claiming that Catholics wanted to remove religion—including Bible reading—from the public schools (Billington 1938).

They also spread stories of former nuns who, upon leaving their convents, exposed what went on behind closed doors. One such episode was said to have involved an "escaped nun" named Rebecca Theresa Reed, whose real life was the subject of conflicting reports, but whose expose, *Six Months in a Convent*, became a best seller here and in England (Billington 1938, 90). Another involved a real nun, Elizabeth Harrison, who left her convent overnight and returned the very next day, but whose harmless violation of house rules was made out to be much more than it really was (Billington 1938, 72). The most famous tale of all appeared in Maria Monk's book *Awful Disclosures of the Hotel Dieu Nunnery of Montreal*. Monk's account of her own life was contradicted by her mother, and her book included fictional stories of nuns being obliged to have sexual intercourse with priests, then strangling their babies to guarantee the infants' place in heaven. Although the book ultimately was discredited, it sold over 300,000 copies (Billington 1938, 108).

Protestants also sponsored public lectures debunking Catholicism, debates in which Catholic spokespeople were to defend their church against criticisms lodged by Protestant leaders, and new magazines and newspapers such as the *Protestant Banner* in Philadelphia and the *National Protestant* (Billington 1938, 170). They also participated in violent attacks on Catholics and their property. After listening to a "revivalistic preacher" in 1829, a mob of Protestants "attacked the homes of Irish Catholics in Boston and stoned them for three days" (Billington 1938, 70). But this was not an isolated incident. Similar attacks occurred again in December 1833, also resulting in death (Menendez 1996). In the words of a noted historian of this period: "In New England, where people had a taste for rioting, mob attacks on Catholic churches became so frequent that many congregations posted armed guards to patrol and protect their property, and insurance companies refused to place a policy upon Catholic buildings which were not constructed of inflammable materials" (Billington 1938, 89).

The most famous incident took place in 1834 at the Ursuline Convent in Charlestown, Massachusetts (Billington 1938, 68–76, 85–90). The Ursuline sisters ran a very successful school for the daughters of wealthy Bostonians, including some prosperous Protestants. A mob of lower class Protestants set fire to the school and a nearby farmhouse owned by the sisters. On each of the next three nights, unruly gangs burned what was left of the school, roamed the streets of Boston, and torched a building housing thirty-five Irish Catholics. Although a group of Protestant publishers and clergy condemned the attack, "they were quick to add that the Ursuline convent and all convents should be done away with to prevent the conversion of Protestant girls to Catholicism, and the spread of immorality throughout the United States" (Billington 1938, 86). Those responsible for the convent fire were acquitted (Menendez 1996).

Matters only got worse in the 1840s, when a potato famine caused millions of Irish Catholics to leave their homeland and head for the New World. As the influx of uneducated and unskilled Irish Catholic immigrants increased the size of the Lower stratum, more American Protestants became concerned. They felt it was their duty to protect and defend the society and culture that they and their ancestors had forged (Albanese 2007; Marty 1986). The Episcopal, Congregational, and Presbyterian churches, along with other Protestant denominations, formed "a virtually united front against Catholicism" (Billington 1938, 181). In addition, the learned classes formed a number of new interdenominational groups, such as the Society for the Promotion of Collegiate and Theological Education in the West (1843) and the American Protestant Society (1844). Their goals, basically, were to protect the new nation's largely Protestant way of life from millions of lower class Irish immigrants whose Catholic faith—it was alleged—was incompatible with America's democratic values (Billington 1938; Perlmutter 1999).

Smoldering tensions between Protestant and Catholic workers turned violent as anti-Catholic riots broke out again in Philadelphia in 1844. This conflict occurred not just because of fears that the Irish were taking away jobs from native born residents and driving down wages, but also because Protestants were angry that school officials allowed the Catholic Bible to be read in public schools along with the King James version (Dinnerstein, Nichols, and Reimers 1990). The city of brotherly love "was beset with riots from May through July, and militant nativists threatened to burn down all Catholic churches. By July 8th, twenty people were dead, two Catholic churches and schools and hundreds of homes had been burned to the ground" (Billington 1938, 234; Menendez 1996).

As Perlmutter (1999) has noted:

> Intergroup conflict was frequent from the 1830s to 1850s, with at least thirty-five major riots in Baltimore, Philadelphia, New York, and Boston. In one three-year period, 1834–37, some 157 acts of mob violence occurred. In Philadelphia, in 1834, Protestants invaded an Irish-Catholic neighborhood and burned down over thirty homes and two churches, killing or injuring some fourteen people. A few months later, a similar clash left thirteen dead and more than fifty wounded. (70)

Had such incidents occurred in the colonial period, the small and powerless population of Catholics might not have responded. But, with their numbers and their increasing resources, Catholics did react to this propaganda and these riots. Perlmutter (1999, 70) reports that "in Boston, a diocesan paper castigated Protestant critics as 'mendacious tract-mongers, mercenary Bible-mongers, peculating missionaries, and modern Pharisees . . . foul libelers, scurrilous scribblers and unprincipled calumniators." Catholics also fought back, both physically and verbally. For example, Catholics attending a Protestant-Catholic debate in Baltimore in 1834 became so enraged that they attacked, and hurt, the Protestant spokesman (Billington 1938, 60). Archbishop John Hughes of New York criticized Protestantism so vehemently from the pulpit in 1850 that nativists responded by desecrating Catholic parishes (Billington 1938, 290–91).

But Protestant-Catholic tensions were not limited to the East Coast (Billington 1938, 322–344). Leaders of Protestant denominations and nativist groups put issues related to alcohol consumption, illiteracy, poverty, political corruption, and crime at the top of the public agenda. The political discourse related to these issues was laced with racism, anti-Catholicism, and anti-Semitism. For example, following a decade of interfaith tension in Louisville, the lid finally blew off in 1855. On election day, "Know-Nothing hoodlums patrolled the polls, 'protecting democracy' from peacefully voting foreign-born citizens. Mobs roamed the streets, assaulting German and Irish citizens. When the furor finally subsided, twenty-two lay dead and countless others were wounded" (Boles as quoted in Menendez 1996).

This period also saw the development of one of the most successful third party political movements in American history—the Know Nothing movement. During the 1850s the Know Nothings (aka the American Party) waved the banner of anti-Catholicism, and, like all nativist movements, found its greatest support among working class Americans who needed someone to blame for their own economic hardships. This is a recurrent pattern throughout American history: during periods of economic adversity and instability, hostility toward immigrants grows. The Know Nothing movement achieved considerable success in the elections of 1854 and 1855, sending sixty-four representatives to Congress, and claiming a former president, Millard Fillmore, as their chief spokesman. The Know Nothings used physical intimidation of voters to ensure political victories. However, the movement collapsed after 1856 when the slave controversy took precedence over concerns about immigration.

As the immigration of Jews from Germany continued, it increased the size of the Jewish population. It also led to the dispersal of Jews, some of whom settled in Midwestern cities such as Cincinnati and Chicago, while others went farther west to places like Denver and San Francisco. With their German roots, many Jews knew of the Germany-based Reform movement and found its liberal policies to their liking. With the Reform movement spreading, the first Sunday school being started in Philadelphia in 1838, and the first Jewish English translation of the Bible (by Isaac Lesser) being printed in 1853, Jewish assimilation was well under way. For the time being at least, Jewish-Christian relations were relatively benign.

As the fervor of the Second Great Awakening died down, so did tensions between liberal elite denominations and more evangelical groups. However, there were increasing tensions between liberal Protestants and the newly founded Church of Jesus Christ of Latter-day Saints. The founding prophet of Mormonism, Joseph Smith, offered revelations that went against the grain of mainstream Christianity, the most notable of which was a revelation that sanctioned polygamy. In addition, the Mormon claim that it was the one true church heightened tensions between Mormons and Christians.

Because Mormon customs were not acceptable to the mainstream population, and expulsion was viewed as justifiable, Mormons were forced to move from New York, to Ohio, to Missouri, and then to Commerce, Illinois, which they renamed Nauvoo, hoping it would become their permanent home. However, the governor of Missouri issued an order mandating that all Mormons leave the state or be exterminated. In June 1844, angry mobs arrested and killed Joseph Smith and his brother Hyrum in nearby Carthage, Illinois (Perlmutter 1999, 70–71). Under the leadership of Brigham Young, survivors left Nauvoo in 1846 and moved on until they finally settled in Salt Lake City in 1847.

By 1850, Nones were about two-thirds of the population (Finke and Stark 1992). Although they were still clearly social outsiders relative to religious adherents, their status did not provoke overt or violent hostilities that disrupted daily life at that time.

So far, the data are consistent with the expectations we depicted in figure 6.1. Religious inequality during the early part of this period was so severe and so ingrained in the culture that neither elites nor nonelites were likely to change it. For the most part, the destabilizing effects of religious stratification were limited. However, the last thirty years of this period included increasing indications that the gap between elites and nonelites was narrowing and that stratification's negative effects were becoming more disruptive.

THE MID-1800s TO THE PRESENT

The second period in our analysis extends over 150 years. Following the timeline we used in chapters 4 and 5, we have divided it into four categories: 1860–1899, 1900–1929, 1930–1959, and 1960–2010.

1860–1899

With the Civil War, immigration slowed down, but it did not stop. German Catholics and German Jews were settling on the East Coast but also in the Midwest, largely in a triangular area between Cincinnati on the east, St. Louis on the west, and Milwaukee on the north (Dolan 2002, 94–95; Albanese 1999, 86). For the most part, these newcomers wanted to assimilate. Archbishop John Ireland led the effort to align the Catholic Church with American culture. The Reform movement was the means by which German Jews tried to accomplish the same goal. The strength of this movement is seen in the formation of the Union of American Hebrew Congregations in 1873 and the founding of Hebrew Union College in 1875.

Elite Protestant groups and their more evangelical Protestant allies responded by forming nativist groups, such as the Ku Klux Klan (which directed its venom at Catholics and Jews as well as blacks) and lesser known groups with names like the Black Snakes, Tigers, Rough Skins, Red Necks, and Thunderbolts (Billington 1938, 420). There also was an increase in scapegoating. For example, when Lincoln was assassinated in 1865 by John Wilkes Booth (reputedly a recent convert to Catholicism), theories of a Catholic takeover increased.[2]

New York City's "orange riots" of 1870 and 1871 are another good example of how religious stratification led to physical violence (Gordon 1993). New York's prosperous Scotch-Irish (Protestant) population wanted to reaffirm America's Anglo-Saxon Protestant way of life, which they believed was being threatened by the influx of lower class Irish Catholics and other immigrants. A good way to do so, they thought, was to celebrate the anniversary of Anglo-Protestantism's triumph over Irish Catholicism at the Battle of the Boyne, which took place in Ireland in 1690. On July 12, 1870, a group called the Loyal Orange Institution (aka the Orangemen) marched through the streets of New York. Angry Irish Catholics opposed the parade. The violence that resulted left eight people dead and many others injured (Gordon 1993, 1). When plans for a similar parade on July 12, 1871, became known, Irish Catholics objected once again. Mayor A. Oakey Hall sided with the Catholics, but Governor John T. Hoffman overruled him and called out the National Guard for the event. On the day of the parade, Irish Catholics threw bricks and stones as the Orangemen marched by. The National Guard responded by firing into the crowd. When all was said and done, over sixty people were dead and many more were injured (Gordon 1993, 2).

Reflecting on how widespread religious violence had become, historian Carleton Beales (as quoted in Menendez 1996) wrote: "All over the country Catholic churches were stoned, dynamited, burned, wrecked. Crosses were stolen, windows smashed, altars were torn out. . . . Everywhere priests were threatened, spat upon, their robes torn off. Everywhere nuns, because of their reputed immorality, were propositioned grossly on the streets, and the police frequently had to rescue them from assault."

There also were flashpoints in Protestant-Jewish relations. For example, in 1862, when illegal trading for cotton became a widespread problem during the Civil War, General Ulysses Grant singled out the Jews, expelling them from units in western Tennessee until his order was rescinded by President Lincoln (Perlmutter 1999, 98–99). In another case, Jews lobbied against, and overturned, a military regulation requiring that a Civil War chaplain be a "regularly ordained minister of some Christian denomination."

However, religious hostilities increased along virtually all axes in the 1880s. One reason was that a new wave of immigrants over the next forty years included about 250,000 Japanese, about 250,000 Chinese, about 2 million Jews from eastern Europe, and 5–6 million Catholics from Italy and Poland. The nation's elite religious groups and their allies didn't know what to make of this huge increase in people who were not Protestants, not Christians, and—in many cases—not even Judeo-Christian. Another reason was the economic depression of the 1870s. Banks failed, money for new construction dried up, and the stock market shut down for ten days. Many new immigrants could not find work. Those who could often worked for low wages in deplorable conditions.

Catholics, Jews, and Others began to organize and demand change. In Philadelphia, workers created the Knights of Labor, a relatively small and secretive organization, which used strikes and boycotts to achieve better working conditions and fairer treatment of women and children employees. Despite the Knights' spotty record on racial matters and its ties to violence, its membership grew to nearly 750,000, about half of whom were Catholic. However, external opposition, internal mismanagement, and the formation of other unions—notably the American Federation of Laborers in 1886—led to the Knights' decline in the mid-1880s.

Although these nonelite groups did not all speak with one voice, they agreed with Pope Pius XIII's 1891 papal encyclical (*Rerum Novarum*) affirming workers' rights to organize and demand just wages. Thus, the labor movement and the disruptive behaviors it endorsed were at least partly a consequence of religious stratification (Smith 2003).

Elite religious groups responded in very different ways. One way was to prohibit immigration from China by supporting the Naturalization Act of 1870 and the Chinese Exclusion Act in 1882. Their desire to restrict Japanese immigration was growing, too, but that goal was not realized until the passage of the Gentlemen's Agreement in 1907. These actions had the effect of reducing the presence of Taoism, Buddhism, and Shintoism in America's religious landscape.

Another way seemed more conciliatory. As concerns about the society's social and moral foundation increased, the "social gospel movement" arose in the late 1800s. Led by Washington Gladden, Walter Rauschenbush, and Horace Bushnell, this movement addressed urban social problems and the spiritual needs of people affected by them. Echoing earlier Protestant concerns about immigrants' impact on the society, new groups—especially the Women's Christian Temperance Union (1874) and the Anti-Saloon League (1895)—reenergized the temperance movement. The renewal of the movement was tied to other factors as well (such as the rise of the women's rights movement and its concern about the link between drinking and sexual abuse), but it also drew strength from the xenophobia and anti-Catholicism of the early 1900s (Jenkins 2004, 31).

But, as much as these groups sought to address urban social problems, they also believed in capitalism and the American way of life. After all, their members included some of the wealthiest "robber barons," such as J. P. Morgan, an Episcopalian, and Andrew Carnegie, a Presbyterian. Thus, while elite groups supported social ministry programs designed to help the poor, they opposed unions, which they saw as trying to restructure the nation's capitalist economy. The religious as well as class differences between elite Protestants, Catholics, Jews, and Others were very apparent in the boycotts, strikes, and protests that became so frequent during this period.

The tensions between mainline and evangelical Protestants also grew. The Third Great Awakening brought their theological differences to the forefront once again. On top of that, the social, economic, and political gaps between these groups were compounded when the groups splintered along regional and racial lines. Mainline white churches and evangelical black churches often clashed. One such incident took place in Wilmington, North Carolina, in 1898.

> It was the Sunday after thousands of white men brandishing guns marched the streets of Wilmington, burning a black newspaper, killing and banishing blacks from town and overturning the city's government.
>
> From his pulpit at First Presbyterian Church, The Rev. Peyton Hoge triumphantly defended the racial violence. "Since we last met in these walls we have taken a city. . . . It has been redeemed for civilization, redeemed for law and redeemed for decency and respectability. . . . For these things, let us give God the glory."

But, Reverend Hoge was not alone. A number of other white clergy expressed similar views in their churches. These actions scarred relationships between black and white churches for many years (www.starnewsonline.com/article/20081106/ARTICLES/811060271?Title=1898-riots-still-resonate-with-Wilmington-s-black-churches).

Finally, selected individuals with no religious preference (e.g., Abraham Lincoln and Chester Arthur) were able to find their way to the top of the political ladder, but Nones as a group remained on the outside looking in at a society controlled by religious adherents. However, their subordinate status was not associated with incidents of public disorder. Such incidents were much more likely to involve elite and nonelite religious groups.

Thus, from the mid-1800s to the end of the nineteenth century, there was a noteworthy increase in social instability. Tensions along all four axes increased. The shift from scenario 1 to scenario 2 was well under way.

1900–1929

As a result of the latest wave of immigrants, Protestant elites felt increasingly threatened. A sure sign of their growing insecurity was the proliferation of nativist organizations (Perlmutter 1999, 122). Many of these groups—such as the Sons of the American Revolution, the Daughters of the American Revolution, the Colonial Dames of America, and the United States Daughters of 1812—had names reflecting their patriotic focus on their Anglo-Saxon Protestant heritage more than their antipathy toward Catholics and Jews, although these two elements were closely linked.

They supported the Eighteenth Amendment, which outlawed the manufacturing, distribution, and sale—but not the consumption—of alcohol. Although the amendment was ratified in 1919, Prohibition proved to be a costly and unenforceable social policy. The "noble experiment" was repealed by the ratification of the Twenty-first Amendment in 1933.

In addition to excluding Jews from elite schools, clubs, and neighborhoods (see chapter 5), and with help from Henry Ford, nativists championed *The Protocols of the Elders of Zion* (1920), a fiercely anti-Semitic publication claiming that Jews wanted to undermine American culture, destroy the nation's infrastructure, and gain world domination.

Although anti-Semitism did not emphasize physical attacks on Jewish people and property, there were some instances when this did occur. One such incident involved the imprisonment of Leo Frank, a Jewish factory superintendent who was accused of raping and killing an employee at his factory in Atlanta (Menendez 1996). In a trial that included largely circumstantial evidence and a heavy dose of anti-Semitism among jurors, Frank was found guilty. When the governor overturned the verdict against Frank, nativists were furious. They threatened the governor and his family, frightened Atlanta's Jewish population, then abducted and lynched Frank.

In response to the rising tide of anti-Semitism, the Independent Order of B'nai B'rith and a Chicago lawyer named Sigmund Livingston founded the Anti-Defamation League (ADL) in 1913. According to the ADL's charter: "The immediate object of the League is to stop, by appeals to reason and conscience and, if necessary, by appeals to law, the defamation of the Jewish people. Its ultimate purpose is to secure justice and fair treatment to all citizens alike and to put an end forever to unjust and unfair discrimination against and ridicule of any sect or body of citizens." The league's strategy was to expose anti-Semitism in the entertainment industry, in hate groups such as the Ku Klux Klan, and in publications such as *The Protocols.*

In the midst of this nativism, social scientist Emory Bogardus (1926) designed a scale to determine how much "social distance" Americans put between themselves and a variety of racial, ethnic, and religious groups. Respondents were asked to place each group at some point on a seven-point scale, ranging from not letting the group into the country (the most social distance) to not letting its members marry members of their family (the least social distance). The results showed a strong preference for white northern European groups, such as the English, the Scots, and the Irish. Italians, Poles, and Jews were farther down the list. The lowest ranked of all were Japanese, Chinese, and Indians from India. Bogardus's findings indicated how much Americans thought of the United States as belonging to white, Anglo-Saxon, Protestants and how they perceived other religious groups as "outsiders."

These insider-outsider perceptions contributed to elite Protestant groups' efforts to limit the influx of nonwhites, non-Anglo-Saxons, and non-Protestants. Earlier, they agitated for, and achieved, the Chinese Exclusion Act of 1882 (which greatly reduced immigration from China). Now, they backed the Gentlemen's Agreement of 1907 (which prohibited passports from Japan to the United States) and the Immigration Act of 1924 (which curtailed immigration from Asian and eastern and southern parts of Europe). As we noted in chapter 5, Albert Johnson (R-WA) and David A. Reed (R-PA) drafted an anti-immigration act, or as it also is known, the National Origins Act. Johnson was a Mason and "an energetic nativist" (Baltzell 1964, 201). Reed was an Episcopalian and a Mason, had "a patrician background," was "a long-respected member of the Duquesne Club," "carried on a Pittsburgh First Family tradition of extreme conservatism," and was "a trustee of Princeton" (Baltzell 1964, 201–2). The two received help from two other "patrician volunteers from New York, Madison Grant and Captain John B. Trevor" (Baltzell 1964, 201–2). Congress passed the bill in 1924. For over forty years, it had the effect of protecting immigration from largely Protestant northern Europe, while greatly reducing immigration from southern and eastern Europe (the sources of most Catholic and Jewish immigrants).

While elites were reducing the inflow of newcomers, some immigrants were deciding to go home. Some had always intended to work in this country for a while and then go back home. Others left their homelands with the intention of never going back but were so estranged by the prejudice and discrimination they experienced that they changed their minds and returned home. Estimates vary, but as many as one of every four people in some groups left the United States and returned home.

An important division also was developing within Protestantism. Some Protestant leaders felt that the social gospel movement put too much focus on resolving social problems, while it neglected the goal of saving individual souls. As a corrective, they attempted to refocus attention to what they considered to be the fundamentals of the Christian faith. The fruits of their labor were published in a twelve-volume series known as *The Fundamentals*. That series provided the framework for a fundamentalist movement that extended into the 1920s. Among the movement's numerous outcomes was the founding of several new Protestant groups, including the Church of the Nazarene.

For many Protestants, the rift between the liberal social gospel movement and the conservative fundamentalist movement overlapped their location on the social hierarchy. High ranking denominations such as Episcopalians, Congregationalists, and Presbyterians tended to align themselves with the social gospel movement, while lower ranking groups such as Baptists were more inclined to identify with the fundamentalist movement. As a result, relations between elite and nonelite Protestant denominations became even more contentious. In 1917, postmillennialist theologians at the University of Chicago Divinity School led attacks on the premillennialism being taught at the Moody Bible Institute. In the context of the Scopes trial in 1925, modernist-fundamentalist antipathies became even more public and virulent, often taking the form of unflattering portrayals in newspaper cartoons, which had devastating effects on the fundamentalist movement.

Overall, this was the period during which religious stratification's destabilizing effects reached their all-time high.

1930–1959

Starting in the mid-1920s, a series of events altered the shape of religious stratification and its negative consequences. The Immigration Act of 1924 greatly reduced the number of non-Protestant immigrants. Although Protestant fundamentalists won the Scopes trial in 1925, the public relations nightmare that accompanied that event took the wind out of fundamentalism's sails. Al Smith's failed attempt to become the nation's first Catholic president in 1928 reassured elite Protestants that a Catholic takeover was not going to happen any time soon. The stock market crash of 1929 and the Great Depression of the 1930s closed the gap between the nation's rich and poor. World War II brought the country together in a unified, and triumphant, struggle against fascism in Europe and Japanese aggression in the Pacific. Between its passage in 1944 and its termination in 1956, the G.I. Bill extended educational opportunities and job training to nearly 8 million veterans of World War II, regardless of their religious affiliations. Catholics increasingly expressed their identification with the society and its religious values. For example, they lobbied for and got the phrase "under God" inserted into the Pledge of Allegiance. Jews fully embraced America's emphasis on religious freedom and worked hard to be accepted. Many "Anglicized" their names, moved to the suburbs, and married Christians.

At the same time, however, other developments intensified religious stratification's negative effects. Expressing the continuing anxieties of the elite Protestant denominations, best-selling author Paul Blanshard (1953) updated old claims that Catholicism was incompatible with American culture by drawing parallels between the Kremlin and the Vatican in terms of their hierarchical power structures, emphases on thought control, management of the truth, and strategies for penetrating—and, ultimately, toppling—American democracy.

The religious landscape also included lower status Protestant "malcontents who zealously seek to promote hate and disruption under the banner of the Christian faith" (Roy 1953, ix). Groups such as Protestants and Other Americans United, Christ's Mission Inc., American Protestant Defense League, and Christian Medical Research League targeted "Americans who are Negro and not white, Jew and not Gentile, Catholic and not Protestant" (Roy 1953, 3). They echoed historical themes of Catholics plotting to take over American society and Jews being Christ killers, "scheming to destroy his church . . . plotting to undermine the American republic . . . [and] conspiring to enslave all mankind under the iron hand of despotism" (Roy 1953 57).

By 1952, Nones were down to 41 percent of the U.S. population. National surveys were indicating that they had successfully worked their way into the Lower Middle stratum. Although laws, customs, and ideologies were still stacked against them, there is no evidence that they were involved—one way or the other—in social problems linked to religious stratification.

Thus, as elite Protestant groups were tightening their control over the nation's resources, there was some overall reduction in hostilities between elite and nonelite religions from the 1930s through the 1950s. This conclusion is in line with scenario 2.

1960 to the Present

Starting in the 1960s, important changes began to take place in America's religious landscape. For one thing, memberships in many mainline Protestant denominations (including the Episcopal Church, the UCC, and the Presbyterian Church) began to decline in the mid-1960s and have continued to fall ever since (Hadaway and Marler 2006, 5). At the same time, membership in evangelical churches has increased. In addition, the latest wave of immigration also has led to the influx of millions of Catholics, Buddhists, Hindus, and Muslims.

These changes have reduced the power differential between elite and nonelite religious. As we saw in chapter 5, this shift has been accompanied by serious attacks on the legal foundations of religious stratification. The importance of these legal advances cannot be overlooked. They have removed legal barriers that have obstructed nonelites' access to resources since colonial days. They also have put wind in the sails of cultural movements toward greater tolerance and more equality.

However, the importance of these legal advances can be overstated. For one thing, laws against any kind of discrimination in the workplace continue to be violated, including laws against religious discrimination. In 2009, for example, the Equal Employment Opportunity Commission (EEOC) processed 93,277 job-related charges. The most frequent charges were based on race and "retaliation" (36 percent each), followed by sex (30 percent), age (24 percent), and disability (23 percent), then national origin (12 percent), religion (4 percent), and equal pay (1 percent).[3] Of the 2,958 religion-related charges that were resolved, 61 percent were found to have no reasonable cause, 20 percent were dismissed for administrative reasons, and 19 percent were resolved through settlement, withdrawal with benefits, or conciliation. Total monetary benefits amounted to $7.6 million. The patterns for 2000–2008 have been essentially the same, with monetary benefits for religion cases alone ranging from a low of $4.3 million in 2002 to a high of $14.1 million in 2001.

Moreover, as we documented in chapter 5, many customs favoring elites and ideological barriers remain intact, religious stratification persists, and so do its destabilizing effects. Its negative impact has ebbed and flowed over the years.

The 1960s was a period when many teenagers and young adults experimented with new forms of religious consciousness. They were attracted to new eastern religions such as Buddhism and contemplative methodologies such as transcendental meditation. For the most part, involvement in these alternatives to the Anglo-Saxon Protestant norm was seen as the dalliance of youth and participants did not become targets of religious hostility. However, when some young people became involved in more cult-like groups such as the Moonies, many parents claimed that their offspring were being brainwashed and kidnapped.

Reflecting pressures from mainstream religious groups, the government became involved on several occasions. In 1978, U.S. Congressman Leo Ryan flew to Jonestown, Guyana, to talk to members of the People's Temple. Viewing the visit as an attack on his community, Jim Jones ordered his followers to take their own lives. Nine hundred and eighteen people died. In 1982, the courts found Reverend Moon guilty of tax fraud. He was sentenced to eighteen months in jail and fined $15,000. In 1993, the U.S. government (specifically, the FBI and the Bureau of Alcohol, Tobacco, Firearms and Explosives) authorized the 1993 assault on the Branch Davidian compound in Waco, Texas, where David Koresh and eighty-two of his followers died.

Like the gilded age of the 1800s and the Roaring Twenties, this period also has been one of large scale immigration involving newcomers who were not Protestant and often were not Christian (Jasso et al. 2003). As in these earlier periods, it also has been a period of increased xenophobia and nativism (Buchanan 2006). Just as we saw increased efforts to reduce immigration in the two earlier periods, a majority of Americans now favor limits on immigration (Chandler and Tsai 2003). Anti-immigration organizations have formed at the national and local levels. The nativist attitudes of their members are reflected in names like the United Patriots of America and Mothers Against Illegal Aliens.

Members of these and other groups have backed an Arizona law that would allow police to stop cars driven by people whom the officers suspect might be undocumented workers. As support for this law has grown, so has opposition to it. In 2010, as thousands of people have rallied in support of cracking down on illegal immigration, thousands more have protested against such actions, and additional police and helicopters have been deployed for their protests and rallies. Opponents have proposed boycotts of Arizona (which is attempting to restrict immigration), while supporters have proposed "buycotts" promoting state businesses.

While some portion of this issue is about immigration and national security, another—less often mentioned—portion of it is about religion. As the Protestant percentage of the U.S. population has declined in recent years (see chapter 5), and the influx of immigrants with other religious affiliations has increased, Protestants and other religious groups have responded in quite different ways. Both mainline and evangelical Protestants have been more in favor of restricting immigration than Catholics and Jews. Once again, clergy and clergy-led organizations in both groups have opposed attempts to restrict immigration and/or deport those who are in this country illegally, but the rank and file members of their churches are in favor of such efforts (www .cnsnews.com/news/article/59164).

Thus, those who see themselves as religious insiders and their allies are attempting to reassert the superiority of Anglo-Protestantism and its way of life, while calling into question the citizenship and lifestyles of people in other religious faiths. Their attempts to do so have extended beyond rallies and protests relating to immigration. They also involve some very traditional forms of interfaith hostility: attacks on nonelite groups' property, the publication of hate literature and hate speech aimed at religious groups, and the use of stereotypes when depicting religious groups and figures in America's popular culture, including movies, television, and music.

These older forms of hate are still very common, and some—such as vandalizing cemeteries—are said to be increasing. One recent example occurred when a member of a neo-Nazi group painted "anti-Semitic slurs, swastikas, and white supremacist slogans . . . on nearly 60 headstones at

[a Jewish cemetery in Illinois] . . . causing $13,000 in damages" (www.adl
.org/learn/extremism_in_the_news/White_Supremacy/Wdziekonski+NSM
.htm?). In California, "vandals defaced the Muslim component of an interfaith
holiday display" (makka.wordpress.com/201001/01/muslim-holiday-display
-vandalized-in-mission-viejo-california/). Windows were broken at a Muslim
mosque in Michigan, and a mosque in Florida was bombed (www.prnews
.com/news-releases/cair-seeks-probe-of-bias-motive-for-vandalism-at-mich
-mosque-93888209.html). In Pennsylvania, "vandals toppled 115 headstones
and ripped up American flags [in a Catholic cemetery] . . . , causing tens
of thousands of dollars damage" (www.pittsburghlive.com/x/pittsburghtrib/
news/pittsburgh/s_631957.html). These incidents don't always get nationwide
media attention, but they are well known in the areas where they take place.

A current example of hate literature and hate speech aimed at religious
groups is California-based Chick Publications, which produces millions of
mean-spirited books, pamphlets, CDs, DVDs, tracts, and cartoons targeting
Catholicism, which Chick claims is not a Christian faith but, rather, a set of
false doctrines and rituals from which its members need to be saved. When it
comes to stereotyping religious groups in pop culture, earlier immigrant religions have been subjected to religious stereotypes in film. Now, Muslims are
experiencing this problem, being depicted as uncivilized and militaristic ag-
gressors who deserve to die (Semmerling 2006; Shaheen 1984, 2008, 2009).

In addition to these more traditional forms of hostility, the Internet has produced a whole new form of hate: cyberhate. The number of websites focusing
on hatred toward religious minorities and outsiders has skyrocketed in recent
years. Some are aimed at specific religious groups that have been part of the
American experience for many years. For example, www.jewwatch.com is
overtly anti-Semitic, and www.chick.com is openly anti-Catholic. Other sites
are more general in nature, spewing hatred aimed at many groups, including the religions of more recent immigrants. Examples of such sites include
www.davidduke.com and www.hatedirectory.com, which provides links to
over 150 hate groups that consider Catholics, Jews, and—lately—Muslims
their favorite target groups.

Much of this hateful behavior is not treated as criminal, but some is
(mostly on a case-by-case basis). According to FBI reports, close to 8,000
hate crimes occur annually. About 1,510 of them (almost one-fifth) are related to religion (www.fbi.gov/ucr/hc2008/data/table_01.html). Thus, crimes
related to religion trail crimes related to race, but are ahead of crimes based
on sexual orientation, ethnicity, and disability. We cannot always tell who
the perpetrators are, but, more often than not, these crimes are directed at
Jews, Muslims, Catholics, and other non-Protestants. Jews always seem to
be the number one target group. Between 1995 and 2008, the percentage of

religious hate crimes against Muslims jumped from 2 percent to 7 percent. The anti-Protestant crimes are probably aimed at evangelicals more often than mainline Protestants.

Members of nonelite groups have responded in predictable fashion: supporting efforts to protect the civil rights of religious outsiders. One pattern of response has been for individuals to make note of times when their religion has been attacked. For example, in the past decade alone, three people have written books documenting anti-Catholicism in American life: Robert Lockwood (*Anti-Catholicism in American Culture*, 2000), Philip Jenkins (*The New Anti-Catholicism*, 2004), and Mark Massa, S.J. (*Anti-Catholicism in America*, 2005). While some people might be tempted to think that books such as these are the rantings of paranoid authors who wish to prolong their suffering by exaggerating the evidence of Catholics' victimization, that is not the case. These books are penned by reasonable and intelligent men who simply call attention to biases that some people would prefer not to talk about but that remain facts of life in our society.

Another type of response is more institutional. The Washington lobbying groups representing Catholics, Jews (especially Reform Jews), and a number of Other Protestant denominations (e.g., American Baptists, Church of the Brethren, Quakers, ELCA Lutherans, and Mennonites) have been outspoken advocates for their groups' values and interests, as indicated by their efforts to support more inclusive and less exclusive immigration policies (Kraus 2005).

In recent decades, the Anti-Defamation League of B'nai B'rith has recorded 1,200–1,600 incidents of anti-Semitism a year, including vandalism, assaults, threats, and harassments. The Catholic League for Religious and Civil Rights tracks incidents of anti-Catholicism, although not as systematically. The Moral Majority, the Christian Coalition, and other forms of the so-called Christian Right express evangelical Protestants' outsider status and their desire to gain more control of their own destinies (Wilcox and Lawson 2006). They rely on the American Center for Law and Justice for data on violations of their members' religious liberties. The new religious movements and new immigrant groups also have formed advocacy groups—such as CAIR (the Council on American-Islamic Relations)—which also have turned to the law for help in identifying cases where their civil rights have been violated (Richardson 2005). CAIR reported that anti-Muslim hate crimes in 2005 included "a December pipe-bombing of a mosque in Cincinnati, an October beating by a group of teenagers of an elderly man leaving a mosque in Arizona, another October assault of a pregnant woman in Virginia by three men who shouted anti-Muslim slurs, and a November shooting of two cars parked near a mosque in the Philadelphia area" (Lobe 2006).

Armed with such data, these organizations issue news releases that describe incidents of religious hostility, identify the perpetrators whenever that is possible, and specify the steps that should be taken to end such incidents. These steps usually include a mixture of lawsuits and collective actions, such as economic boycotts. None of these organizations and actions would be necessary if it were not for religious stratification.

Thus, as we expected, religious stratification's negative effects have been more pronounced in the past 150 years or so (scenario 1) than they were in the colonial period and the early 1800s (scenario 2). Within the last century and a half, they have fluctuated—increasing from the mid-1800s through 1929, then decreasing from the 1930s through the 1950s, then increasing once again from the 1960s to the present. These findings also are consistent with figure 6.1.

CONCLUSION

The evidence in this chapter generally supports our hypotheses that (a) when religious stratification is most severe, its harmful consequences are tempered by the fact that it is highly institutionalized and that (b) when religious stratification is less institutionalized and less severe, its destabilizing effects become more pronounced. Religious stratification's negative effects were rather muted in the colonial period and early 1800s, but have increased rather dramatically since then. Since the mid-1800s, they have fluctuated in relation to the amount of religious stratification. When inequalities based on religion have increased (as they did in the 1930s, 1940s, and 1950s), their negative effects have declined, but when they have declined (such as from the late 1800s through 1929 and from the 1960s to the present), their destabilizing effects have increased.

That completes our presentation of data related to the origins, persistence and change, and consequences of religious stratification in America. It is time to recap our major findings and explore their implications. For that, we turn to chapter 7.

7

Summary and Implications

America is a land of opportunity, yet there have always been conditions that make it easier for some people to realize their dreams. From the very beginning, societal preferences have given rich, white, Anglo-Saxon, Protestant males advantages over other groups. For people with other physiological traits and social backgrounds, the American Dream has often been something of an American nightmare. Racial roadblocks, ethnic hurdles, class conflicts, gender gaps, and religious barriers have made it difficult, if not impossible, for them to improve their lot in life.

This book has focused on inequalities based on religion for four reasons. First, for a variety of reasons that we discussed in chapter 1, researchers have paid far more attention to the advantages and disadvantages attached to race, ethnicity, class, and gender than they have to the favoritism and barricades linked to religion. We believe religious stratification is a prominent part of American society and deserves more attention than it usually gets in the social sciences. Second, social scientists can explain the origins, histories, and consequences of other types of stratification better than they can explain how religious stratification develops, how it persists and changes, and how it impacts our society. We thought that if we approached religious stratification the same way sociologists approach other types of stratification, we might be able to advance scholars' understanding of religious stratification. Third, if we succeeded, we could make contributions to two areas of research. We could suggest a new way of approaching religion in the study of stratification, and we could suggest a new way of approaching stratification in the study of religion. Finally, in addition to being researchers who believe that the search for understanding is an end in itself, we are American citizens who want our work to contribute to the well-being of our society. To that end, we will explore the implications we think our findings might have for Americans interested in public policies related to religious stratification.

We have organized our conclusions around four topics: approaches, origins, persistence and change, and consequences. In each section, we begin with a summary of our findings and end with implications.

APPROACHES

We began by stating five assumptions that limit people's appreciation of religious stratification and showing that these assumptions are seriously flawed. Then we presented the following alternative assumptions:

1. Religion continues to be an important influence in modern society.
2. Religious affiliation is still largely an ascribed and permanent status.
3. Religion is quite visible.
4. Religion has important effects on people's access to resources, even after other factors are taken into account.
5. Religious stratification has always been and continues to be an important part of our society.

After that, we asked three questions about religious stratification in America: (a) how did it develop? (b) how has it persisted and changed over the course of U.S. history? (c) how has it affected our society? We considered the two main theoretical approaches sociologists might use to explore these questions, finally deciding that conflict theory would be more useful than functionalist theory. We then decided that a Weberian version of conflict theory would be more helpful than a Marxian version. We borrowed several key ideas from others who have used this approach to examine other forms of stratification. For example, we imported Noel's (1968) emphasis on the importance of ethnocentrism, competition, and power in the evolution of racial inequality. Our approach embraced the centrality of intergroup power relationships as a force in the perpetuation and alteration of various types of stratification (Feagin and Feagin 2008). From studies of race, ethnicity, class, and gender, we also gained an appreciation of just how institutionalized and, therefore, how permanent inequality is (Rothman 2005). Our analysis also included the idea that changes in laws tend to occur sooner than, and sometimes without much impact on, changes in ideology and customs (Hurst 2007). Finally, like studies of other inequalities, ours emphasized the destabilizing effects of stratification based on religion (Kerbo 2006). This approach led us to a number of hypotheses, which we have examined using a combination of data that we have gleaned from previous research and original data that we have gathered over a period of years.

Implications

We hope our use of this approach encourages other researchers to pay more attention to religious affiliation as a variable affecting people's access to power, privilege, and prestige. We hope they will come to appreciate the fact that "religion" is not simply a means by which elites are able to exploit and oppress women and minorities. It is much more than that. It also is a basis for group affiliation and an important component of people's identities that needs to be addressed with the same care that is given to race, ethnicity, class, and gender. For example, just as researchers distinguish between belonging to a given race and the extent to which members of that race are involved in race-related activities, they also need to distinguish between religious affiliation (e.g., being Protestant) and religious involvement (e.g., being an active or inactive Protestant). Just as there are subgroups within races (e.g., African American and West Indian blacks), there also are subgroups within religions (e.g., Protestants who are Episcopalian and ones who are Presbyterian). And, just as these differences add depth to studies of other types of stratification, they also enhance the quality of research on religious stratification.

While our work has focused on religious stratification in America, similar investigations could be done in other parts of the world. For example, researchers should look at religious stratification in other countries that also have high levels of religious diversity, such as England and Canada. Other studies might be done in countries where one religion outnumbers all others, but where there also are a number of smaller groups. Examples would include countries that are heavily Catholic (e.g., Poland, Mexico), Lutheran (e.g., Sweden, Denmark), Muslim (e.g., Pakistan, Iran), Jewish (i.e., Israel), Buddhist (e.g., Sri Lanka, Thailand), and Hindu (e.g., India, Nepal).

In addition to studying religious stratification at the societal level, researchers could examine the same issues at the meso level. They could reexamine previous research and launch new studies of religious stratification in different regions, states, cities, and small towns. Some good places to start would be landmark studies of places such as "Yankee City" and "Jonesville" (Warner and associates 1942, 1943, 1963), Gastonia, North Carolina (Pope 1942; Earle, Knudsen, and Shriver 1976), "Middletown" (Caplow et al. 1983; Lynd and Lynd 1929, 1937), Indianapolis, Indiana (Farnsley et al. 2004), and Springfield, Massachusetts (Demerath and Williams 1992). Together, these investigations would provide additional insights into the tenacity of entrenched patterns of religious stratification and/or reveal changes in the nature and extent of religious inequality in a variety of local settings. These insights could be incorporated into proposals for research in younger towns and cities in other regions of the country.

We hope colleagues also will give more attention to microlevel issues related to religious stratification. Some good examples of research that explores the extent to which, and the ways in which, religious affiliation affects individuals' access to a variety of resources are Lehrer's work (2008) on access to education, Keister's studies (2005) of access to wealth, and Masci and Miller's (2008) investigation of access to political power. Drawing upon studies such as these, researchers could develop new studies showing exactly how religion increases some people's worldly success, how it becomes a barrier for others, and when it seems to be of little or no consequence. For example, they could explore the link between religious stratification and individuals' views of themselves and their place in the world. Studies could investigate how religious stratification affects people's identities and self-images. For example, do the self-images of Baptists and Episcopalians differ, and if they do, to what degree are these differences an effect of socialization into different status cultures rooted in religion? Is there an association between a religious group's worldly standing and the worldview of its members? Do members of elite and nonelite faiths today embrace different views about the nature of the world, and to what degree are these differences affected by religious influences and to what degree are they affected by social class factors? What are the social consequences of these different value systems? How do theodicies associated with elite and nonelite groups translate to social action or social inaction? Is there a difference in the habitus of affluent and low income church members and how do these differences play out in terms of members' support of egalitarian public policies? Researchers also need to explore the ways in which individuals belonging to various religious groups have been treated by others who might affect their access to resources. For example, have teachers, job placement personnel, and recruiters ever given them opportunities because of their religious affiliation? Have colleagues ever gone out of their way to help them get ahead because of their religion? Can they describe specific incidents in which others have denied them opportunities because of their religion? Can they recall specific people who have ever discriminated against them because of their religion? Do they know of any other people who have been denied access to resources because of their religion? When the results of such research are collated, we will have a much better understanding of how religion's effects on resources compare with the consequences of race, ethnicity, class, and gender.

But, let's return to the macro level. We also hope that people in the sociology of religion will pay more attention to conflict theory. It is much broader than Marxism and well suited to analyses of religion and stratification. Compared to functionalism, it provides more viable explanations of how religious stratification comes into being, perpetuates itself, changes over time, and impacts society. It also gives religion scholars an awareness of the ways in which religious groups and their members pursue their values and worldly self-interests (sometimes in unison, sometimes in direct conflict with one another). The importance of intergroup relations and the role of power in these relationships are additional lessons to be learned—so is the extent to which religion is a source of social problems. In its more Weberian versions, it provides religion scholars with opportunities to link their interests in religious stratification with any interests they might have in stratification based on race, ethnicity, class, and gender.

ORIGINS

We hypothesized that religious stratification would develop when the relationship between religious groups included three conditions: ethnocentrism, competition, and differential power. Ethnocentrism occurs when some groups view themselves as better than others. Competition refers to the interaction between groups that want to gain control of the same scarce resources. Finally, if some groups are larger, have stronger organizational bases, and have more resources, they have more power than others. In the absence of any one or more of these conditions, religious equality would develop, not religious stratification.

In chapter 3, we found that all three conditions were present in the thirteen original colonies. Religious prejudice took several forms. In the broadest sense, there was a division between people who claimed a religion (adherents) and those who did not (Nones). There also was an early bias toward Christians and a discernible element of anti-Semitism. Protestant-Catholic relations also were quite sour, resulting in a bias toward Protestants and the undeniable existence of anti-Catholicism. But there also were antipathies between mainline or liberal Protestant reformers and more radical or evangelical reformers. Thus, there was ill will between insiders (adherents, Christians, Protestants, and especially liberal Protestants) and outsiders (Nones, Jews, Catholics, and evangelical Protestants).

These groups openly competed for political and cultural influence and the right to live as they wished in the new world. Some groups had more resources than others, such as political ties to England and the British crown. In this context, two liberal Protestant groups got the upper hand on all others: Anglicans and Congregationalists. Members of these groups created laws making themselves the established churches in nine colonies. Along with Presbyterians, they also developed an ideology that made their denominations and their beliefs the cultural norm against which all other groups would be evaluated. The greater the differences between their cultural patterns and other groups' ways of life, the more deficient the other groups were thought to be. Thus, evangelical Protestants were seen as inferior, but at least they were Protestant. Catholics, Jews, and Nones were even more culturally different, so they were viewed as the most inferior of all. These groups were expected to surrender their traditions and assimilate into the dominant culture.

The dominant groups also developed customs that allowed them to accumulate resources and pass them on to their children and grandchildren. These customs skewed the allocation of resources in favor of people belonging to their own religious groups and away from members of other religious groups. For example, in the political area, the dominant groups nominated political candidates who belonged to the same religious groups, voted for members of their own groups, appointed people of the same faith to political office, and created their own lobbying groups at the state and national levels. In the economic sphere, they established their own businesses, hired people who shared their religious affiliation, promoted members of their own religious groups more than workers with other religious preferences, and left their businesses and wealth to family members and other members of their own religious groups. In the area of family life, they encouraged their children to marry members of their own religious groups. Within the educational sphere, they founded church-sponsored colleges and universities, hired teachers and administrators on the basis of their religion, and gave preference to students who belonged to the same faith. And, of course, they built their own religious organizations, selected people who shared their beliefs and practices, and interacted with other groups that shared their values and interests.

These conditions led to a highly institutionalized ranking of religious groups. Anglicans, Congregationalists, and Presbyterians were the Upper stratum. Below them was an Upper Middle stratum, which included Quakers and Unitarians, whose influence far exceeded their numbers in the total population. The Lower Middle stratum consisted of all other Protestants, such as Baptists, Dutch and German Reformeds, Lutherans, and Methodists. Catholics, Jews, and Nones were in the Lower stratum.

Implications

We hope that people who investigate religious stratification will explore its origins in whatever settings they choose to study. There is a need to retest the three factors we believe contribute to the rise of religious stratification: religious prejudice, competition, and power. Do these variables behave the same way in all settings, or do they perform differently in different places? Are all three necessary? And, of course, alternative theories, hypotheses, and methodologies might be proposed and tested.

Our findings also challenge an idea that we came across several times: that the group that gets there first gets to be the dominant group (i.e., the development of inequality based on religion is largely a chronological matter). Don't tell Native Americans that. And don't tell the indigenous people of Mexico and in the American Southwest that either. Also, if the first groups to arrive in a particular setting view each other with respect, cooperate with each other, and are similar in terms of their resources, religious stratification is not likely to evolve. It only does so under very specific conditions: when groups dislike each other, compete with one another, and have unequal resources.

PERSISTENCE AND CHANGE

We hypothesized that the power differential between the groups in the Upper stratum (the elites) and all other groups (the nonelites) would determine the permanence of and/or fluctuations in religious stratification over time. This differential is measured in terms of size of membership, organizational capacity, and resources. Liberal Protestant denominations were about 9 percent of the total population in 1776. With recent membership losses, which have garnered a great deal of attention, these elite groups are about 2 percent of today's population. Nonadherents (Nones) have also lost ground, going from 83 percent of colonists to about 37 percent of today's Americans. On the other hand, Catholics, Jews, other Protestants, and new immigrant religions have gone from being only a handful of colonists to being over half of today's population.

More importantly, the organizational bases of historically elite groups have expanded to include many more denominational offices, local congregations, prep schools, private colleges and universities, lobbying offices on Capitol Hill, private foundations and endowments, and ecumenical coalitions. These groups—especially Episcopalians and Presbyterians—have retained a disproportionate share of the nation's social resources, and their members also are linked through a network of business, political, and fraternal organizations. When needed, they have also formed alliances with other mainline denominations and evangelical Protestants who identify with Protestant elites more than they do with nonelites of other religious traditions. They also have forged relationships with those Catholics, Jews, members of other religions, and Nones who aspire to be accepted by the elites.

Nonelites also have expanded their organizational bases and resources. New denominations have evolved, along with thousands of local congregations, schools, and other organizations. Their organizational styles have varied a great deal, with Catholics building an elaborate parochial school system, and Jews choosing not to do so. Their organizational networks have expanded and contracted at different points in time. As the Catholic Church is reducing the number of schools it sponsors, evangelical Protestants' commitment to private schooling is increasing. Overall, nonelites have had fewer resources to work with, but that has varied a great deal. Jews have accumulated more resources than Catholics and Mormons, who, in turn, have accumulated more than black and fundamentalist Protestants.

The net effect is that the power differential between elite and nonelite groups has shrunk. As a result, there have been some important changes in the laws, some additional changes in the ideologies and customs affecting religious stratification, some reduction in the amount of religious stratification, and some changes in the ranking of groups. However, religious stratification persists, and the ranking of many groups has not changed all that much in over 250 years.

Laws

The elite religious groups of the colonial period and their (largely Protestant) allies have won legislative victories, such as the Immigration Act of 1924, when lay members acting on their interests and inegalitarian or "good fortune" values have prevailed over clergy and clergy-led organizations that have often championed laws based on egalitarian or "social justice" values, knowing full well that these actions were contrary to adherents' self-interests. But, overall, elites have not been as effective in supporting laws that would perpetuate their dominance as nonelites have been in opposing them. One reason for this has been the tendency for liberal clergy and clergy-led organizations to prevail over adherents' more conservative values and self-interests. Nonelites also have been quite successful in forming alliances with those elites who are willing to side with the have-nots instead of the haves.

As a result, most of the laws that favored the Protestant Establishment in the colonial period have been struck down by the courts and replaced by ones guaranteeing religious groups equal protection. For example, the First Amendment made it impossible for colonial elites to determine the established religion of the society as a whole. The Fourteenth Amendment put an end to any idea of having religious establishments or imposing limitations on the free exercise of religion at the state level. Although elites and their allies succeeded in shutting off the flow of immigrants in the 1920s, nonelites and their allies were able to reopen the doors of immigration in 1965. The civil rights acts of the past several decades have made it illegal to discriminate against anyone on the basis of "race, color, religion, sex, or national origin." Thus, it is against the law to consider religious affiliation when advertising employment opportunities, hiring and firing personnel, testing and training, and promoting and paying people. Thus, many legal props have been knocked out from under religious stratification.

However, that doesn't mean that religious groups are now on a level playing field. The enforcement of these laws is a never-ending problem, as indicated by Equal Employment Opportunity Commission (EEOC) data documenting thousands of claims of religious discrimination, about one-fifth of which have merit, resulting in millions of dollars in settlements. And, as recent attempts to restrict immigration suggest, laws are subject to serious modification or even reversal. Besides, laws are only one of three factors that need to be considered.

Ideologies

Ideologies are another. In the colonial period, elites promoted ideologies of racism, ethnocentrism, classism, sexism, and Anglo-Protestantism. These ideologies distinguished between ingroups and outgroups. Rich, white, Anglo-Saxon, male, Anglicans, Congregationalists, and Presbyterians were the insiders; the poor, people of color, people of other ethnicities, women, and people belonging to other religious groups were the outsiders. These ideologies also asserted that the cultures of the dominant groups were preferable to the cultures of the subordinate groups. The religious ideology of the time took the form of a pro-Protestant (especially mainline or liberal Protestant) bias that viewed other religious traditions as undesirable or even inferior. Although this ideology always contained a discordant element of egalitarianism, in the main it insisted that the way for outsiders to overcome this stigma was to shed their own traditions and adopt the insiders' way of life (in other words, assimilate).

Most scholars agree that these ideologies extended into the early twentieth century. However, some writers believe they have lost their potency since then. The loss, they say, is the result of many factors, including the legal changes we just outlined and the social movements of the past forty to fifty years. They argue that these ideologies have been superseded by a more inclusive and egalitarian one known as "cultural pluralism" or "multiculturalism." This ideology questions the primacy or superiority of any one set of religious values and insists that all groups have a right to their distinctive ways of life and that these differences shouldn't affect their access to power, privilege, and prestige.

Although pluralism has made some inroads into our culture, racism, ethno-centrism, classism, sexism, and Anglo-Protestantism persist, but in modified form. Without going into the evidence connected to the ideologies related to race, ethnicity, class, and gender, we can say the following about Anglo-Protestantism. First, in terms of the ideology's affiliation component, insider status is no longer reserved for members of the three establishment denomi-nations. The boundaries have been extended to include other mainline Protes-tants, Unitarians, Jews, and Catholics. However, other groups remain outside the boundaries. These include evangelical Protestants, Mormons, Hindus, Buddhists, Muslims, and Nones. These groups are still different enough that they are not welcome in elite circles.[1]

Second, in terms of the dominant ideology's belief component, liberal Protestant values remain the societal norm. The values of individualism, vol-untarism, rationality, tolerance, and democracy are still the cultural standard against which all other religious traditions are judged. This standard puts lots of pressure on other groups to adapt, which some groups have done more than others. Catholics with European roots, Reform Jews, and Unitarians have embraced enough of the dominant ideology that they are now seen as acceptable by members of elite Protestant denominations. On the other hand, evangelical Protestants, Mormons, Latino Catholics, Orthodox Jews, and the new immigrant religions are still thought to be undesirable or even inferior.

In short, the Anglo-Protestant ideology has been impacted by multicultur-alism, but it has not been supplanted or replaced by it.

Customs

The third factor is customs affecting groups' access to resources. As we noted earlier, colonial elites engaged in a variety of behaviors that favored insid-ers over outsiders. A number of these customs (e.g., discrimination against minority groups in areas such as employment, property ownership, and use of public facilities) are now illegal. The reduction in such customs certainly has increased nonelites' access to power, privilege, and prestige.

However, many other long-standing elite customs persist, and a number of new ones have been introduced over the years. With regard to power, members of elite Protestant groups do not vote for their own kind quite as automatically as they used to, but—as we showed in chapter 5—they still vote for them-selves more often than they do for others, and when they have the opportunity to appoint their own kind to cabinet posts and seats on the Supreme Court, they still have a tendency to do that. With regard to privilege, elites who start their own businesses often pass them on to their sons and daughters. They are more constrained by laws against religious discrimination in the workplace, but they still tend to recruit prospective employees at schools where religious elites are overrepresented in the graduating classes. Inheritance laws allow them to pass their wealth down to their children and grandchildren. From the pool of qualified candidates, they are still more likely to select those who share their characteristics than those who do not. Avenues for advancement certainly are more open than they used to be, but elites still promote their own kind at a higher rate than they promote others, especially in corporate careers where social acceptability is an important consideration. With regard to prestige, elite prep schools, colleges, and universities are not as exclusive as they used to be, but religious elites are still more likely to be admitted to and graduate from these schools due to relatively new and widespread customs such as legacy admissions. In short, elite religions created organizations and policies that were more private than public, more exclusive than inclusive, and more segregated than integrated along the lines of religious affiliation.[2]

But nonelites also have customs of their own. Some groups—especially Catholics and Jews—have been more willing than others—such as evangelical or Black Protestants—to assimilate into the dominant culture. The willingness to assimilate tends to reinforce the hegemony of mainline Protestant groups, but increases nonelites' chances for upward mobility within traditional social structures. One way nonelite religions have tried to assimilate has been to participate in organizations that that have been owned and operated by elite religions (such as prep schools, colleges, and universities). Another way has been to use publicly owned and operated institutions (such as public high schools and state colleges and universities). A third way has been to develop organizations owned and operated by nonelites (such as parochial schools and private colleges and universities). Minority religions have used all three methods. For example, Massachusetts Catholics have gone to Harvard, University of Massachusetts, and Holy Cross; New York Jews have gone to Columbia, the City University of New York (CUNY), and Yeshiva. But groups have done so in varying degrees. For example, Catholics have developed a vast network of their own schools; Jews have been less inclined to do so. All three approaches have worked, as long as the goal has been assimilation. When the goal of retaining minority distinctiveness has prevailed, all three approaches have led to the perpetuation of lower status.[3]

Religious Stratification

Through it all, religious stratification has persisted in some important ways and changed in others. Today's Upper stratum includes Episcopalians, Jews, Presbyterians, and Unitarians. The Upper Middle stratum includes Catholics, Hindus, Methodists, Mormons, Quakers, and UCCs. The Lower Middle stratum includes Buddhists, Reformeds, Lutherans, and Nones. The Lower stratum includes the Assemblies of God and a variety of other pentecostal groups, Southern and independent Baptists and other fundamentalist groups, black Methodists and black Baptists, and Muslims. This profile is similar to, but not identical with, other recent rankings.

When we compare the twelve groups that were part of America's colonial history and are still part of America's religious landscape, there is considerable continuity over time, especially toward the top. Two of the three groups that were in the Upper stratum during the colonial period are still members of that stratum (Anglicans/Episcopalians and Presbyterians). Five of the twelve groups are in the same strata they've always been in: Anglicans/Episcopalians, Lutherans, Presbyterians, Quakers, and Reformeds. Five of the original twelve groups are within one stratum of where they were in the colonial period: Unitarians, Methodists, and Nones have moved up a notch, and Baptists and UCC/Congregationalists have gone down one. Given the fact that we are covering over 250 years of history, these continuities are striking.

However, there also have been noteworthy changes. Two colonial groups have moved two or more strata: Jews and Catholics. Jews have made it all the way from the bottom to the top. With the notable exception that the United States has never had a Jewish president, Jews are now equal to or surpass liberal Protestants on most measures of power, privilege, and prestige. Irish, Italian, and other European Catholics have moved into the Upper Middle stratum. Mormons also have moved up from the bottom to the Upper Middle stratum.

There also has been some closing of the gap between elite and nonelite religions. It is useful to distinguish between an early period in which religious stratification was highly institutionalized and highly pronounced (the colonial period through the mid-1800s) and a later period in which it was less institutionalized and less pronounced (the mid-1800s to the present). There are fluctuations within each period, including a measurable narrowing of the gap between elites and nonelites in recent decades.

Implications

Future research on religious stratification should retest the four factors we hypothesized would affect its persistence and change: power relations, laws, ideologies, and customs. We need to see if these variables behave the same way in all settings, or if they perform differently in different places. For example, do the components of power (group size, organizational capacity, and resources) function differently in first, second, and third world countries? But in addition to retesting our hypotheses, scholars also should extend and revise our approach to include other variables and explore other hypotheses.

For example, we have not paid much attention to global economic and political events, such as the 2009–2010 financial crisis and continuing threats of global terrorism. To what extent and in what ways might these influences affect the trajectory of religious stratification? And, once again, alternative theories, hypotheses, and methodologies might be proposed and tested.

In the meantime, our findings call attention to the remarkable continuities we have found over the course of U.S. history. In such a religiously diverse society as the United States, a society in which there is so much emphasis on the future and willingness to change, we are impressed by two facts: (a) that many of the religious groups that date back to the colonial period are still in the same stratum or have moved up or down no more than one stratum in over 250 years, and (b) that two of the groups that made up the Protestant Establishment in the colonial period (Episcopalians and Presbyterians) are still in the Upper stratum, and the third (UCC/Congregationalists) is still overrepresented among leaders in many spheres of American life. As far as we are concerned, these are striking findings that need to be explained. We have taken a step in that direction and hope others also will pursue this line of inquiry.

But we also are impressed with the changes that have taken place in the rankings and the fact that religious inequalities are not as severe as they were in colonial times. Jews, Catholics, and Mormons have made great progress in gaining access to resources, and the gap between elite and nonelite groups has narrowed. The religious composition of today's Supreme Court may be the most dramatic sign of these changes. For the first time in history, there are no Protestant justices on the Court. Instead of being dominated by Episcopalians, Presbyterians, and Congregationalists, it is now made up entirely of Catholics and Jews.

These findings speak to ongoing debates. One debate concerns the point at which the Protestant Establishment began to decline. Some people contend that the decline began with the ratification of the First Amendment. Others suggest that the decline started in the 1920s. Others point to somewhere between the 1930s and 1960s. Still others say the decline has happened in the past fifty years or so. Our analysis (especially figure 5.1) suggests that the decline was well under way by the mid-1800s.

Another debate has to do with how steep the decline has been. Some suggest that it has been a gradual linear process, while others say it has been linear and precipitous. Our analysis suggests that it has not been a linear process. Rather, it declined quite rapidly in the 1800s and early 1900s, then increased between the 1930s and 1959, and has declined again since 1960.

A third debate is about how close America is to achieving religious equality. Some people believe that the decline of the Protestant Establishment has been so complete that religious groups are now on a level playing field.

They believe that the nation's laws don't favor any groups any more, that Anglo-Protestantism is dead, that exclusive customs have been replaced by inclusive ones, that resources are so widely shared that there are no dominant or minority religious any more, and that religious stratification is a thing of the past. Others disagree. They say that civil rights laws are still violated, that Anglo-Protestant values are still the heart and soul of the nation's religious ideology, that many customs favoring elite Protestant groups are still very much in place, that some members of the old Protestant Establishment still have more access to resources than other groups do, and that religious stratification is still a fact of life in America. Our findings are more compatible with the second view than the first one.

From this vantage point, the religious composition of today's Supreme Court is a sign of the decline of the Protestant Establishment, but it does not signal the end of religious stratification. Religious affiliation still matters in Americans' access to seats on the Court. With the Protestant base of the GOP declining, Republican presidents Ronald Reagan, George Herbert Walker Bush, and George W. Bush nominated candidates who would be acceptable to their largely Protestant base but also might attract new people to the Republican Party. Their choices were conservative Catholics: Chief Justice John Roberts and Associate Justices Samuel Alito, Anthony Kennedy, Antonin Scalia, and Clarence Thomas. Democratic presidents Clinton and Obama have nominated people who represent their party's largely non-Protestant base. Their choices have been liberal Catholics (Associate Justice Sonia Sotomayor) and Jews (Associate Justices Stephen Breyer, Ruth Bader Ginsberg, and Elena Kagan). Thus the current composition of the Court reflects the decline of the Protestant Establishment and the ascendancy of Catholics and Jews. The lack of support for George W. Bush's nominee Harriet Miers also reflects the difficulty evangelical Protestants historically have had gaining access to the Supreme Court.

According to our theory, fluctuations in the amount and form of religious stratification can be traced back to changes in the power differential between elites and nonelites. When the differential shrinks, the laws, customs, and ideologies supporting religious stratification are likely to change, and the amount of inequality is likely to decline. When the differential widens, elites are able to reassert their interests in laws, customs, and ideologies, and religious stratification surges.

This interpretation calls into question two very common views of the future. One view, which is functionalist in spirit, goes something like this. The United States is gradually and inexorably moving toward being a more just and equal society. It has made progress on all fronts. As part of that progress, America is slowly but surely moving toward religious equality. Steps already have been taken in this direction (such as knocking out the legal foundations of religious stratification), and religious inequalities are less pronounced these days than they were earlier in U.S. history (for example, Protestants no longer dominate the Supreme Court the way they used to). Assuming that the past foreshadows the future, the United States is on an irreversible journey toward religious equality and social stability.

There is no denying the facts just cited. Religious discrimination is no longer legal, and religious stratification is not as extreme as it was in the colonial period. There is no question that, in terms of religion's effects on people's access to resources, America is a more open and egalitarian society than it was at its birth in the later 1700s.

But these conditions are not the result of some evolutionary process that is gradually producing a society in which people's access to resources is based on merit and not ascription. They are the result of power struggles between elite and nonreligious groups. Nonelites certainly have made some gains (sometimes with help from elites), but elite groups have won more battles than they have lost (sometimes with assistance from nonelites). Through it all, America's historically elite religions still have far more access to most resources than other groups do.

The second view recognizes the importance of power struggles. It is Marxian in tone and goes like this. The United States has a long history of social inequalities based on race, ethnicity, class, and gender. Religious affiliation is not an important basis of inequality, but religious ideas have been an effective means by which elite groups have been able to oppress others. Religion suggests that inequality is God's will—that elites are more righteous people and deserve more blessings than nonelites. Ideas such as this have the effect of justifying the wealth and power of elites and perpetuating the plight of the less fortunate. If we are ever going to build a just and equal society, we must get rid of religion.

There is no denying that some religious ideas and practices legitimate and perpetuate inequality. But this view overlooks two things. One is that—like race, ethnicity, class, and gender—religious affiliation also has affected people's access to resources. Quite independent of these other factors, it is a reason why some people have more power, privilege, and prestige than others. The other thing this view overlooks is that some religious ideas actually promote equality. As we have shown, a theodicy of social justice has contributed to the reduction of inequality over the course of U.S. history. Thus, this view fails to address an important basis of social inequality, and does not recognize the role that justice-oriented religious beliefs have played in the struggle for religious equality.

Our analysis suggests a third view. It suggests that the future will be the result of ongoing struggles between whites and people of color, Anglo-

Saxons and people of other ancestries, rich and poor, men and women, and the four religious groups in the New Upper stratum and other religious groups. The outcome of this struggle will depend on membership trends, organizational trends, and resource trends. With regard to religion, it seems likely that the groups in the New Upper stratum will continue to lose ground to nonelites in terms of membership size. However, they may very well retain their advantages in organizational capacity and resources. If so, we should expect more continuity than change in religious stratification in the foreseeable future.

CONSEQUENCES

Just as stratification based on race, ethnicity, class, and gender destabilizes society by producing a variety of social problems, so does religious stratification. It fosters tensions between elites and nonelites and cultivates a tendency to think in terms of "ingroup virtues and outgroup vices." It is only a short step from there to nativist groups and self-defensive organizations; hate groups, hate literature, and hate crimes; marches, protests, and riots; and the wanton destruction of life and property.

Research on other forms of stratification indicates that these harmful effects are muted when inequality is most severe and most highly institutionalized. They are most pronounced when inequality is less severe and less institutionalized. The same is true for religious stratification. Its destabilizing effects were muted during the colonial period and early 1800s, when elite groups clearly dominated and nonelites had no choice but to cope with their lowly status. Since religion-based inequality has become less institutionalized and the gap between elites and nonelites has narrowed, religious stratification's destabilizing effects have increased. Without denying the importance of earlier incidents and flashpoints, it is fair to say that problems intensified in the mid-1800s. Nativist groups such as the Know Nothings, the American Protective Association, and the Ku Klux Klan arose in the mid to late 1800s and the early 1900s. There was violence against Jews in Georgia and Louisiana in the 1880s, attacks on Catholics in Montana and Kansas City in 1894, the lynching of Leo Frank (a Jew) in Georgia in 1915, and Henry Ford's widely circulated anti-Semitic publications in the 1920s. These days, nativist groups have websites, where they preach hate against religious outsiders. Millions of mean-spirited books, pamphlets, CDs, DVDs, tracts, and cartoons targeting religious outgroups are produced and sold every year. And, according to FBI reports, hate crimes related to religion account for about one-fifth of all hate crimes—trailing race, but ahead of sexual orientation, ethnicity, and disability. We cannot always tell who the perpetrators are, but, more often than not, these crimes are directed at Jews, Muslims, Catholics, and other non-Protestants. Since 1995, attacks on Muslims have increased as a percentage of all religious hate crimes.

It is no wonder that religious outsiders have created self-defense organizations to monitor and respond to such attacks. Groups such as the Anti-Defamation League of B'nai B'rith, the Catholic League for Religious and Civil Rights, the American Center for Law and Justice, and the Council on American-Islamic Relations gather data on violations of religious liberties, issue news releases, and conduct press conferences calling for an end to such violations.

These findings align themselves with scenario 1 (high inequality-medium instability) in the colonial period and early 1800s and scenario 2 (medium inequality-high instability) since the mid-1800s. They also provide no empirical evidence for scenario 3 (low inequality-low instability)—at least not yet.

Implications

One implication of our analysis is to raise Americans' awareness of religious stratification's destabilizing effects. This is not an entirely new insight. Other scholars have made essentially the same point. Albanese (1999, 504), for example, put it this way:

> At least in the first three centuries in the land, the response of the dominant and public tradition [Anglo-Protestantism] was more negative than positive toward the religions of the many. And because the one religion was dominant—in power—this tended to mean various kinds of discrimination and disability for non-Protestant and non-mainstream religions. In contrast, the response of the many religious traditions toward public Protestantism was more evenly divided between those who wanted to maintain a separate identity as a community and those who wanted to "Americanize" by becoming more like mainstream Protestants. Lastly, the response of members of the many religions toward one another was more often negative than positive.

The question then is: how can we reduce religious stratification and its negative consequences? Our answer is: the same way we strive to reduce other forms of stratification and their harmful effects. That means forming social movement organizations aimed at creating a society in which religious stratification and its destabilizing effects are virtually nonexistent. These organizations would include people who believe it is important to expose and oppose laws, customs, and ideologies that support the use of religious affiliation as a factor in the allocation of social rewards and benefits. In terms of legal issues, these groups should increase people's awareness of civil rights laws making it illegal to use religious affiliation as a factor in granting or denying people access to resources in all spheres of life. They also should target settings in which violations of such laws are most likely to occur and offer assistance to persons who have reason to believe that their rights have been violated. In the process, these groups might learn that violations are even more common than the EEOC statistics reported in chapter 6 suggest.

In terms of ideologies, coalitions should scour American culture looking for ways in which it asserts—or at least implies—the superiority of some religious groups and the inferiority of others. In the course of this research, we have observed a tendency for Americans to assume that the liberal Protestant experience applies to everyone, even when it does not. For example, the widespread belief that religious affiliation is and should be voluntary grows out of Protestantism and is imposed on all religions, even those that view religion as something one is born into. Another example is the tendency to apply the Protestant concept of "denomination" to other religious groups, even those that do not use that term to describe their religious organizations. A third example is the uncritical assumption that the Protestant term "congregation" applies equally well to Catholic parishes, Jewish synagogues, and Muslim mosques, even though these language differences point to very different views of what it means to be a worshipping community at the local level. Such cultural biases need to be identified and challenged if a more just and equal society is to be created.

Finally, social movement groups should look for customs that favor elite religions over others. One example growing out of our research is legacy admission policies in colleges and universities. These policies started out as means by which Ivy League schools protected the status of their elite Protestant alumni as their sons and daughters competed with increasing numbers of Jewish and Catholic applicants in the 1920s. These policies were given new justifications related to fund-raising and spread quickly—to the point where they are "givens" in the admissions processes at many schools. Reform groups should call attention to the roots and ramifications of these policies and, wherever there is evidence that they perpetuate religious stratification, urge school officials to drop them.

Whatever people do to expose and challenge such legal violations, cultural biases, and customs would be important steps toward reducing religious stratification and its destabilizing consequences. Any progress along these lines would be an important contribution to the creation of a more just and equal society.

CONCLUSION

In the past twenty years, we have conducted several studies of how religious groups rank in terms of their members' access to power, privilege, and prestige. In the course of these projects, we have reviewed many other studies that have shown how religious groups rank according to the socioeconomic status of their members, their representation among the nation's elites, and their concentration among the nation's poor. This book summarizes what we have learned about the conditions under which religious stratification developed in the thirteen original colonies, under which it has both persisted and changed since then, and under which its effects have been most pronounced. We hope this effort has advanced readers' understanding of these issues. There is much more to be learned about just how deeply rooted religious stratification is in our society, just how enduring yet volatile it has been, and just how profound its ramifications have been, so religious stratification deserves a prominent place in scholars' research priorities. But based on what we know already, Americans wanting a more just and equal society should add religious stratification to their list of conditions that need to be overcome.

Appendixes

Appendix 1. Data on American Elites*

Elites	Data	Years
All Types	Listees in *Who's Who*	1910, 1930–31, 1950–51, 1970–71, 1992–93[a]
Economic, Business	Industrial Elites	1870s[b]
	Business Leaders	1901–10[c]
	Business Elites	1976–77[d]
Political	Speakers	1690–1776[e]
	Signers, Dec. of Indep.	1776[f]
	Delegates, Const. Conv.	1787[g]
	Presidents USA	1800–49, 1850–99, 1900–59, 1960–2010[h]
	Presidents USA	1789–1839, 1840–1929, 1930–2003[i]
	Cabinet Officers	1789–1839, 1840–1929, 1930–2003[j]
	Supreme Court Justices	1789–1839, 1840–1929, 1930–2003[k]
	Political Leaders	1901–1910[l]
	Political Elites	1976–77[m]
Economic, Political	Power Elites in *Who's Who*	1930–31, 1950–51, 1970–71, 1992–93[n]
Education, Cultural	Cultural Elites in *Who's Who*	1930–31, 1950–51, 1970–71, 1992–93[o]
	Ivy League Presidents	1636–1788, 1789–1839, 1840–1929, 1930–64, 1965–2009[p]
	Ivy League Presidents	1800–49, 1850–1899, 1900–59, 1960–2009[q]
	Intellectual Elites	1976–77[r]
	College Graduates	2001[s]

* As collected by coauthors and colleagues or by others and cited in this book
[a] Fry (1933b), Davidson, Pyle, and Reyes (1995), Pyle (1996), Pyle and Koch (2001)
[b] Gregory and Neu (1962)
[c] Miller (1962)
[d] Davidson (1994)
[e] Wendel (1986)
[f] Davidson and Pyle (2003)
[g] Davidson and Pyle (2003)
[h] Chapter 1
[i] Davidson, Kraus, and Morrissey (2005)
[j] Davidson, Kraus, and Morrissey (2005)
[k] Davidson, Kraus, and Morrissey (2005)
[l] Miller (1962)
[m] Davidson (1994)
[n] Davidson, Pyle, and Reyes (1995), Pyle (1996), Pyle and Koch (2001)
[o] Davidson, Pyle, and Reyes (1995), Pyle (1996), Pyle and Koch (2001)
[p] Coe and Davidson (2010)
[q] Chapter 1
[r] Davidson (1994)
[s] Davidson (2008)

Appendix 2. Data Points Used to Estimate Amount of Religious Stratification (percent)*

Stratum, Period	Economic Elite	Political Elite	Educational, Cultural Elite	All Elites
*Old Upper Stratum***				
1636–1788			97[p]	
1690–1776		78[e]		
1776		95[f]		
1787		85[g]		
1789–1839		61[i], 64[k]	71[p]	
1800–1849		63[h]		
1840–1929		46[i], 51[k]	62[p]	
1850–1899		46[h]		
1870s	61[b]			
1901–1910	46[c]	29[l]		
1910				47[a]
1900–1959		44[h]		
1930–1931				53[n,o]
1930–1964			78[p]	
1950–1951				50[n,o]
1930–2003		42[i], 36[k]		
1965–2009			24[p]	
1960–2010		30[h]		
1970–1971				46[n,o]
1976–1977	50[d]	29[m]	27[r]	
1992–1993				35[n,o]
2001			55[s]	
*New Upper Stratum****				
1965–2009			70[p]	
1960–2010		20[h]		
1970–1971				50[n,o]
1976–1977	48[d]	35[m]	40[r]	
1992–1993				47[n,o]
2001			59[s]	

*Superscripts match superscripts in appendix 1
**Elites who are Episcopalian, UCC/Congregationalist, or Presbyterian
***Elites who are Episcopalian, Jewish, Presbyterian, or Unitarian-Universalist

Notes

CHAPTER 1

1. Judaism, Catholicism, and conservative Protestant bodies are more successful than mainline Protestant denominations when it comes to retaining members (Kosmin and Keysar 2006; Fischer and Hout 2006). Keister (2005), for example, shows that the correlations between childhood religion and adult religion are higher for Jews (.87), Catholics (.77), and Baptists (.76) than they are for Lutherans (.71), Episcopalians (.65), Methodists (.61), Presbyterians (.58), and Other Protestants (.56). They are lowest for Others (.54) and Nones (.36).

2. There is a sharp difference between the "total population" and "total religious adherents." The total population includes all persons, whether they belong to a religious group or not. Religious adherents are all of those people who belong to a religious group. Thus, whenever there are lots of people with no religious affiliation (as there were in the colonial period), any religious group will be a larger percentage of all religious adherents than the total population. To illustrate, in 1776, Episcopalians, Congregationalists, and Presbyterians together accounted for about 9 percent of the total population, but they represented 55 percent of all religious adherents. Occasionally, we report a group's membership as a percentage of the total population, although we will also consider a group's "market share," or its size relative to the number of religious adherents.

3. These findings are based on Coe and Davidson's (2010) data. The number of presidents whose religious affiliations are unknown jumped from four in 1900–1959 to fourteen in 1960–2009. Excluding these eighteen cases, the 1900–1959 figure for Episcopalians, Presbyterians, and Congregationalists is 73 percent, and the 1960–2009 figure is 27 percent.

4. Table 1.5 is from Davidson, Pyle, and Reyes (1995). Also see Davidson and Pyle (2005) and Pyle and Koch (2001).

5. Numerous reviews of the research on Weber's Protestant ethic thesis show that there is little or no empirical support for it (Bouma 1973, Greeley 1964, Samuelson 1993, Schuman 1971, Winter 1977). This thesis also presumes the superiority of Protestant theology and blames other groups for their lower status, something that is not tolerated in studies of stratification based on race, ethnicity, class, and gender. In our view, a sociological explanation of religious stratification should focus on the relationships between dominant and subordinate religious groups, not on the characteristics of any one group (see chapter 2).

CHAPTER 2

1. Ryan (1981) substitutes the term "fair play" theory for functionalism and the term "fair shares" theory for conflict theory. We have used these terms in some of our work on religious stratification, but we have decided to stick with the language of "functionalism" and "conflict theory" in this book.

2. As these approaches have been applied to different topics, they have been given labels such as "feminist" theory, "power elite" theory, "ruling class" theory, "social reproduction" theory, and "dual labor market" theory.

3. For other discussions of our theoretical approach, see Davidson (1985, 1994, 2008), Davidson and Pyle (2005), Davidson, Pyle, and Reyes (1995), Pyle (1996, 2006), and Pyle and Davidson (2003).

4. There is a difference between adherence rates based on membership figures provided by religious groups and adherence rates based on religious identification as reported by individuals. For example, in 2000–2001, the adherence rate based on membership data was 63 percent (making the nonadherence rate at 37 percent), while the adherence rate based on self-identification was 85 percent (making the nonadherence rate 15 percent). When we calculate a group's access to a given resource (such as the presidency of the United States) relative to its representation in the total population, the ratio is based on membership statistics unless otherwise indicated.

5. At any point in time, the relationships among the groups within each stratum can range from very cohesive to not very cohesive. The more the groups think of one another as a single unit, see themselves as pitted against groups in other strata, take one another into account when they make decisions, and interact with one another on a regular basis, the more cohesive they are. As we will show, the degree of cohesiveness within any stratum also can vary from high to low over time.

6. Other societal factors also can dampen or stoke the flames of instability (Hurst 2007, Juster 2005). For example, religious stratification's negative impacts are likely to be muted when the population is sparse and there are few visible symbols of religious differences in the public square. They are likely to be more prominent when the population is dense and religious icons are highly visible.

CHAPTER 3

1. The first reliable census of the population was not conducted until fourteen years later in 1790. It showed a total population of 3,929,214 (including slaves). The rank order of states from largest to smallest was as follows: Virginia (747,610), Pennsylvania (434,373), North Carolina (393,751), Massachusetts (378,787), New York (340,120), Maryland (319,728), South Carolina (249,073), Connecticut (237,946), New Jersey (184,139), New Hampshire (141,885), Maine (96,540), Vermont (85,425), Kentucky (73,677), Rhode Island (68,825), Delaware (59,096), and Tennessee (35,691). For more details, see www.census.gov/population/www/censusdata/files/table-16.pdf.

CHAPTER 4

1. Unfortunately, we don't have hard numbers with respect to immigration before 1820. It wasn't until 1819 that Congress enacted a system for keeping statistics on the immigrant population.

2. Outbreaks of revivalism also occurred in New England in the 1790s along with a Congregationalist revival at Yale and other northeastern colleges (McLoughlin 1978). But this more intellectual strain of revivalism in the North stood in contrast to the camp meeting revivalism in the South and Midwest, which was characterized by periods of unrestrained emotionalism spurred on by enthusiastic and plain-speaking preachers who energized crowds caught up in the moment of religious fervor.

3. The Constitution was adopted in 1787 and needed to be ratified by the states before it could become law. However, it became evident that many states would not ratify the Constitution as adopted because they believed it did not adequately protect individual liberties. Seven states at their ratifying conventions recommended that a specific guarantee of religious liberty be added to the constitution (Sweet 1952). The first ten Amendments of the Constitution (the Bill of Rights) were subsequently added and ratified by three-quarters of the states in 1791.

4. One symbol of this superiority was the prime real estate on which elite religious groups built their churches and schools (e.g., on the highest hills in small towns and the most desirable land in urban areas).

5. John Tyler, Millard Fillmore, and Martin Van Buren held two posts (president and vice president) but are counted only once.

6. This new wave of immigration was propelled by a number of factors, including overpopulation in Europe, persecution of Jews in Russia, the advent of direct steamship service between Mediterranean and American ports, and the promise of jobs and economic betterment in an expanding American economy.

7. Other African American groups that formed during this time included the Colored Primitive Baptist Church (1866), the African Union First Colored Methodist Protestant Church (1866), the First Colored Methodist Protestant Church (1866), the Second Cumberland Presbyterian Church (1868), the Reformed Zion Union Apos-

tolic Church (1869), the Christian Methodist Episcopal Church (1870), the Reformed
Zion Union Apostolic Church (1881), the Reformed Methodist Union Episcopal
Church (1885), the Independent African Methodist Episcopal Church (1885), and the
African Union Church of the Living God (1889). Most of these faiths were reorganized in subsequent years.

8. To be listed in the *Register*, one needs letters of recommendation from five
individuals who are already listed, and then the advisory committee makes a decision about admission. According to Thomas Lee Jones, a spokesman for the advisory
committee, "A 25-member advisory board simply asks themselves this question when
evaluating a candidate: Would one want to have dinner with this person on a regular
basis?" (Sargent 1997). It appears that very few members of the committee prefer to
dine with Jews, thus illustrating the perpetuation of policies of religious exclusion that
were enacted by the *Social Register* over one hundred years ago.

CHAPTER 5

1. By the early 1920s, Jews made up 9 percent of the student body in all American colleges and universities (Howe 1976, 167).

2. These figures were obtained by dividing the average percentage for Episcopalians and Presbyterians by the average percentage for all other groups (e.g., for
business leaders: 23/8.1= 2.8).

3. Although Miller does not provide a separate listing for Congregationalists, it
is likely that Congregationalists were among the 24 percent of business elites and 45
percent of political elites who were classified as "Other Protestant" or "Protestant,
unspecified." However, given their relatively small numbers in the total population,
their being in one of these two groups rather than in the elite category would not
throw the overall picture off by very much at all.

4. Huntington and Whitney (1927) and Ament (1927) also conducted studies of
the religious affiliations of *Who's Who* listees in the 1920s, and their findings mirror
those of Fry.

5. See Meade, Hill, and Atwood (2005).

6. In 1990s the NAE changed its policy and allowed denominations in the NCC
or World Council of Churches to hold dual membership with the NAE.

7. Rosen and Bell (1966) also looked at patterns of mate selection in the upper
class, but they did not analyze the religious affiliation of the couples.

8. Finke and Stark (1992) argue that mainline Protestant churches started to experience a decline in their market share, if not their absolute membership, after the
American Revolution.

9. In 2008 Cizik was forced to resign after he publicly affirmed support for same-sex civil unions.

10. Two of our favorite examples of nonelites appointing elites have to do with
President Lyndon Johnson's nomination of Thurgood Marshall to be the first black
justice on the Supreme Court and President Ronald Reagan's nomination of Sandra
Day O'Connor to be the first female justice on the Court. Johnson and Reagan were

both Disciples of Christ and, therefore, nonelites in terms of their religious affiliations. Although their two nominees were minorities in terms of race and gender, they also were Episcopalians. Thus, the nominations of Marshall and O'Connor to the highest court in the land were breakthroughs in terms of racial and gender stratification, but they had the effect of reproducing the original pattern of religious stratification.

11. This only includes presidents whose religious affiliation is known.

CHAPTER 6

1. According to the *Hartford Courant*: "The individual Catholic votes as the priest dictates; the priest follows the dictates of the prelate, and he so controls the elections as shall best serve the interests of the Pope, the establishment of the Church, and its subsequent complete rule over the country" (Perlmutter 1999, 88).

2. According to Lipset (1964, 82), Protestants were more responsible for Lincoln's political success in 1864 than Catholics, Jews, and Others, who were more inclined to support his Democratic opponent.

3. Percentages exceed 100 percent because some charges involve more than one type of discrimination.

CHAPTER 7

1. In a June 2006 poll, 10 percent of Americans said they wouldn't vote for a presidential candidate who was Catholic, 15 percent wouldn't vote for a Jew, 21 percent wouldn't vote for an evangelical Christian, 37 percent wouldn't vote for a Mormon, and 54 percent would not vote for a Muslim. Several other polls show much the same thing.

2. The elite customs that persist are so ingrained in our culture that we take them for granted and do not think much about their consequences. Thus, it is not necessary to assume that elites who support these policies and practices do so because they have selfish motives or that they are prejudiced against minorities. All that is necessary is to document their behavior.

3. To date, evangelical Protestants have tended to rely on public schools, but in recent years, they have begun to develop "Christian" colleges and universities. It remains to be seen if this shift in emphasis will lead to assimilation and improve their lot in life, or if they will reinforce evangelical distinctiveness and the lower status of evangelical Protestants.

References

Adamczyk, Amy, John Wybraniec, and Roger Finke. 2004. "Religious Regulation and the Courts: Documenting the Effects of Smith and RFRA." *Journal of Church and State* 46: 237–62.

Aguirre, Adalberto, Jr., and Jonathan H. Turner. 2001. *American Ethnicity*. Boston: McGraw-Hill.

Aguirre, Adalberto, Jr., and David V. Baker (editors). 2008. *Structured Inequality in the United States* (second edition). Upper Saddle River, NJ: Pearson/Prentice-Hall.

Ahlstrom, Sidney E. 1972. *A Religious History of the American People*. New Haven, CT: Yale University Press.

Albanese, Catherine L. 1999. *America: Religions and Religion* (third edition). Belmont, CA: Wadsworth Publishing.

———. 2007. *America: Religions and Religion* (fourth edition). Belmont, CA: Thomson.

Ament, Jonathan. 2005. American Jewish Religious Denominations. Report 10. New York: United Jewish Communities/National Jewish Population Survey. www.jewishdatabank.org/Archive/NJPS2000_American_Jewish_Religious_Denominations.pdf.

Ament. William S. 1927. "Religion, Education, and Distinction." *School and Society* 26(665): 399–406.

American Jewish Yearbook. 1968. Philadelphia: American Jewish Committee.

American Jewish Yearbook. 2009. Philadelphia: American Jewish Committee.

Ammerman, Nancy T. 2003. "Religious Identities and Religious Institutions," Pp. 207–24 in Michelle Dillon (editor), *Handbook of the Sociology of Religion*. New York: Cambridge University Press.

Anderson, Charles H. 1970. *White Protestant Americans*. Englewood Cliffs, NJ: Prentice-Hall.

Anderson, Elijah, and Douglas S. Massey. 2004. *Racial Stratification in the United States*. New York: Russell Sage Foundation.

Anderson, Elin. 1937. *We Americans*. Cambridge, MA: Harvard University Press.

Baer, Hans A. 1998. "African American Religious Experience," Pp. 7–11 in William H. Swatos, Jr. (editor), *Encyclopedia of Religion and Society*. Walnut Creek, CA: Sage.

Baltzell, E. Digby. 1958. *Philadelphia Gentlemen*. Glencoe, IL: The Free Press.

———. 1964. *The Protestant Establishment*. New York: Random House.

———. 1976. "The Protestant Establishment Revisited." *American Scholar* 45: 499–518.

———. 1982. *Puritan Boston and Quaker Philadelphia*. Boston: Beacon Press.

———. 1986. "Foreword." Pp. ix–xiii in Murray Freidman (editor), *Philadelphia Jewish Life, 1940–1985*. Ardmore, PA: Seth Press Inc.

Barck, Oscar Theodore, and Hugh Talmage Lefler. 1958. *Colonial America*. New York: Macmillan.

Barro, Robert, and Joshua Mitchell. 2004. "Religious Faith and Economic Growth: What Matters Most—Belief or Belonging?" www.heritage.org/Reseach/Lecture.

Beeghley, Leonard. 2005. *The Structure of Social Stratification in the United States* (fourth edition). Boston: Allyn and Bacon.

Bell, Daniel. 1972. "On Meritocracy and Equality." *The Public Interest* 29 (Fall): 29–68.

Bellah, Robert N. 1970. "Christianity and Symbolic Realism." *Journal for the Scientific Study of Religion* 9: 89–115.

Berger, Peter. 1967. *The Sacred Canopy*. Garden City, NY: Doubleday.

———. 1986. "Religion in Post-Protestant America." *Commentary* 81 (May): 41–46.

Beyerlein, Kevin. 2004. "Specifying the Impact of Conservative Protestantism on Educational Attainment." *Journal for the Scientific Study of Religion* 43: 505–18.

Billings, Warren B., John E. Selby, and Thad W. Tate. 1986. *Colonial Virginia*. White Plains, NY: KTO Press.

Billington, Ray Allen. 1938. *The Protestant Crusade, 1800–1860*. New York: The Macmillan Company.

Blanshard, Paul. 1953. *Apostles of Discord*. Boston: Beacon Press.

Bogardus, Emory. 1926. "Social Distance in the City." *Proceedings and Publications of the American Sociological Society,* vol. 20: 40–46 (also see James Vander Zanden, *American Minority Relations*. New York: Ronald Press).

Boger, John Charles, and Judith Welch Wegner. 1996. *Race, Poverty, and American Cities*. Chapel Hill: University of North Carolina Press.

Bonomi, Patricia V. 1986. *Under the Cope of Heaven*. New York: Oxford University Press.

Bouma, Gary D. 1973. "Beyond Lenski: A Critical of Recent 'Protestant Ethic' Research." *Journal for the Scientific Study of Religion* 12: 141–55.

Braverman, Harold, and Louis Krapin. 1967. "A Study of Religious Discrimination by Social Clubs." Pp. 211–21 in Milton L. Barron (editor), *Minorities in a Changing World*. New York: Knopf.

Brewer, Mark. 2003. *Relevant No More? The Protestant Divide in American Electoral Politics*. Lanham, MD: Lexington Books.

Bridenbaugh, Carl. 1962. *Mitre and Sceptre*. New York: Oxford University Press.

Brilliant, Richard. 1997. *Facing the New World*. New York: Jewish Theological Seminary of America.

Brodkin, Karen. 1998. *How Jews Became White Folks and What That Says About Race in America*. New Brunswick, NJ: Rutgers University Press.

Brookhiser, Richard. 1991. *The Way of the WASP*. New York: Free Press.

———. 1993. "III Cheers for the WASPs." *Time*, Special Issue, Fall: 78–79.

Brooks, Clem, and Jeff Manza. 2004. "A Great Divide? Religion and Political Change in U.S. National Elections, 1972–2000." *Sociological Quarterly* 45: 421–50.

Buchanan, Patrick J. 2006. *State of Emergency*. New York: St. Martin's Griffin.

Bureau of the Census. 1894. *Eleventh Census of the United States, 1890. Vol. 9: Report on Statistics of Churches in the United States*. Washington, DC: Government Printing Office.

———. 1910. *Religious Bodies: 1906*. Washington, DC: Government Printing Office.

———. 1919. *Religious Bodies 1916*. Part I. Washington, DC: Government Printing Office.

———. 1930. *Religious Bodies: 1926*. Washington, DC: Government Printing Office.

———. 2010. "Self Described Religious Identification of Adult Population, 1990–2008." www.U.S.Census.gov/compendia/statab/2010/tables/10s0075.pdf.

Burstein, Paul. 2007. "Jewish Educational and Economic Success in the United States: A Search for Explanations." *Social Perspectives* 50: 209–28.

Butler, Jon. 1978. *Power, Authority, and the Origins of the American Denominational Order*. Philadelphia: American Philosophical Society.

———. 1990. *Awash in a Sea of Faith*. Cambridge, MA: Harvard University Press.

Butts, R. Freeman, and Lawrence A. Cremin. 1953. *A History of Education in American Culture*. New York: Henry Holt and Company.

Cantril, Hadley. 1943. "Educational and Economic Composition of Religious Groups." *American Journal of Sociology* 47: 574–79.

Caplow, Theodore, Howard M. Bahr, Bruce A. Chadwick, and Dwight W. Hoover. 1983. *All Faithful People: Change and Continuity in Middletown's Religion*. Minneapolis: University of Minnesota Press.

Carr, James H., and Nandinee K. Kutty. 2008. *Segregation: The Rising Cost for America*. New York: Routledge.

Carroll, Jackson, and Wade Clark Roof. 1993. *Beyond Establishment*. Louisville, KY: Westminster/John Knox Press.

Carter, Gregg Lee. 2007. "The 1960s Black Riots Revisited: City Level Explanation of the Severity." *Sociological Inquiry* 56: 210–18.

Chandler, Charles, and Yung-mei Tsai. 2003. "Social Factors Influencing Immigration Attitudes: An Analysis of Data from the General Social Survey." *The Social Science Journal* 38: 177–88.

Chickering, George L. 1986. "Founders of an Oligrarchy: The Virginia Council, 1692–1722." Pp. 255–74 in B. C. Daniels (editor), *Power and Status*. Middletown, CT: Wesleyan University Press.

Chin, Gabriel J. 1996. "The Civil Rights Revolution Comes to Immigration Law: A New Look at the Immigration and Nationality Act of 1965." *North Carolina Law Review* 75: 273–345.

Christiano, Kevin J., William H. Swatos, Jr., and Peter Kivisto. 2008. *Sociology of Religion* (second edition). Walnut Creek, CA: AltaMira Press.

Christiansen, Terry, and Tom Hogen-Esch. 2006. *Local Politics*. Armonk, NY: M.E. Sharpe.

Christopher, Robert C. 1989. *Crashing the Gates*. New York: Simon and Schuster.

Cimino, Richard, and Don Lattin. 2002. *Shopping for Faith*. New York: Jossey-Bass.

Clark, Terry Nichols. 1975. "The Irish Ethic and the Spirit of Patronage." *Ethnicity* 2: 305–59.

Cobb, Sanford H. 1968. *The Rise of Religious Liberty in America*. New York: Cooper Square Publishers.

Coe, Deborah A., and James D. Davidson. 2010. "The Religious Affiliations of Ivy League Presidents." Paper presented at annual meeting of the Society for the Scientific Study of Religion, Baltimore.

———. Forthcoming. "The Social Origins of Legacy Admissions." *Review of Religious Research*.

Coleman, James S. 1956. "Social Cleavage and Religious Conflict." *Journal of Social Issues* 12: 44–56.

Cooke, George Willis. 1910. *Unitarianism in America*. Boston: American Unitarian Association.

Coreno, T. 2002. "Fundamentalism as a Class Culture." *Sociology of Religion* 63: 335–60.

Cornelison, Isaac A. 1970. *The Relation of Religion to Civil Government in the United States of America.* New York: DaCapo Press.

Cremin, Lawrence A. 1970. *American Education: The Colonial Experience, 1607–1783*. New York: Harper and Row.

Crompton, Rosemary, and Michael Mann (editors). 1986. *Gender and Stratification*. New York: Blackwell.

Crosby, Faye J., Margaret S. Stockdale, and S. Ann Ropp (editors). 2007. *Sex Discrimination in the Workplace*. Hoboken, NJ: Wiley-Blackwell.

Curran, Francis X., S.J. 1963. *Catholics in Colonial Law*. Chicago: Loyola University Press.

Dahrendorf, Ralf. 1959. *Class and Class Conflict in Industrial Society*. Stanford, CA: Stanford University Press.

Daniels, Bruce C. (editor). 1986. *Power and Status: Officeholding in Colonial America*. Middletown, CT: Wesleyan University Press.

D'Antonio, William V., James D. Davidson, Dean R. Hoge, and Katherine Meyer. 2001. *American Catholics*. Walnut Creek, CA: AltaMira Press.

Darnell, Alfred, and Darren E. Sherkat. 1997. "The Impact of Protestant Fundamentalism on Educational Attainment." *American Sociological Review* 62: 306–15.

Davidson, James D. 1977. "Socio-economic Status and Ten Dimensions of Religious Commitment." *Sociology and Social Research* 61: 462–85.

————.1985. "Theories and Measures of Poverty: Toward a Holistic Approach." *Sociological Focus* 18: 177–98.

————. 1994. "Religion Among America's Elite: Persistence and Change in the Protestant Establishment." *Sociology of Religion* 55: 419–40.

————. 2005. *Catholicism in Motion*. Ligouri, MO: Ligouri/Triumph.

————. 2008. "Religious Stratification: Its Origins, Persistence, and Consequences." *Sociology of Religion* 69: 371–95.

Davidson, James D., and Jerome R. Koch. 1998. "Beyond Mutual and Public Benefits: The Inward and Outward Orientations of Nonprofit Organizations." Pp. 292–306 in N. J. Demerath III, Peter Dobkin, Terry Schmitt, and Rhys H. Williams (editors), *Sacred Companies*. New York: Oxford University Press.

Davidson, James D., Rachel Kraus, and Scott Morrissey. 2005. "Presidential Appointments and Religious Stratification in the United States, 1789–2003." *Journal for the Scientific Study of Religion* 44: 485–95.

Davidson, James D., Alan K. Mock, and C. Lincoln Johnson. 1997. "Through the Eye of a Needle: Social Ministry in Affluent Churches." *Review of Religious Research* (March): 247–62.

Davidson, James D., and Ralph E. Pyle. 1999. "Public Religion and Economic Inequality." Pp. 101–14 in William H. Swatos and James K. Wellman (editors), *The Power of Religious Publics*. Westport, CT: Praeger.

————. 2005. "Social Class." Pp. 185–205 in Helen Rose Ebaugh (editor), *Handbook on Religion and Social Institutions*. New York: Springer.

Davidson, James D., Ralph E. Pyle, and David V. Reyes. 1995. "Persistence and Change in the Protestant Establishment, 1930–1992." *Social Forces* 74: 157–75.

Davidson, James D., Andrea Williams, Richard A. Lamanna, Jan Stenftenagel, William J. Whalen, Kathleen Maas Weigert, and Patricia Wittberg. 1997. *The Search for Common Ground*. Huntington, IN: Our Sunday Visitor.

Davis, Beverly. 1953. "Eminence and Level of Social Origin." *American Journal of Sociology* 59: 11–18.

Davis, Kingsley, and Wilbert E. Moore. 1945. "Some Principles of Stratification." *American Sociological Review* 10: 242–49.

DeJong, Gordon F. 1978. *The Dutch Reformed Church in the American Colonies*. Grand Rapids, MI: Eerdmans.

Demerath, N. J. 1965. *Social Class in American Protestantism*. Chicago: Rand McNally.

Demerath, N. J. III, and Rhys Williams. 1992. *A Bridging of Faiths: Religion and Politics in a New England City*. Princeton, NJ: Princeton University Press.

Dershowitz, Alan. 1998. *The Vanishing American Jew*. New York: Touchstone Books.

Dillon, Michele (editor). 2003. *Handbook of the Sociology of Religion*. Cambridge: Cambridge University Press.

Dinnerstein, Leonard, Roger L. Nichols, and David M. Reimers. 1990. *Natives and Strangers*. New York: Oxford University Press.

Dobbelaere, Karel. 1981. *Secularization: A Multidimensional Concept*. London: Sage.

Dolan, Jay P. 1985. *The American Catholic Experience*. Garden City, NY: Image Books.
———. 2002. *In Search of American Catholicism*. New York: Oxford University Press.
Eagles, Charles W. 1990. *Democracy Delayed*. Athens: University of Georgia Press.
Earle, John R., Dean D. Knudsen, and Donald W. Shriver. 1976. *Spindles and Spires*. Atlanta: John Knox Press.
Ebaugh, Helen Rose (editor). 2005. *Handbook of Religion and Social Institutions*. New York: Springer.
Ellis, John Tracy. 1956. *American Catholics*. Chicago: University of Chicago Press.
Erskine, Hazel Gaudet. 1965. "The Polls: Religious Prejudice, Part 2: Anti-Semitism." *Public Opinion Quarterly* 29: 649–64.
Fallows, James. 1988. "A Talent for Disorder." *U.S. News and World Report* (February 8): 83–84.
Farnsley, Arthur E. II, N. J. Demerath III, Etan Diamond, Mary L. Mapes, and Elfriede Wedam. 2004. *Sacred Circles, Public Squares*. Bloomington: Indiana University Press.
Feagin, Joe R., and Clairece Booher Feagin. 2008. *Racial and Ethnic Relations* (eighth edition). Upper Saddle River, NJ: Prentice Hall.
Finke, Roger. 1997. "The Consequences of Religious Competition: Supply-side Explanations for Religious Change. Pp. 46–65 in Larry A. Young (editor), *Rational Choice Theory and Religion*. New York: Routledge.
Finke, Roger, and Rodney Stark. 1986. "Turning Pews into People: Estimating Nineteenth-Century Church Membership." *Journal for the Scientific Study of Religion* 25: 180–92.
———. 1992. *The Churching of America, 1776–1990*. New Brunswick, NJ: Rutgers University Press.
Fischer, Claude S., and Michael Hout. 2006. *Century of Difference*. New York: Russell Sage Foundation.
Friedman, Murray. 1986. "Introduction: From Outsiders to Insiders." Pp. 3–29 in *Philadelphia Jewish Life, 1940–1985*. Ardmore, PA: Seth Press Inc.
Fry, Luther C. 1933a. "The Reported Religious Affiliations of the Various Classes of Leaders Listed in Who's Who, 1930–31 Edition." Pp. 311–14 in *Yearbook of American Churches, 1933*. New York: Round Table Press.
———. 1933b. "The Reported Religious Affiliations of American Leaders." *Scientific Monthly* 36: 241–49.
Gallup Organization. 2010. "In U.S., Religious Prejudice Stronger Against Muslims." January 21. Retrieved January 22, 2010, from www.gallup.com/poll/125312/Religious-Prejudice-Stronger-Against-Muslims.aspx.
Gaustad, Edwin. 1962. *Historical Atlas of Religion in America*. New York: Harper and Row.
———. 1966. *A Religious History of America*. New York: Harper and Row.
Gergen, Kenneth, 2009. *An Invitation to Social Construction*. Thousand Oaks, CA: Sage.

Geschwender, James A. 1978. *Racial Stratification in America*. Dubuque, IA: W.C. Brown.

Glenn, Norval D., and Ruth Hyland. 1967. "Religious Preferences and Worldly Success: Some Evidence from National Surveys." *American Sociological Review* 32: 73–85.

Glock, Charles Y. 1964. "The Role of Deprivation in the Origin and Evolution of Religious Groups." Pp. 24–36 in R. Lee and M. Marty (editors), *Religion and Social Conflict*. New York: Oxford University Press.

Glock, Charles Y., and Rodney Stark. 1965. *Religion and Society in Tension*. Chicago: Rand McNally.

———. 1966. *Christian Beliefs and Anti-Semitism*. New York: Harper and Row.

Goldberg, A. 1970. "Jews in the Legal Profession: A Case of Adjustment to Discrimination." *Jewish Social Studies* 32 (April): 148–61.

Goldstein, S. 1969. "Socioeconomic Differentials among Religious Groups in the United States." *American Journal of Sociology* 74: 612–31.

Gordon, Michaell A. 1993. *The Orange Riots: Irish Political Violence in New York City, 1870 and 1871*. Ithaca, NY: Cornell University Press.

Grant, Madison. 1918. *The Passing of the Great Race*. New York: Charles Scribner's Sons.

Greeley, Andrew M. 1964. "The Protestant Ethic: Time for a Moratorium." *Sociological Analysis*. 25: 20–33.

———. 1981. "Catholics and the Upper Middle Class." *Social Forces* 59: 824–30.

Green, John C. 2004. "The American Religious Landscape and Political Attitudes." Pew Forum Publications. Retrieved August 28, 2009, from pewforum.org/publications/surveys/green-full.pdf.

Gregory, Frances, and Irene Neu. 1962. "The American Industrial Elite of the 1870s." Pp.193–212 in William Miller (editor), *Men in Business*. Santa Barbara, CA: Greenwood Publishing Group.

Griffin, Edward. 1980. *Old Brick: Charles Chauncy of Boston, 1705–1787*. Minneapolis: University of Minnesota Press.

Griffin, John Howard. 1976. *Black Like Me*. New York: Signet Books.

"Grosse Pointe's Gross Points." 1960. *Time* (April 25): 25.

Hadaway, C. Kirk, and Penny Long Marler. 2006. "Growth and Decline in the Mainline." Pp. 1–24 in Charles H. Lippy (editor), *Faith in America: Changes, Challenges, New Directions*. Westport, CT: Praeger Publishers.

Hadden, Jeffrey K. 1987. "Toward Desacralizing Secularization Theory." *Social Forces* 65: 587–611.

Hadden, Jeffrey K., and Charles E. Swann. 1981. *Prime Time Preachers*. Reading, MA: Addison-Wesley.

Hammond, Philip. 1992. *The Protestant Presence in America*. Albany: State University of New York Press.

Handlin, Oscar, and Mary F. Handlin. 1949. "A Century of Jewish Immigration to the United States." *American Jewish Yearbook* 50: 1–83.

Handy, Robert T. 1984. *A Christian America*. New York: Oxford University Press.

Hartford, Danny. 2009. "The National Association of Evangelicals' Latest Blunder?" *Vital Signs* (October 22). Retrieved February 13, 2010, from vitalsignsblog .blogspot.com/2009/10/national-association-of-evangelicals.html.

Hatch, David L., and Mary A. Hatch. 1947. "Criteria of Social Status as Derived from Marriage Announcements in the *New York Times.*" *American Sociological Review* 12 (April): 396–403.

Hatch, Nathan O. 1989. *The Democratization of American Christianity.* New Haven, CT: Yale University Press.

Heiner, Robert. 2009. *Social Problems: An Introduction to Critical Constructionism.* New York: Oxford University Press.

Hennesey, James, S.J. 1981. *American Catholics.* New York: Oxford University Press.

Herberg, Will. 1960. *Protestant-Catholic-Jew.* Garden City, NY: Anchor Books.

Hertel, Bradley R., and Michael Hughes. 1987. "Religious Affiliation, Attendance, and Support for Pro-Family Issues." *Social Forces* 65: 858–82.

Hertzberg, Arthur. 1989. *The Jews in America.* New York: Simon and Schuster.

Higham, John. 1988. *Strangers in the Land* (second edition). New Brunswick, NJ: Rutgers University Press.

Higley, Stephen Richard. 1995. *Privilege, Power, and Place.* Lanham, MD: Rowman & Littlefield.

Hoge, Dean R., William Dinges, Mary Johnson, and Juan Gonsalez. 2001. *Young Adult Catholics.* Notre Dame, IN: University of Notre Dame Press.

Hoge, Dean, and David A. Roozen. 1979. *Understanding Church Growth and Decline, 1950–1978.* New York: Pilgrim Press.

Homola, Michael, Dean Knudsen, and Harvey Marshall. 1987. "Religion and Socio-Economic Achievement." *Journal for the Scientific Study of Religion* 26: 201–17.

Housely, Norman. 2003. *Religious Warfare in Europe 1400–1538.* New York: Oxford University Press.

Hout, M., and C. S. Fischer. 2002. "Why More Americans Have No Religious Preference: Politics And Generations." *American Sociological Review* 67: 165–90.

Howe, Irving. 1976. *World of Our Fathers.* New York: Simon and Schuster.

Huber, Joan. 1986. "A Theory of Gender Stratification." Pp. 110–19 in Laurel Richardson and Vera Taylor (editors), *Feminist Frontiers II: Rethinking Sex, Gender, and Society.* New York: Random House.

Hunsberger, Bruce, and Lynne M. Jackson. 2005. "Religion, Meaning, and Prejudice." *Journal of Social Issues* 51: 113–29.

Huntington, Ellsworth, and Leon F. Whitney. 1927. "Religion and 'Who's Who.'" *American Mercury* 11(44): 438–43.

Hurst, Charles E. 2007. *Social Inequality* (sixth edition). Boston: Allyn and Bacon.

Hutchison, William R. 1989. "Protestantism as Establishment." Pp. 3–18 in William R. Hutchison (editor), *Between the Times.* Cambridge: Cambridge University Press.

Isaac, Rhys. 1974. "Evangelical Revolt: The Nature of the Baptists' Challenge to the Traditional Order in Virginia, 1765–1775." *William and Mary Quarterly* 31: 345–68.

———. 1982. *Transformation of Virginia, 1740–1790.* Chapel Hill: University of North Carolina Press.

Jacquet, Constant H. (editor). 1976. *Yearbook of American and Canadian Churches 1976.* Nashville: Abingdon Press.

Jaher, Frederic Cople. 1982. *The Urban Establishment.* Urbana: University of Illinois Press.

Jasso, G., D. S. Massey, M. R. Rosenzweig, and J. P. Smith. 2003. "Exploring the Religious Preferences of Recent Immigrants to the United States." Pp. 217–53 in Y. Haddad (editor), *Religion and Immigration.* Walnut Creek, CA: AltaMira Press.

Jeffreys, Daniel. 1999. "No Jews on Their Golf Courses." *New Statesman* (August 23): 8–9.

Jenkins, Philip. 2004. *The New Anti-Catholicism.* New York: Oxford University Press.

Johnstone, Ronald L. 2007. *Religion in Society* (eighth edition). Upper Saddle River, NJ: Pearson Prentice Hall.

Jones, Jeffrey M. 2007. "Some Americans Reluctant to Vote for Mormon, 72-Year-Old Presidential Candidates." Gallup News Service (February 20). Retrieved May 31, 2010, from www.gallup.com/poll/26611/Some-Americans-Reluctant-Vote-Mormon-72Yearold-Presidential-Candidates.aspx.

———. 2008. "Americans Have Net Positive Views of U.S. Catholics." Gallup News Service (April 15). Retrieved July 19, 2009, from www.gallup.com/poll/106516/Americans-NetPositive-View-US-Catholics.aspx.

Juster, Susan. 2005. "What's 'Sacred' about Violence in Early America?" *Common-Place* 6:1 www.common-place.org.

Kalmijn, Matthijs. 1991. "Shifting Boundaries: Trends in Religious and Educational Homogamy." *American Sociological Review* 56 (December): 786–800.

———. 1998. "Intermarriage and Homogamy: Causes, Patterns, and Trends." *Annual Review of Sociology* 24: 395–421.

Karabel, Jerome. 1984. "Status-Group Struggle, Organizational Interests, and the Limits of Institutional Autonomy: The Transformation of Harvard, Yale, and Princeton, 1918–1940." *Theory and Society* 13: 1–40.

———. 2005. *The Chosen.* New York: Mariner Books.

Katznelson, Ira. 2005. *When Affirmative Action Was White.* New York: W.W. Norton and Co.

Kaufmann, Eric P. 2004. *The Rise and Fall of Anglo-America.* Cambridge, MA: Harvard University Press.

Keeter, Scott. 2006. "Evangelicals and the GOP: An Update." Pew Research Center Publications, October 18. Washington, DC: Pew Research Center. Retrieved February 14, 2010, from pewresearch.org/pubs/78/evangelicals-and-the-gop-an-update.

Keister, Lisa A. 2000. *Wealth in America: Trends in Wealth Inequality.* New York: Cambridge University Press.

———. 2003. "Religion and Wealth: The Role of Religious Affiliation and Participation in Early Adult Asset Accumulation." *Social Forces* 82: 173–205.

———. 2005. *Getting Rich: America's New Rich and How They Got That Way.* Cambridge: Cambridge University Press.

———. 2007. "Upward Wealth Mobility: Exploring the Roman Catholic Advantage." *Social Forces* 85: 1195–1226.

———. 2008. "Conservative Protestants and Wealth: How Religion Perpetuates Asset Poverty." *American Journal of Sociology* 113: 1237–71.

Kelley, Dean. 1972. *Why Conservative Churches Are Growing*. New York: Harper and Row.

Kennedy, Ruby Jo Reeves. 1944. "Single or Triple Melting Pot? Intermarriage Trends in New Haven, 1870–1940." *American Journal of Sociology* 49: 331–39.

Kerbo, Harold R. 2006. *Social Stratification and Social Inequality* (sixth edition). Boston: McGraw-Hill.

Kiester, Edwin, Jr. 1968. *The Case of the Missing Executive*. New York: Institute of Jewish Relations, American Jewish Committee.

Klausner, Samuel Z. 1989. "Jews in the Executive Suite: The Ambience of Jewish and Gentile Firms." Pp. 147–79 in Harold J. Bershady (editor), *Social Class and Democratic Leadership*. Philadelphia: University of Pennsylvania Press.

Koppelman, Kent L., and Lee Goodhart. 2008. *Understanding Human Differences: Multicultural Education for a Diverse America* (second edition). Boston: Allyn and Bacon.

Kosmin, Barry A., and Ariela Keysar. 2006. *Religion in a Free Market*. Ithaca, NY: Paramount Market Publishing.

———. 2009. *American Religious Identification Survey*. Hartford, CT: Trinity College. Retrieved May 7, 2010, from www.americanreligionsurvey-aris.org/.

Kraus, Rachel M. 2005. "God's (Not So) Quiet Hand: The Political Advocacy of Liberal and Conservative Washington Offices." Doctoral dissertation. West Lafayette, IN: Purdue University Department of Sociology and Anthropology.

Labaree, Leonard W. 1967. *Instructions to British Colonial Governors, 1670–1776*. New York: Octagon Books.

Landry, Bart (editor). 2007. *Race, Gender, and Class: Theory and Methods of Analysis*. Upper Saddle River, NJ: Pearson/Prentice-Hall.

Larew, John. 1991. "Why are Droves of Unqualified, Unprepared Kids Getting into Our Top Colleges?" *Washington Monthly* (June): 10–14.

Lazerwitz, B. 1964. "Religion and Social Structure of the United States." Pp. 426–39 in L. Schneider (editor), *Religion, Culture, and Society*. New York: Wiley.

Lefler, Hugh T., and Albert R. Newsome. 1973. *The History of a Southern State: North Carolina*. Chapel Hill: University of North Carolina Press.

Lehrer, Evelyn L. 1999. "Religion as a Determinant of Educational Attainment: An Economic Perspective." *Social Science Research* 28: 358–79.

———. 2008. *Religion, Economics, and Demography: The Effects of Religion on Education, Work, and the Family*. New York: Routledge.

Lemann, Nicholas. 1992. "Ruling by Degree: Why the New Meritocracy Is Bad for America." *Washington Monthly* 24 (Jan-Feb): 41–46.

Levine, David B. 1986. *The American College and the Culture of Aspiration, 1915–1940*. Ithaca, NY: Cornell University Press.

Levine, Steven B. 1980. "The Rise of American Boarding Schools and the Development of a National Upper Class." *Social Problems* 28: 63–94.

Lewis, G. R. 2008. "Buddhism in America." Buddhist Faith Fellowship of Connecticut. Retrieved May 7, 2010, from bffct.net/id65.html.

Lind, Michael. 1995. *The Next American Nation.* New York: The Free Press.

Lindner, Eileen W. (editor). 2010. *Yearbook of American and Canadian Churches 2010.* Nashville: Abingdon Press.

Lindsay, D. Michael. 2007. *Faith in the Halls of Power.* New York: Oxford University Press.

———. 2008. "Evangelicals in the Power Elite: Elite Cohesion Advancing a Movement." *American Sociological Review* 73: 60–83.

Lipset, Seymour Martin. 1964. "Religion and Politics in the American Past and Present." Pp. 69–126 in Robert Lee and Martin Marty (editors), *Religion and Society in Conflict.* New York: Oxford University Press.

Lobe, Jim. 2006. "Big Jump Found in US Anti-Muslim Incidents." www.commondreams.org (September 19).

Longmore, Paul K. 1996. "All Matters and Things Relating to Religion and Morality: The Virginia Burgesses' Committee for Religion, 1769–1775." *Journal of Church and State* 38: 775–97.

Lynd, Robert S., and Helen M. Lynd. 1929. *Middletown: A Study of Modern American Culture.* New York: Harcourt, Brace, Jovanovich.

———. 1937. *Middletown in Transition.* New York: Harcourt, Brace and Company.

Maisel, L. Sandy, and Ira N. Forman (editors). 2001. *Jews in American Politics.* Lanham, MD: Rowman & Littlefield.

Marcus, Jacob R. 1970. *The Colonial American Jew, 1492–1776.* Volume 1. Detroit, MI: Wayne State University Press.

Marger, Martin. 2009. *Racial and Ethnic Relations* (eighth edition). Belmont, CA: Wadsworth.

Marnell, William H. 1964. *The First Amendment.* Garden City, NY: Doubleday.

Marty, Martin. 1984. *Pilgrims in Their Own Land.* New York: Penquin.

Marx, Karl, and Freidrich Engels. 1959. *Basic Writings on Politics and Philosophy.* Lewis Feuer (editor). Garden City, NY: Doubleday.

———. 1964. *Selected Writings.* T. B. Bottomore (editor). New York: McGraw-Hill.

Masci, David, and Tracy Miller. 2008. "Faith on Capitol Hill: The Religious Affiliations of Members of Congress." www.pewforum/docs/?DocID=379.

Massengill, Rebekah Peeples. 2008. "Educational Attainment and Cohort Change Among Conservative Protestants, 1972–2004." *Journal for the Scientific Study of Religion* 47: 545–62.

Massey, Douglas. 2009. "The Psychology of Social Stratification." Pp. 385–96 in Jeff Manza and Michael Sauder (editors), *Inequality and Society.* New York: W.W. Norton and Company.

McCloud, Sean. 2007. *Divine Hierarchies.* Chapel Hill: University of North Carolina Press.

McCloud, Sean, and William A. Mirola (editors). 2009. *Religion and Class in America: Culture, History, and Politics.* Boston: Brill.

McLoughlin, William G. 1978. *Revivals, Awakenings, and Reform*. Chicago: University of Chicago Press.

McKinley, Albert. E. 1969. *The Suffrage Franchise in the Thirteen English Colonies in America.* New York: Burt Franklin.

McLoughlin, William G. 1978. *Revivals, Awakenings, and Reform*. Chicago: University of Chicago Press.

Meade, Frank, Samuel S. Hill, and Craig D. Atwood. 2005. *Handbook of Denominations* (twelfth edition). Nashville: Abingdon Press.

Menendez, Albert J. 1977. *Religion at the Polls*. Philadelphia: Westminster Press.

———. 1985. *Religious Conflict in America*. New York: Garland.

———. 1996. "Religious Violence—American Style." *Freedom Writer*. Retrieved June 3, 2010, from www.publiceye.org/ifas/fw/9606/violence.html.

Merton, Robert K. 1957. *Social Theory and Social Structure*. Glencoe, IL: Free Press.

Metress, Samuel B. 1985. "The History of Irish-American Care of the Aged." *Social Service Review* 59: 18–31.

Meyers, John. 2003. *Dominant-Minority Relations in America* (second edition). Boston: Allyn and Bacon.

Mihesuah, Devon A. 1996. *American Indians: Stereotypes and Realities*. Atlanta, GA: Clarity Press.

Miller Frank. H. 1900. "Legal Qualification for Office in America, 1619–1899." *Annual Report of the American Historical Association* 1: 87–153.

Miller, William. 1962. *Men in Business*. Santa Barbara, CA: Greenwood Publishing Group.

Mills, C. Wright. 1956. *The Power Elite*. New York: Oxford University Press.

Moore, David W. 2003. "Little Prejudice Against a Woman, Jewish, Black or Catholic Presidential Candidate." Gallup News Service (June 10). Retrieved July 19, 2009, from www.gallup.com/poll/8611/Little-Prejudice-Against-Woman-Jewish-Black-Catholic-Presidential-Candidate.aspx.

Moore, Gwen. 1987. "Women in the Old-Boy Network: The Case of New York State Government." In G. William Domhoff and Thomas R. Dye (editors), *Power Elites and Organizations.* Newbury Park, CA: Sage.

Morris, Aldon. 1984. *The Origins of the Civil Rights Movement*. New York: Free Press.

Myers, Gustavus. 1943. *History of Bigotry in the United States*. New York: Random House.

Nash, Gary B. 1968. *Quakers and Politics*. Princeton, NJ: Princeton University Press.

———. 1986. *Race, Class, and Politics*. Urbana: University of Illinois Press.

National Association of Evangelicals. 2009. "History." Retrieved February 20, 2010, from www.nae.net/about-us/history/62.

Nelsen, Hart M. 1988. "The Religious Identification of Children of Interfaith Marriages." *Review of Religious Research* 32: 122–34.

Nerad, Maresi. 1999. *The Academic Kitchen: A Social History of Gender Stratification at the University of California at Berkeley*. Albany: State University of New York Press.

Niebuhr, H. Richard. 1929. *The Social Sources of Denominationalism*. New York: Henry Holt.

Noel, Donald L. 1968. "A Theory of the Origin of Ethnic Stratification." *Social Problems* 16: 157–72.

Nordstrom, Justin. 2006. *Danger on the Doorstep*. Notre Dame, IN: University of Notre Dame Press.

Official Catholic Directory. 1912. New York: P.J. Kenedy.

O'Grady, Joseph P. 1973. *How the Irish Became Americans*. New York: Twayne.

Olmstead, Clifton E. 1960. *History of Religion in the United States*. Englewood Cliffs, NJ: Prentice-Hall.

Ostby, Gundrun. 2005. "Inequality, Institutions, and Instability: Horizontal Inequalities, Political Instituttions, and Civil Conflict in Developing Countries, 1986–2003." Paper presented at the Political Institutions, Development, and a Domestic Civil Peace Workshop, Oxford.

———. 2007. "Horizontal Inequalities, Political Environment, and Civil Conflict: Evidence from 55 Developing Countries, 1986–2003." World Bank Policy Research Working Paper. Available at papers.ssrn/sol3papers.cfm?abstract id=979665.

O'Toole, James M. 2003. *Passing for White*. Amherst: University of Massachusetts Press.

Park, Jerry Z., and S. H. Reimer. 2002. "Revisiting the Social Sources of American Christianity 1972–1988." *Journal for the Scientific Study of Religion* 41: 733–46.

Parrillo, Vincent N. 2006. *Strangers to These Shores* (eighth edition). Boston: Allyn and Bacon.

Parsons, Talcott. 1971. *The System of Modern Societies*. Englewood Cliffs, NJ: Prentice-Hall.

Paullin, Charles O. 1975. *Atlas of the Historical Geography of the United States*. Westport, CT: Greenwood Press.

Perlmutter, Philip. 1999. *Legacy of Hate*. Armonk, NY: M.E. Sharpe.

Pew Forum on Religion and Public Life. 2008. *The U.S. Religious Landscape Survey*. Washington, DC. Pew Organization. Retrieved August 28, 2009, from religions.pewforum.org/reports.

Pew Research Center. 2010. *Millennials: Confident, Connected, Open to Change*. pewresearch.org.

Pointer, Richard W. 1988. *Protestant Pluralism and the New York Experience*. Bloomington: Indiana University Press.

Pope, Liston. 1942. *Millhands and Preachers*. New Haven, CT: Yale University Press.

———. 1948. "Religion and the Class Structure." *Annals of the American Academy of Political and Social Science* 256: 84–91.

Powell, R. M. 1969. *Race, Religion, and the Promotion of the American Executive*. Columbus: Ohio State University Press.

Pratt, John Webb. 1967. *Religion, Politics, and Diversity*. Ithaca, NY: Cornell University Press.

Prendergast, William B. 1999. *The Catholic Voter in America*. Washington, DC: Georgetown University Press.

Purvis, Thomas L. 1980. "High-Born, Long-Awaited Families: Social Origins of New Jersey Assemblymen, 1703–1776." *William and Mary Quarterly* 37: 542–615.

———. 1986. "A Beleaguered Elite: The New Jersey Council, 1702–1776." Pp. 232–54 in Bruce C. Daniels (editor), *Power and Status*. Middletown, CT: Wesleyan University Press.

Pyle, Ralph E. 1996. *Persistence and Change in the Protestant Establishment*. Westport, CT: Praeger.

———. 2006. "Trends in Religious Stratification: Have Religious Group Socioeconomic Distinctions Declined in Recent Decades?" *Sociology of Religion* 67: 61–79.

Pyle, Ralph E., and James D. Davidson. 2003. "The Origins of Religious Stratification in Colonial America." *Journal for the Scientific Study of Religion* 42: 57–75.

Pyle, Ralph E., and Jerome R. Koch. 2001. "The Religious Affiliation of American Elites, 1930s to 1990s: A Note on the Pace of Disestablishment." *Sociological Focus* 34: 125–37.

Ribuffo, L. P. 1997. "Henry Ford and the International Jew." Pp. 201–18 in J. Sarna (editor), *The American Jewish Experience* (second edition). New York: Holmes and Meier.

Richardson, James T. 2005. "Law." Pp. 227–40 in Helen Rose Ebaugh (editor), *Handbook of Religion and Social Institutions*. New York: Springer.

Ritzer, George. 2010. *Sociological Theory* (eighth edition). New York: McGraw-Hill.

Roach, Marilynne K. 2002. *The Salem Witch Trials: A Day-by-Day Chronicle of a Community Under Siege*. New York: Cooper Square Press.

Roberts, Keith. 2004. *Religion in Sociological Perspective* (fourth edition). Belmont, CA: Wadsworth.

Roof, Wade Clark. 1979. "Socioeconomic Differences among White Socioreligious Groups in the United States." *Social Forces* 58: 280–89.

Roof, Wade Clark, and William McKinney. 1987. *American Mainline Religion*. New Brunswick, NJ: Rutgers University Press.

Rosen, Lawrence, and Robert R. Bell. 1966. "Mate Selection in the Upper Class." *Sociological Quarterly* 7: 157–66.

Rossides, Daniel W. 1997. *Social Stratification* (second edition). Upper Saddle River, NJ: Prentice-Hall.

Rothman, Robert A. 2005. *Inequality and Stratification* (fourth edition). Upper Saddle River, NJ: Prentice Hall.

Roy, Ralph Lord. 1953. *Apostles of Discord*. Boston: Beacon Press.

Ryan, William. 1981. *Equality*. New York: Pantheon Books.

Ryerson, Richard A. 1986. "Portrait of a Colonial Oligarchy: The Quaker Elite in the Pennsylvania Assembly, 1729–1776." Pp. 106–35 in B. C. Daniels (editor), *Power and Status*. Middletown, CT: Wesleyan University Press.

Samuelson, Kurt. 1993. *The Protestant Ethic, the Spirit of Capitalism, and the Abuses of Scholarship*. Toronto: University of Toronto Press.

Sargent, Allison Ijams. 1997. "The Social Register: Just a Circle of Friends." *New York Times,* December 21. Retrieved February 13, 2009, from query.nytimes.com/

gst/fullpage.html?res=9902E4DC1F3FF932A15751C1A961958260&scp=1&sq= Social%20Register&st=cse.

Schick, Marvin. 2005. *A Census of Jewish Day Schools in the United States, 2003–2004.* New York: Avi Chai Foundation.

Schrag, Peter. 1971. *The Decline of the WASP.* New York: Simon and Schuster.

Schultze, Quentin J. 1991. *Televangelism and American Culture.* Grand Rapids, MI: Baker Book House.

Schuman, Howard. 1971. "The Religious Factor in Detroit: Review, Replication, Reanalysis." *American Sociological Review* 36: 30–48.

Schwartz, Sally. 1987. *A Mixed Multitude.* New York: New York University Press.

Semmerling, Tim Jon. 2006. *"Evil" Arabs in American Popular Film.* Austin: University of Texas Press.

Shaheen, Jack G. 1984. *The TV Arabs.* Bowling Green, OH: Bowling Green State University Press.

———. 2008. *Guilty.* New York: Olive Branch Press.

———. 2009. *Reel Bad Arabs.* New York: Olive Branch Press.

Shannon, William V. 1989. *The American Irish* (second edition). Amherst: University of Massachusetts Press.

Sherkat, Darren E. 2007. "Religion and Higher Education: The Good, the Bad, and the Ugly." religion.ssrc.reforum/sherkat.pdf.

Sheskin, Ira M. 2000. "American Jews." Pp. 227–61 in Jesse O. Mckee (editor), *Ethnicity in Contemporary America* (second edition). Lanham, MD: Rowman & Littlefield.

Silberman, Charles E. 1985. *A Certain People.* New York: Summit Books.

Silk, Mark. 1984. "Notes on the Judeo-Christian Tradition in America." *American Quarterly* 36: 65–85.

Smigel, Edwin O. 1969. *The Wall Street Lawyer.* Bloomington: Indiana University Press.

Smith, Christian, and Robert Faris. 2005. "Socioeconomic Inequality in the American Religious System: An Update and Assessment." *Journal for the Scientific Study of Religion* 44: 95–104.

Smith, Christian, and Melinda Lundquist Denton. 2005. *Soul Searching.* New York: Oxford University Press.

Smith, Gary Scott. 2003. "Protestant Churches and Business in Gilded-Age America." *Theology Today*, October.

Snell, Ronald K. 1986. "Ambition of Honor and Places: The Magistracy of Hampshire County, Massachusetts, 1692–1760." Pp. 17–34 in B. C. Daniels (editor), *Power and Status.* Middletown, CT: Wesleyan University Press.

Stark, Rodney. 2003. "Upper Class Asceticism: Social Origins of Ascetic Movements and Medieval Saints." *Review of Religious Research* 45: 5–19.

Stark, Rodney, and Charles Y. Glock. 1968. *American Piety.* Berkeley: University of California Press.

Stokes, Anson Phelps. 1950. *Church and State in the United States.* Volume 1. New York: Harper and Brothers.

Stout, Harry S. 1974. "University Men in New England, 1620–1660: A Demographic Analysis." *Journal of Interdisciplinary History* 4: 375–400.

208   *References*

Sweet, William Warren. 1952. *Religion in the Development of American Culture,*
1765–1840. New York: Scribner's.
———. 1965. *Religion in Colonial America.* New York: Cooper Square Publishers.
Synnott, Marcia Graham. 1979. *The Half-Opened Door: Discrimination and Admissions*
at Harvard, Yale, and Princeton, 1900–1970. Westport, CT: Greenwood Press.
Taylor, Stephanie. 2009. *Narratives of Identity and Place.* New York: Routledge.
Thorpe, Francis N. 1909. *The Federal and State Constitutions.* Washington, DC:
Government Printing Office.
Tolles, Frederick B. 1948. *Meeting House and Counting House.* Chapel Hill: Univer-
sity of North Carolina Press.
Tumin, Melvin. 1953. "Some Principles of Stratification: A Critical Analysis."
American Sociological Review 18: 387–94.
Turner, Jonathan H. 2002. *The Structure of Sociological Theory* (seventh edition).
Belmont, CA: Wadsworth.
Turner, Jonathan H., and Royce Singleton. 1978. "A Theory of Ethnic Oppression."
Social Forces 56: 1001–1008.
U.S. Department of Commerce. 1976. *Historical Statistics of the United States: Colonial*
Times to 1970 (Bicentennial Edition). Washington DC: U.S. Bureau of the Census.
———. 2005. "Facts for Features." (cb05-ff.09–2). Washington DC: U.S. Bureau of
the Census (July 27).
U.S. Senate Commission on Immigration. 1911. *Abstract of Reports of the Immigra-*
tion Commission, vol. 1. Washington, DC: Government Printing Office.
Varady, David P. 1979. *Ethnic Minorities in Urban Areas.* Boston: Martinus Nijhoff
Publishing.
Vine, Phyllis. 1978. "The Social Function of Eighteenth-Century Higher Education."
History of Education Quarterly 16: 409–24.
Waldman, Lois. 1955. "Employment Discrimination Against Jews in the United
States—1955." *Jewish Social Studies* 18: 211–14.
Warner, R. Stephen. 1993. "Work in Progress toward a New Paradigm in the Socio-
logical Study of Religion." *American Journal of Sociology* 83: 144–1093.
Warner, W. Lloyd. 1942. *The Status System of a Modern Community.* New York:
Oxford University Press.
———. 1943. *Democracy in Jonesville: A Study of Quality and Inequality.* New
York: Harper.
Warner, W. Lloyd, and Paul S. Hunt. 1941. *Social Life of a Modern Community.* New
Haven, CT: Yale University Press.
Warner, W. Lloyd, J. O. Low, Paul S. Hunt, and Leo Srole. 1963. *Yankee City.* New
Haven, CT: Yale University Press.
Warner, W. Lloyd, Marchia Meeker, and Kenneth Eels. 1949. *Social Class in Amer-*
ica. Chicago, IL: Science Research Associates.
Weber, Max. 1946a. "Class, Status, Party." Pp. 180–95 in H. H. Gerth and C. W.
Mills (editors), *From Max Weber.* New York: Oxford University Press.
———. 1946b. "The Social Psychology of the World Religions." Pp. 267–301 in H.
H. Gerth and C. W. Mills (editors), *From Max Weber.* New York: Oxford Univer-
sity Press.

————. 1958. *The Protestant Ethic and the Spirit of Capitalism.* Talcott Parsons, translator. New York: Charles Scribner's Sons.

————. 1968. *Economy and Society,* vol. I. Guenther Roth and Claus Wittich (editors). New York: Bedminster Press.

Wendel, Thomas. 1986. "At the Pinnacle of Elective Success: The Speaker of the House in Colonial America." Pp. 173–201 in B. C. Daniels (editor), *Power and Status.* Middletown, CT: Wesleyan University Press.

Wilcox, Clyde, and Carin Lawson. 2006. *Onward Christian Soldiers.* Boulder, CO: Westview Press.

Wilson, Bryan R. 1966. *Religion and Secular Society.* London: Watts.

Winter, J. Alan. 1977. *Continuities in the Sociology of Religion.* New York: Harper & Sons.

Wuthnow, Robert. 1988. *The Restructuring of American Religion.* Princeton, NJ: Princeton University Press.

————. 2005. *America and the Challenges of Religious Diversity.* Princeton: Princeton University Press. www.adherents.com.

Zweigenhaft, Richard L., and G. William Domhoff. 1991. *Blacks in the White Establishment?* New Haven, CT: Yale University Press.

————. 2006. *Diversity in the Power Elite.* Lanham, MD: Rowman & Littlefield.

Index

139–161, 178–179; defined, vii–viii, 32; institutionalization of, 34–35, 38–39; not addressed by stratification researchers, 2; origins, 6–11, 33–35, 43–62, 167–169; persistence and change, 35–39, 169–170; suggestions for future studies of, 165–67, 168–69, 174–75; trends, 90, 135–138, 140–41, 161; ways to reduce, 179–180; 1787–1899, 11–16, 71–72, 78–79, 89–91; 1900–2010, 16–21, 100, 104–106, 113–114, 173–174
religious switching, 3–4, 5
religious tests for public office, 68–69

Salvation Army, 81
school prayer issue, 119–120
Second Great Awakening, 64, 65, 66, 144, 148
secularization thesis, 2–3
Seventh-day Adventists, 19–20, 80, 95, 145
Slavs, 80
slaves and religion, 66
Smith, Al, 102, 155
social distance, 153
social gospel movement, 151, 154–55
social justice theodicy, 30–31, 37–38, 170, 177
Social Register, 85–86, 102, 111, 190n8
Society for the Propagation of the Gospel in Foreign Parts, 49, 51, 64
socioeconomic ranking of religious groups, 19–21, 127–133
socioeconomic status, vii
southern and eastern Europeans, 83, 86, 88, 93, 94, 96, 98, 99, 100
Southern Baptist Convention, 73
Southern Baptists, 95, 115, 127
Speakers of the House, colonial period, 59–61
state churches. *See* religious establishments.
St. Grottlesex, 100. *See also* boarding schools

stratification: conflict view, viii–ix, 22–23, 25–27; definition of, vii; functionalist view, viii, 22, 25–26; and social instability, 140–141; types of, vii–viii, 1, 139. *See also* religious stratification
suggestions for future studies of religious stratification, 165–67, 168–69, 174–75
Supreme Court justices, 69, 71–72, 78–79, 89, 103, 127, 175–76
Supreme Court rulings, 119–120, 121

Temperance movement, 97, 151
Third Great Awakening, 152
Third Plenary Council of Baltimore, 86
toleration of religious dissent in colonies, 52–56
trends in religious stratification, 90, 135–138, 140–41, 161
triple melting pot, 36, 111, 124
Tumin, Melvin, 26, 40

upper-class Anglo-Saxonism, 83–86
Unitarians: in colonies, 7, 61; 1789–1899, 66, 72, 78, 79, 89, 90; 1900–2010, 103, 105, 113, 127, 133, 134, 135, 136, 137
Unitarian-Universalist Association, 115
Unitarian-Universalists, 19–21
United Brethren, 115
United Brethren of Christ, 67, 78
United Church of Christ, 19–21, 29, 106, 115, 116, 133, 134, 135, 136, 137
United Lutheran Church in America, 95
United Methodist Church, 29, 115, 116
United Presbyterian Church, 106
Universalists, 66–67
U.S. Constitution, 68, 76, 189n3

vestry, 46–47
Vice Presidents, U.S., 78–79
Virginia bill for religious freedom, 68
visibility of religion, 4
voting restrictions and religion, 53–56
Voting Rights Act, 121

Washington National Cathedral, 95
WASP, 36, 39, 83–86, 87, 89, 102, 112,
    124, 125, 127
wealth, concentration of, 12
Weber, Max, 111; Protestant ethic, viii,
    22, 187–88n4; perspective on stratifi-
    cation, 31–32

white shoe law firms, 85
Wisconsin Evangelical Synod, 95
Who's Who in America, 6, 17–19,
    129
Who's Who in the East, 113
*Why Conservative Churches Are Grow-
    ing*, 114

About the Authors

James D. Davidson is emeritus professor of sociology at Purdue University. He is author or coauthor of ten books, including *American Catholics Today* (2007), *Catholicism in Motion* (2005), and *The Search for Common Ground* (1997). He has been president of the Association for the Sociology of Religion, the Religious Research Association, and the North Central Sociological Association, as well as editor of the *Review of Religious Research* and executive officer of the Society for the Scientific Study of Religion. He has won CARA's Rev. Louis Luzbetak Award for Exemplary Church Research, NCSA's Distinguished Service Award, the state of Indiana's Distinguished Hoosier Award, and his department's Excellence in Teaching Award.

Ralph E. Pyle is visiting assistant professor in the Department of Sociology at Michigan State University. His research interests include racial and ethnic relations, social stratification, and religion. He is the author of *Persistence and Change in the Protestant Establishment* and has contributed articles to the *Journal for the Scientific Study of Religion, Sociology of Religion, Social Forces*, and *Review of Religious Research*. He teaches courses in social theory, research methods, American diversity, religion, and introductory sociology. He also has received teaching awards from his department.